Love, Freedom, Aloneness

Love, Freedom, Aloneness

THE KOAN OF RELATIONSHIPS

Osho

St. Martin's Griffin
New York

Edited by Sarito Carol Neiman

www.stmartins.com

ISBN 0-312-26227-2 (hc)
ISBN 0-312-29162-0 (pbk)

10   9   8   7

Contents

Preface

In Plato's *Symposium*, Socrates says:

A man who practices the mysteries of love will be in contact not with a reflection, but with truth itself. To know this blessing of human nature, one can find no better helper than love.

I have been commenting my whole life on love, in thousands of different ways, but the message is the same. Just one fundamental thing has to be remembered: It is not the love that you think is love. Neither is Socrates speaking about that love nor am I speaking about it.

The love you know is nothing but a biological urge; it depends on your chemistry and your hormones. It can be changed very easily—a small change in your chemistry and the love that you thought was the "ultimate truth" will simply disappear. You have been calling lust "love." This distinction should be remembered.

Socrates says, "A man who practices the mysteries of love . . ." Lust has no mysteries. It is a simple biological game; every animal, every bird, every tree knows about it. Certainly the love that has mysteries is going to be totally different from the love with which you are ordinarily acquainted.

A man who practices the mysteries of love will be in contact not with the reflection, but with truth itself.

This love that can become a contact with truth itself arises only out of your consciousness—not out of your body, but out of your innermost being. Lust arises out of your body, love arises out of your consciousness. But people don't know their consciousness, and the misunderstanding goes on and on—their bodily lust is taken for love.

Very few people in the world have known love. Those are the people who have become so silent, so peaceful . . . and out of that silence and peace they come in contact with their innermost being, their soul. Once you are in contact with your soul, your love becomes not a relationship but simply a shadow to you. Wherever you move, with whomsoever you move, you are loving.

Right now, what you call love is addressed to someone, confined to someone. And love is not a phenomenon that can be confined. You can have it in your open hands, but you cannot have it in your fist. The moment your hands are closed, they are empty. The moment they are open, the whole of existence is available to you.

Socrates is right: One who knows love also knows truth, because they are only two names of one experience. And if you have not known the truth, remember that you have not known love, either.

To know this blessing of human nature, one can find no better helper than love.

PART ONE

Love

You will be surprised to know that the English word *love* comes from a Sanskrit word *lobha; lobha* means greed. It may have been just a coincidence that the English word *love* grew out of a Sanskrit word that means greed, but my feeling is that it cannot be just coincidence. There must be something more mysterious behind it, there must be some alchemical reason behind it. In fact, greed digested becomes love. It is greed, *lobha*, digested well, which becomes love.

Love is sharing; greed is hoarding. Greed only wants and never gives, and love knows only giving and never asks for anything in return; it is unconditional sharing. There may be some alchemical reason that *lobha* has become *love* in the English language. *Lobha* becomes love as far as inner alchemy is concerned.

CHAPTER ONE

Lovey-Dovey

Love is not what is ordinarily understood by the word. The ordinary love is just a masquerade; something else is hiding behind it. The real love is a totally different phenomenon. The ordinary love is a demand, the real love is a sharing. It knows nothing of demand; it knows the joy of giving.

The ordinary love pretends too much. The real love is nonpretentious; it simply is. The ordinary love becomes almost sickening, syrupy, drippy, what you call "lovey-dovey." It is sickening, it is nauseating. The real love is a nourishment, it strengthens your soul. The ordinary love only feeds your ego—not the real you but the unreal you. The unreal always feeds the unreal, remember; and the real feeds the real.

Become a servant of real love—and that means becoming a servant of love in its ultimate purity. Give, share whatsoever you have, share and enjoy sharing. Don't do it as if it is a duty—then the whole joy is gone. And don't feel that you are obliging the other, never, not even for a single moment. Love never obliges. On the contrary, when somebody receives your love, *you* feel obliged. Love is thankful that it has been received.

Love never waits to be rewarded, even to be thanked. If the thankfulness comes from the other side, love is always surprised—it is a pleasant surprise, because there was no expectation.

You cannot frustrate real love, because there is no expectation in the first place. And you cannot fulfill unreal love because it is so rooted in expectation that whatsoever is done always falls short. Its expectation is too great, nobody can fulfill it. So the unreal love always brings frustration, and the real love always brings fulfillment.

And when I say, "Become a servant of love," I am not saying to become a servant of somebody whom you love, no, not at all. I am not saying to become a servant of a lover. I am saying become a servant of *love*. The pure idea of love should be worshipped. Your lover is only one of the forms of that pure idea, and the whole existence contains nothing but millions of forms of that pure idea. The flower is one idea, one form, the moon another, your lover still another . . . your child, your mother, your father, they are all forms, all waves in the ocean of love. But never become a servant of a lover. Remember always that your lover is only one tiny expression.

Serve love through the lover, so that you never become attached to the lover. And when one is not attached to the lover, love reaches its highest peaks. The moment one is attached, one starts falling low. Attachment is a kind of gravitation—unattachment is grace. Unreal love is another name for attachment; real love is very detached.

Unreal love shows so much concern—it is always concerned. Real love is considerate but has no concern. If you really love a man you will be considerate of his true need but you will not show unnecessary concern for his foolish, stupid fantasies. You will take every care of his needs, but you are not there to fulfill his fictitious desires. You will not fulfill anything that is really going to harm him. For example, you will not fulfill his ego, although his ego will be demanding. The person who is too concerned, attached, will fulfill the ego demands—that means you are poisoning your beloved. Consideration means you will see that this is not a real need but an ego need; you will not fulfill it.

Love knows compassion but no concern. Sometimes it is hard, because sometimes it is needed to be hard. Sometimes it is very aloof. If it helps to be aloof, it is aloof. Sometimes it is very cold; if it is needed to be cold then it is cold. Whatever the need, love is considerate—but not concerned. It will not fulfill any unreal need; it will not fulfill any poisonous idea in the other.

Search into, meditate on love, experiment. Love is the greatest experiment in life, and those who live without experimenting with love energy will never know what life is. They will only remain on the surface without going into the depth of it.

My teaching is love-oriented. I can drop the word *God* very easily—there is no problem—but I cannot drop the word *love*. If I have to choose between the words *love* and *God*, I will choose love; I will forget all about God, because those who know love are bound to know God. But it is not vice versa: Those who think about God and philosophize about God may never know about love—and will never know about God, either.

CHAPTER TWO

Real and Unreal—The First Step

Love yourself and watch—today, tomorrow, always.

We begin with one of the most profound teachings of Gautama the Buddha:

Love yourself.

Just the opposite has been taught to you by all the traditions of the world—all the civilizations, all the cultures, all the churches. They say: *Love others, don't love yourself.* And there is a certain cunning strategy behind their teaching.

Love is the nourishment for the soul. Just as food is to the body, so love is to the soul. Without food the body is weak, without love the soul is weak. And no state, no church, no vested interest has ever wanted people to have strong souls, because a person with spiritual energy is bound to be rebellious.

Love makes you rebellious, revolutionary. Love gives you wings to soar high. Love gives you insight into things, so that nobody can deceive you, exploit you, oppress you. And the priests and the politicians survive only on your blood; they survive only on exploitation.

All the priests and politicians are parasites. To make you spiritually weak they have found a sure method, one hundred percent guaranteed, and that is to teach you not to love yourself. Because if a man cannot love himself he cannot love anybody else, either. The teaching is very tricky—they say, "Love others" . . . because they know that if you cannot love yourself you cannot love at all. But they go on saying, "Love others, love humanity, love God. Love nature, love your wife, your husband, your children, your parents." But don't love yourself—because to love oneself is selfish according to them. They condemn self-love as they condemn nothing else.

And they have made their teaching look very logical. They say, "If you love yourself you will become an egoist; if you love yourself you will become narcissistic." It is not true.

A man who loves himself finds that there is no ego in him. It is by loving others *without* loving yourself, *trying* to love others, that the ego arises. The missionaries, the social reformers, the social servants have the greatest egos in the world—naturally, because they think themselves to be superior human beings. They are not ordinary—ordinary people love themselves. They love others, they love great ideals, they love God.

And all their love is false, because all their love is without any roots.

A man who loves himself takes the first step toward real love. It is like throwing a pebble into a silent lake: The first, circular ripples will arise around the pebble, very close to the pebble—naturally, where else can they arise? And then they will go on spreading; they will reach the farthest shore. If you stop those ripples arising close to the pebble, there will be no other ripples at all. Then you cannot hope to create ripples reaching to the farthest shores; it is impossible.

And the priests and the politicians became aware of the phenomenon: Stop people loving themselves and you have destroyed their capacity to love. Now whatsoever they think is love will be only pseudo. It may be duty, but not love—and duty is a four-letter dirty word. Parents are fulfilling their duties toward their children and then in return, children will fulfill their duties toward their parents. The wife is dutiful toward her husband and the husband is dutiful toward his wife. Where is love?

Love knows nothing of duty. Duty is a burden, a formality. Love is a joy, a sharing; love is informal. The lover never feels that he has done enough; the lover always feels that more was possible. The lover never feels, "I have obliged the other." On the contrary, he feels, "Because my love has been received, I am obliged. <u>The other has obliged me by receiving my gift, by not rejecting it</u>."

The man of duty thinks, "I am higher, spiritual, extraordinary. Look how I serve people!" These servants of the people are the most pseudo people in the world, and the most mischievous, too. If we can get rid of the public servants, humanity will be unburdened, will feel very light, will be able to dance again, sing again.

But for centuries your roots have been cut, poisoned. You have been made afraid of ever being in love with yourself—which is the first step of love, and the first experience. <u>A man who loves himself respects himself</u>. <u>And a man who loves and respects himself respects others, too</u>, because he knows: "Just as I am, so are others. <u>Just as I enjoy love, respect, dignity, so do others</u>." He becomes aware that <u>we are not different as far as the fundamentals are concerned; we are one</u>. We are under the same law. Buddha says we live under the same eternal law— *aes dhammo sanantano*. <u>In the details we may be a little bit different from each other—that brings variety, that is beautiful</u>—but in the foundations we are part of one nature.

The man who loves himself enjoys the love so much, becomes so blissful, that the love starts overflowing, it starts reaching others. It *has* to reach! If you live love, you have to share it. You cannot go on loving yourself forever, because one thing will become absolutely clear to you: that if loving one person, yourself, is so tremendously ecstatic and beautiful, how much more ecstasy is waiting for you if you start sharing your love with many, many people!

Slowly the ripples start reaching farther and farther. You love other people, then you start loving animals, birds, trees, rocks. You can fill the whole universe with your love. A single person is enough to fill the whole universe with love, just as a single pebble can fill the whole lake with ripples—a small pebble.

Only a Buddha can say *Love yourself*. No priest, no politician can agree with it, because this is destroying their whole edifice, their whole structure of exploitation. If a man is not allowed to love himself, his spirit, his soul, becomes weaker and weaker every day. His body may grow but he has no inner growth because he has no inner nourishment. He remains a body almost without a soul or with only a potentiality, a possibility, of a soul. The soul remains a seed—and it will remain a seed if you cannot find the right soil of love for it. And you will not find it if you follow the stupid idea, "Don't love yourself."

I also teach you to love yourself first. It has nothing to do with ego. In fact, love is such a light that the darkness of the ego cannot exist in it at all. If you love others, if your love is focused on others, you will live in darkness. Turn your light toward yourself first, become a light unto yourself first. Let the light dispel your inner darkness, your inner weakness. Let love make you a tremendous power, a spiritual force.

And once your soul is powerful, you know you are not going to die, you are immortal, you are eternal. Love gives you the first insight into eternity. Love is the only experience that transcends time—that's why lovers are not afraid of death. Love knows no death. A single moment of love is more than a whole eternity.

But love has to begin from the very beginning. Love has to start with this first step:

Love Yourself

Don't condemn yourself. You have been condemned so much, and you have accepted all that condemnation. Now you go on doing harm to yourself. Nobody thinks himself worthy enough, nobody thinks himself a beautiful creation of God; nobody thinks that he is needed at all. These are poisonous ideas, but you have been poisoned. You have been poisoned with your mother's milk—and this has been your whole past. Humanity has lived under a dark, dark cloud of self-condemnation. If you condemn yourself, how can you grow? How can you ever become mature? And if you condemn yourself, how can you worship existence? If you cannot worship existence within you, you will become incapable of worshipping existence in others; it will be impossible.

You can become part of the whole only if you have great respect for the God that resides within you. You are a host, God is your guest. By loving yourself you will know this: that God has chosen you to be a vehicle. In choosing you to be a vehicle he has already respected you, loved you. In creating you he has shown his love for you. He has not made you accidentally; he has made you with a certain destiny, with a certain potential, with a certain glory that you have to attain. Yes, God has created man in his own image. Man has to become a God. Unless man becomes a God there is going to be no fulfillment, no contentment.

But how can you become a God? Your priests say that you are a sinner. Your priests say that you are doomed, that you are bound to go to hell. And they make you very much afraid of loving yourself. This is their trick, to cut the very root of love. And they are very cunning people. The most cunning profession in the world is that of the priest. Then he says, "Love others." Now it is going to be plastic, synthetic, a pretension, a performance.

They say, "Love humanity, your mother country, your motherland, life, existence, God." Big words, but utterly meaningless. Have you ever come across humanity? You always come across human beings— and you have condemned the first human being that you came across, that is *you*.

You have not respected yourself, not loved yourself. Now your whole life will be wasted in condemning others. That's why people are such great fault-finders. They find fault with themselves—how can they avoid finding the same faults in others? In fact, they will find them and they will magnify them, they will make them as big as possible. That seems to be the only way out; somehow, to save face, you have to do it. That's why there is so much criticism and such a lack of love.

I say this is one of the most profound sutras of Buddha, and only an awakened person can give you such an insight.

He says, *Love yourself* . . . This can become the foundation of a radical transformation. Don't be afraid of loving yourself. Love totally, and you will be surprised: The day you can get rid of all self-condemnation, self-disrespect—the day you can get rid of the idea of original sin, the day you can think of yourself as worthy and loved by existence—will be a day of great blessing. From that day onward you will start seeing people in their true light, and you will have compassion. And it will not be a cultivated compassion; it will be a natural, spontaneous flow.

And a person who loves himself can easily become meditative, because <u>meditation means being with yourself</u>. If you hate yourself—as you do, as you have been told to do, and you have been following it religiously—if you hate yourself, how can you be with yourself? And meditation is nothing but enjoying your beautiful aloneness. Celebrating yourself; that's what meditation is all about.

Meditation is not a relationship; the other is not needed at all, one is enough unto oneself. One is bathed in one's own glory, bathed in one's own light. <u>One is simply joyous because one is alive, because one *is*.</u>

The greatest miracle in the world is that you are, that I am. <u>To *be* is the greatest miracle</u>—and meditation opens the doors of this great miracle. <u>But only a man who loves himself can meditate;</u> otherwise you are always escaping from yourself, avoiding yourself. Who wants to look at an ugly face, and <u>who wants to penetrate into an ugly being?</u> Who wants to go deep into one's own mud, into one's own darkness? Who wants to enter into the hell that you think you are? You want to keep this whole thing covered up with beautiful flowers and you want always to escape from yourself.

Hence people are continuously seeking company. They can't be with themselves; they want to be with others. People are seeking any type of company; if they can avoid the company of themselves, anything will do. They will sit in a movie house for three hours watching something utterly stupid. They will read a detective novel for hours, wasting their time. They will read the same newspaper again and again just to keep themselves engaged. They will play cards and chess just to kill time— as if they have too much time!

<u>We don't have too much time</u>. <u>We don't have time enough to grow, to be, to rejoice.</u>

But this is one of the basic problems created by a wrong upbringing: <u>you avoid yourself</u>. People are sitting in front of their TVs glued to their chairs, for four, five, even six hours. The average American is watching TV five hours per day, and this disease is going to spread all over the world. And what are you seeing? And what are you getting? Burning your eyes . . .

But this has always been so; even if the TV was not there, there are other things. The problem is the same: how to avoid oneself because one feels so ugly. And who has made you so ugly?—your so-called religious people, your popes, your *shankaracharyas*. They are responsible for distorting your faces—and they have succeeded; they have made everybody ugly.

Each child is born beautiful and then we start distorting his beauty, crippling him in many ways, paralyzing him in many ways, distorting his proportion, making him unbalanced. Sooner or later he becomes so disgusted with himself that he is ready to be with anybody. He may go to a prostitute just to avoid himself.

Love yourself, says Buddha. And this can transform the whole world. It can destroy the whole ugly past. It can herald a new age, it can be the beginning of a new humanity.

Hence my insistence on love—but love begins with you yourself, then it can go on spreading. It goes on spreading of its own accord; you need not do anything to spread it.

Love yourself, says Buddha, and then immediately he adds, *and watch*. That is meditation—that is Buddha's name for meditation. But the first requirement is to love yourself, and *then* watch. If you don't love yourself, and start watching, you may feel like committing suicide! Many Buddhists feel like committing suicide because they don't pay attention to the first part of the sutra. They immediately jump to the second: "Watch yourself." In fact, I have never come across a single commentary on *The Dhammapada,* on these sutras of the Buddha, which has paid any attention to the first part: *Love yourself.*

Socrates says, "Know thyself." Buddha says, "Love thyself" and Buddha is far more true, because unless you love yourself you will never know yourself—knowing comes only later on. Love prepares the ground. Love is the possibility of knowing oneself; love is the right way to know oneself.

I was staying once with a Buddhist monk, Jagdish Kashyap; he is now dead. He was a good man. We were talking about *The Dhammapada* and we came across this sutra, and he started talking about watching, as if he had not read the first part at all. No traditional Buddhist ever pays any attention to the first part; he simply bypasses it.

I said to Bhikshu Jagdish Kashyap, "Wait! You are overlooking something very essential. Watching is the second step and you are making it the first step. It cannot be the first step."

Then he read the sutra again and he said, with mystified eyes, "I have been reading *The Dhammapada* my whole life and I must have read this sutra millions of times. It is my everyday morning prayer to go through *The Dhammapada*, I can repeat it simply from memory, but I have never thought that *'Love yourself'* is the first part of meditation, and watching is the second part."

And this is the case with millions of Buddhists all over the world—and this is the case with neo-Buddhists, also, because in the West Buddhism is now spreading. The time for Buddha has come in the West—now the West is ready to understand Buddha, and the same mistake is being made there, too. Nobody thinks that loving yourself has to be the foundation of knowing yourself, of watching yourself . . . because unless you love yourself you cannot face yourself. You will avoid. Your watching may itself be a way of avoiding yourself.

First: *Love yourself and watch—today, tomorrow, always.*

Create loving energy around yourself. Love your body, love your mind. Love your whole mechanism, your whole organism. By "love" is meant, accept it as it is. Don't try to repress. We repress only when we hate something, we repress only when we are against something. Don't repress, because if you repress, how are you going to watch? And we cannot look eye to eye at the enemy; we can look only in the eyes of our beloved. If you are not a lover of yourself you will not be able to look into your own eyes, into your own face, into your own reality.

Watching is meditation, Buddha's name for meditation. *Watch* is Buddha's watchword. He says: Be aware, be alert, don't be unconscious. Don't behave in a sleepy way. Don't go on functioning like a machine, like a robot. That's how people are functioning.

Mike had just moved into his apartment and decided he should get acquainted with his across-the-hall neighbor. When the door was opened he was delightfully surprised to see a beautiful young blonde bulging out of a skimpy see-through negligee.

Mike looked her squarely in the eye and ad-libbed, "Hi! I am your new sugar across the hall—can I borrow a cup of neighbor?"

People are living unconsciously. They are not aware of what they are saying, what they are doing—they are not watchful. People go on guessing, not seeing; they don't have any insight, they *can't* have. Insight arises only through great watchfulness; then you can see even with closed eyes. Right now you can't see even with open eyes. You guess, you infer, you impose, you project.

Grace lay on the psychiatrist's couch.

"Close your eyes and relax," said the shrink, "and I will try an experiment."

He took a leather key case from his pocket, flipped it open and shook the keys. "What did that sound remind you of?" he asked.

"Sex," she whispered.

Then he closed his key case and touched it to the girl's upturned palm. Her body stiffened.

"And that?" asked the psychiatrist.

"Sex," Grace murmured nervously.

"Now open your eyes," instructed the doctor, "and tell me why what I did was sexually evocative to you."

Hesitantly, her eyelids flickered open. Grace saw the key case in the psychiatrist's hand and blushed scarlet.

"Well—er—to begin with," she stammered, "I thought that first sound was your zipper opening . . ."

Your mind is constantly projecting—projecting itself. Your mind is constantly interfering with reality, giving it a color, shape, and form that are not its own. Your mind never allows you to see that which is; it allows you to see only that which it *wants* to see.

Scientists used to think that our eyes, ears, nose, and our other senses, and the mind, were nothing but openings to reality, bridges to reality. But now the whole understanding has changed. Now they say our senses and the mind are not really openings to reality but guards against it.

Only two percent of reality ever gets through these guards into you; ninety-eight percent of reality is kept outside. And the two percent that reaches you and your being is no longer the same. It has to pass through so many barriers, it has to conform to so many mind things, that by the time it reaches you it is no longer itself.

Meditation means putting the mind aside so that it no longer interferes with reality and you can see things as they are.

Why does the mind interfere at all? Because the mind is created by society. It is society's agent within you; it is not in your service, remember! It is your mind, but it is not in your service; it is in a conspiracy against you. It has been conditioned by society; society has implanted many things in it. It is your mind but it no longer functions as a servant to you, it functions as a servant to society. If you are a Christian then it functions as an agent of the Christian church, if you are a Hindu then your mind is Hindu, if you are a Buddhist your mind is Buddhist. And reality is neither Christian nor Hindu nor Buddhist; reality is simply as it is.

You have to put these minds aside: the communist mind, the fascist mind, the Catholic mind, the Protestant mind . . . There are three thousand religions on the earth—big religions and small religions and very small sects and sects within sects—three thousand in all. So there exist three thousand minds, types of mind—and reality is one, and existence is one, and truth is one!

Meditation means: Put the mind aside and watch. The first step— *love yourself*—will help you tremendously. By loving yourself you will have destroyed much that society has implanted within you. You will have become freer from the society and its conditioning.

And the second step is, *watch*—just watch. Buddha does not say what has to be watched—everything! Walking, watch your walking. Eating, watch your eating. Taking a shower, watch the water, the cold water falling on you, the touch of the water, the coldness, the shiver that goes through your spine—watch everything, *today, tomorrow, always.*

A moment finally comes when you can watch even your sleep. That is the ultimate in watching. The body goes to sleep and there is still a watcher awake, silently watching the body fast asleep. That is the ultimate in watching. Right now just the opposite is the case: Your body is awake but *you* are asleep. Then, *you* will be awake and your body will be asleep.

The body needs rest, but your consciousness needs no sleep. Your consciousness *is consciousness;* it is alertness, that is its very nature. The body tires because the body lives under the law of gravitation. It is gravitation that makes you tired—that's why running fast, you will be tired soon, going upstairs, you will be tired soon, because the gravitation pulls you downward. In fact, to stand is tiring, to sit is tiring—when you lie down flat, horizontal, only then is there a little rest for the body because now you are in tune with the law of gravitation. When you are standing, vertical, you are going against the law; the blood is going toward the head, against the law; the heart has to pump hard.

But consciousness does not function under the law of gravitation; hence it never gets tired. Gravitation has no power over consciousness; it is not a rock, it has no weight. It functions under a totally different law: the law of grace, or, as it is known in the East, the law of levitation. Gravitation means pulling downward, levitation means pulling upward.

The body is continuously being pulled downward—that's why finally it will have to lie down in the grave. That will be the real rest for it, dust unto dust. The body has returned back to its source, the turmoil has ceased, now there is no conflict. The atoms of your body will have real rest only in the grave.

The soul soars higher and higher. As you become more watchful you start having wings—then the whole sky is yours.

Man is a meeting of the earth and the sky, of body and soul.

CHAPTER THREE

The Virtues of Selfishness

If you are not selfish you will not be altruistic, remember. If you are not selfish you will not be unselfish, remember. Only a very deeply selfish person can be unselfish. But this has to be understood because it looks like a paradox.

What is the meaning of being selfish? The first basic thing is to be self-centered. The second basic thing is always to look for one's blissfulness. If you are self-centered, you will be selfish whatsoever you do. You may go and serve people but you will do it only because you enjoy it, because you love doing it, you feel happy and blissful doing it—you feel *yourself* doing it. You are not doing any duty; you are not serving humanity. You are not a great martyr; you are not sacrificing. These are all nonsensical terms. You are simply being happy in your own way— it feels good to you. You go to the hospital and serve the ill people there, or you go to the poor and serve them, but you *love* it. It is how you grow. Deep down you feel blissful and silent, happy about yourself.

A self-centered person is always seeking his happiness. And this is the beauty of it, that the more you seek your happiness the more you will help others to be happy. Because that is the only way to be happy in the world. If everybody else around you is unhappy, you cannot be happy, because man is not an island. He is part of the vast continent. If you want to be happy, you will have to help others who surround you to be happy. Then—and only then—can you be happy.

You have to create the atmosphere of happiness around you. If everybody is miserable, how can you be happy? You will be affected. You are not a stone, you are a very delicate being, very sensitive. If everybody is miserable around you, their misery will affect you. Misery is as infectious as any disease. Blissfulness is also infectious as any disease. If you help others to be happy, in the end you help yourself to be happy. A person who is deeply interested in his happiness is always interested in others' happiness also—but not for them. Deep down he is interested in himself, that's why he helps. If in the world everybody is taught to be selfish, the whole world will be happy. There will be no possibility for misery.

Teach everybody to be selfish—unselfishness grows out of it. Unselfishness is, ultimately, selfishness—it may look unselfish in the beginning, but finally it fulfills *you*. And then happiness can be multiplied: As many as are the people around you that are happy, that much happiness goes on falling on you. You can become superbly happy.

And a happy person is so happy, he wants to be left alone to be happy. He wants his own privacy to be preserved. He wants to live with the flowers and the poetry and the music. Why should he bother to go to wars, be killed and kill others? Why should he be murderous and suicidal? Only unselfish people can do that, because they have never known the bliss that is possible to them. They have never had any experience of what it is to *be*, what it is to celebrate. They have never danced, they have never breathed life. They have not known any divine glimpse; all those glimpses come from deep happiness, from deep satiety, contentment.

An unselfish person is uprooted, uncentered. He is in deep neurosis. He is against nature; he cannot be healthy and whole. He is fighting against the current of life, being, existence—he is trying to be unselfish. He *cannot* be unselfish—because only a selfish person can be unselfish.

When you have happiness you can share it; when you don't have it, how can you share it? To share, in the first place one must have it. An unselfish person is always serious, deep down ill, in anguish. He has missed his own life. And remember, whenever you miss your life you become murderous, suicidal. Whenever a person lives in misery, he would like to destroy.

Misery is destructive; happiness is creative. There is only one creativity and that is of blissfulness, cheerfulness, delight. When you are delighted you want to create something—maybe a toy for children, maybe a poem, maybe a painting, something. Whenever you are too delighted in life, how to express it? You create something—something or other. But when you are miserable you want to crush and destroy something. You would like to become a politician, you would like to become a soldier—you would like to create some situation in which you can be destructive.

That's why every now and then war erupts somewhere on the earth. It is a great disease. And all politicians go on talking about peace—they prepare for war and they talk for peace. In fact they say, "We are preparing for war to preserve peace." Most irrational! If you are preparing for war, how can you preserve peace? To preserve peace one should prepare for peace.

That's why the new generation all over the world is a great danger to the establishment. They are interested only in being happy. They are interested in love, they are interested in meditation, they are interested in music, dance . . . Politicians have become very alert all over the world. The new generation is not interested in politics—rightist or leftist. No, they are not interested at all. They are not communists; they don't belong to any -ism.

A happy person belongs to himself. Why should he belong to any organization? That is the way of an unhappy person: to belong to some organization, to belong to some crowd. Because he has no roots within himself, he does not belong—and that gives him a very, very deep anxiety: He should belong. He creates a substitute belonging. He goes and becomes part of a political party, of a revolutionary party, or anything—a religion. Now he feels he belongs: A crowd is there in which he is rooted.

One should be rooted in oneself because the way from oneself moves deep down into existence. If you belong to a crowd you belong to an impasse; from there no further growth is possible. There comes the end, a cul-de-sac.

So I don't teach you to be unselfish because I know if you are selfish you will be unselfish automatically, spontaneously. If you are not selfish you have missed yourself; now you cannot be in contact with anybody else—the basic contact is missing. The first step has been missed.

Forget about the world and the society and the utopias and Karl Marx. Forget about all this. You are just here for a few years to be. Enjoy, delight, be happy, dance, and love; and out of your love and dancing, out of your deep selfishness will start an overflowing of energy. You will be able to share with others.

Love, I say, is one of the most selfish things.

CHAPTER FOUR

Attached to Nothing

Love is the only freedom from attachment. When you love everything you are attached to nothing.

. . . Man made prisoner by the love of a woman and woman made prisoner by the love of a man are equally unfit for freedom's precious crown. But man and woman made as one by love, inseparable, indistinguishable, are verily entitled to the prize.

—from *The Book of Mirdad*, Mikhail Naimy

The *Book of Mirdad* is my most loved book. Mirdad is a fictitious figure, but each statement and act of Mirdad is tremendously important. It should not be read as a novel, it should be read as a holy scripture— perhaps the only holy scripture.

And you can see in this statement just a glimpse of Mirdad's insight, awareness, understanding. He is saying, *Love is the only freedom from attachment . . .* and you have always heard that love is the only attachment! All the religions agree on that point, that love is the only attachment.

I agree with Mirdad:

Love is the only freedom from attachment. When you love everything you are attached to nothing.

In fact, one has to understand the very phenomenon of attachment. Why do you cling to something? Because you are afraid you will lose it. Perhaps somebody may steal it. Your fear is that what is available to you today may not be available to you tomorrow.

Who knows about what is going to happen tomorrow? The woman you love or the man you love—either movement is possible: You may come closer, you may become distant. You may become again strangers or you may become so one with each other that even to say that you are two will not be right; of course there are two bodies, but the heart is one, and the song of the heart is one, and the ecstasy surrounds you both like a cloud. You disappear in that ecstasy: You are not you, I am not I. Love becomes so total, love is so great and overwhelming, that you cannot remain yourself; you have to drown yourself and disappear.

In that disappearance who is going to be attached, and to whom? Everything *is*. When love blossoms in its totality, everything simply is. The fear of tomorrow does not arise; hence there is no question of attachment, clinging, marriage, of any kind of contract, bondage.

What are your marriages except business contracts? "We commit to each other before a magistrate"—you are insulting love! You are following law, which is the lowest thing in existence, and the ugliest. When you bring love to the court you are committing a crime that cannot be forgiven. You make a commitment before a magistrate in a court that "We want to be married and we will remain married. It is our promise, given to the law: We will not separate and we will not deceive each other." Do you think this is not a great insult to love? Are not you putting law above love?

Law is for those who do not know how to love. Law is for the blind, not for those who have eyes. Law is for those who have forgotten the language of the heart and only know the language of the mind. Mirdad's statement is of such great value that it should be deeply understood— not only intellectually, not only emotionally, but in your totality. Your whole being should drink it:

Love is the only freedom from attachment . . . because when you love you cannot even think of anything else. *When you love everything you are attached to nothing.* Each moment comes with new splendor, new glory, new songs; each moment brings new dances to dance. Perhaps partners may change, but love remains.

Attachment is the desire that the partner should never change. For that you have to commit to the court, to the society—all stupid formalities. And if you go against those formalities you will lose all respect and honor in the eyes of the people amongst whom you have to live.

Love knows nothing of attachment because love knows no possibility of falling from dignity. Love is the very honor itself, the very respectability itself; you cannot do anything against it. I am not saying that partners cannot change, but that it does not matter. If partners change but love remains like a river, flowing, then in fact the world will have much more love than it has today. Today it is just like a tap—drip, drip, drip. It is not able to quench anybody's thirst. Love needs to be oceanic, not the drip, drip of a public tap. And all marriages are public.

Love is universal. Love does not invite only a few people to celebrate, love invites the stars and the sun and the flowers and the birds; the whole existence is welcome to celebrate.

Love does not need anything else—a night full of stars, what more can you ask for? Just a few friends . . . and the whole universe is friendly. I have never come across a tree who was against me. I have been to many mountains, but I have never found any mountain antagonistic. The whole existence is very friendly.

Once your own understanding of love blossoms there is no question of attachment at all. You can go on changing your partners, that does not mean you are deserting anybody. You may come back again to the same partner, there is no question of any prejudice.

Man should understand himself to be just like a child playing on the sea beach, collecting seashells, colored stones, and immensely enjoying, as if he has found a great treasure. If a person can enjoy small things of life, can live in freedom and can allow others to live in freedom, this whole world can become a totally different kind of world. Then it will have a quality of beauty, grace; it will have great luminosity, every heart on fire. And once you know the fire, the flames go on growing. Flames of love grow just like trees grow; flames of love bring flowers and fruits, just as trees do.

But what you think is love is not love. That's why such strange experiences happen. Somebody says to you, "How beautiful you look! I love you so much, there is no woman like you in the whole universe." And you never object, "You have no right to say such things, because you don't know all the women of the whole universe." When such beautiful things are said, one forgets completely the irrationality of them.

These things people learn from films, from novels—all these dialogues and they don't mean anything. They simply mean, "Just come to bed!" But because we are civilized people, without making some introductory remarks, a little preface, you cannot say directly to someone, "Let's go to the bed." The woman will run to the police station to report, "This man is saying something very ugly to me!" But if you go in a civilized way, offer some ice cream first—that cools the heart—bring some roses, talk some sweet nothings . . . Then both understand that finally it has to end up in a morning hangover, a headache, a migraine, and in the morning both will look awkwardly at each other: What were they doing in the bed? One will hide behind the newspaper, as if he is really reading it, and the other will start preparing the tea or coffee, just somehow to forget what happened.

And later on Mirdad says:

Man made prisoner by the love of a woman and woman made prisoner by the love of a man are equally unfit for freedom's precious crown.

The moment love becomes attachment, love becomes a relationship. The moment love becomes demanding, it is a prison. It has destroyed your freedom; you cannot fly in the sky, you are encaged. And one wonders . . . particularly I wonder myself. People wonder about me, what I go on doing alone in my room. And I wonder about them— what do these two people go on doing together? Alone I am at least at ease. If somebody else is there, there is trouble; something is going to happen. If the other is there, the silence cannot remain. The other is going to ask something, say something, do something, or force *you* to do something. Moreover, if the same person goes on continuously, day after day . . .

The man who invented the double bed was one of the greatest enemies of humanity. Even in the bed, no freedom! You cannot move; the other is by the side. And mostly the other takes most of the space. If you can manage a small space you are fortunate—and remember, the other goes on growing. It is a very strange world, where women go on growing and men go on shrinking. And the whole fault is of the man— he makes those women grow fatter, pregnant. More trouble is ahead. Once you put two persons together, a male and a female, soon the third will arrive. If it does not arrive, the neighbors become anxious: "What is the matter? Why is the child not coming?"

I have lived with many people, in many places. I was surprised—why are people so anxious to create trouble for other people? If somebody is unmarried they are worried: "Why don't you get married?"—as if marriage is some universal law that has to be followed. Tortured by everybody, one thinks it is better to get married—at least these people will stop the torture. But you are wrong: Once you get married they start asking, "When is the child coming?"

Now, this is a very difficult problem. It is not in your hands; the child may come, may not come—and will come in its own time. But the people will harass you . . . "A home is not a home without a child." It is true—because a home seems to be a silent temple without a child; with a child, the home seems to be a madhouse! And with many children, troubles go on multiplying.

I am sitting, silent in my room, my whole life. I am not bothering anybody, I have never asked anybody, "Why are you not married, why have you not produced a child?" Because I don't think it is civilized to ask such questions, to make such queries; it is interfering in somebody's freedom.

And people go on living with their wives, with their children—and because the presence of every new member that enters your family is going to disturb many things, you automatically become less and less sensitive. You hear less, you see less, you smell less, you taste less.

You are not using all your senses in their intensity. That's why when somebody falls in love for the first time, you can see his face glow. You can see his walk has a new freshness, a dance in it; you can see his tie is rightly tied, his clothes are well pressed. Something has happened. But it does not last long. Within a week or two the same boredom settles; you see the dust has started gathering again. The light is gone; again he is dragging, not dancing. Flowers are still flowering, but he does not see any beauty. Stars go on provoking him, but he does not look at the sky.

There are millions of people who have never looked upward; their eyes are glued on the earth as if they are afraid that some star will fall on them. There are very few people who would like to sleep under the sky with all the stars—the fear of vastness, aloneness, darkness.

And millions of people go on, deep down feeling that if they had remained alone, if they had never bothered about love and marriage . . . but now nothing can be done. You cannot go back; you cannot be a bachelor again. In fact you may have become so much accustomed to the prison that you cannot leave the prison. It is a kind of safety; it is cozy, although miserable. The blanket is rotten, but the double bed— at least you are not alone in your misery, somebody is sharing it. The fact is, somebody is creating it for you and you are creating it for him or her.

Love has to be of the quality that gives freedom, not new chains for you; a love that gives you wings and supports you to fly as high as possible.

Man and woman made as one by love, inseparable, indistinguishable, are verily entitled to the prize.

This *Book of Mirdad* is one of those books that will live eternally, as long as a single human being survives on the earth. But the man who wrote the book is completely forgotten. Mirdad is a fiction, Mirdad is the name of the hero. The man who wrote the book . . . his name was Mikhail Naimy, but his name does not matter. His book is so great, greater than himself. He himself tried his whole life to create something similar again, but he failed. He has written many other books, but the *Book of Mirdad* is the Everest. The others are small hills, they don't matter much.

If love is understood as the meeting of two souls—not just a sexual, biological meeting of male and female hormones—then love can give you great wings, it can give you great insights into life. And lovers can become for the first time friends. Otherwise they have always been enemies in disguise.

The religions and the so-called saints who have escaped from the world, cowards who cannot face and encounter life, have poisoned the whole idea of love as the only spirituality. They have condemned sex, and with their condemnation of sex they have also condemned love, because people think sex and love are synonymous. They are not. Sex is a very small part of your biological energy. Love is your whole being, love is your soul. You have to learn that sex is simply a need of the society, of the race, to continue itself—you can participate if you want. But you cannot avoid love. The moment you avoid love all your creativity dies and all your senses become insensitive; great dust gathers around you. You become the living dead.

Yes, you breathe and you eat and you talk and you go to the office every day till death comes and releases you from the boredom that you were carrying your whole life.

If sex is all that you have then you don't have anything; then you are just an instrument of biology, of the universe, to reproduce. You are just a machine, a factory. But if you can conceive love as your real being, and loving another person as a deep friendship, as a dance of two hearts together with such synchronicity that they become almost one, you don't need any other spirituality. You have found it.

Love leads to the ultimate experience—called God, called the Absolute, called the Truth. These are only names. In fact the ultimate has no name; it is nameless, but love leads toward it.

If you think only of sex and never become aware of love, then you are going down the drain. Yes, you will produce children and you will live in misery and you will play cards and you will go to see the movie and you will watch football matches and you will have great experiences of utter futility, boredom, war, and a constant undercurrent of anxiety, called by the existentialists, "angst." But you will never know the real beauty of existence, the real silence and peace of the cosmos.

Love can make it possible.

But remember, love knows no boundaries. Love cannot be jealous, because love cannot possess. It is ugly, the very idea that you possess somebody because you love. You possess somebody—it means you have killed somebody and turned him into a commodity.

Only things can be possessed. Love gives freedom. Love is freedom.

QUESTIONS

• *Will you please speak about the difference between a healthy love of oneself and egoistic pride?*

There is a great difference between the two, although they both look very alike. The healthy love of oneself is a great spiritual value. The person who does not love himself will not be able to love anybody else, ever. The first ripple of love has to rise in your heart. If it has not risen for yourself it cannot rise for anybody else, because everybody else is further away from you.

One has to love one's body, one has to love one's soul, one has to love one's totality. And this is natural; otherwise you would not be able to survive at all. And it is beautiful because it beautifies you. The person who loves himself becomes graceful, elegant. The person who loves himself is bound to become more silent, more meditative, more prayerful than the person who does not love himself.

If you don't love your house you will not clean it; if you don't love your house you will not paint it; if you don't love it, you will not surround it with a beautiful garden, with a lotus pond. If you love yourself you will create a garden around yourself. You will try to grow your potential, you will try to bring out all that is in you to be expressed. If you love, you will go on showering yourself, you will go on nourishing yourself.

And if you love yourself you will be surprised: Others will love you. Nobody loves a person who does not love himself. If you cannot even love yourself, who else is going to take the trouble?

And the person who does not love himself cannot remain neutral. Remember, in life there is no neutrality. The man who does not love himself, hates—will have to hate; <u>life knows no</u> <u>neutrality</u>. <u>Life is always a choice</u>. <u>If you don't love, that does not</u> <u>mean that you can simply remain in that not-loving state</u>. <u>No, you</u> <u>will hate</u>. And the person who hates himself becomes destructive. The person who hates himself will hate everybody else—he will be so angry and violent and continuously in rage. The person who hates himself, how can he hope that others will love him? His whole life will be destroyed. To love oneself is a great spiritual value.

I teach self-love. But remember, self-love does not mean egotistical pride, not at all. In fact it means just the opposite. The person who loves himself finds there is no self in him. Love always melts the self—that is one of the alchemical secrets to be learned, understood, experienced. <u>Love always melts the self</u>. Whenever you love, the self disappears. You love a woman, and at least in the few moments when there is real love for the woman, there is no self in you, no ego.

Ego and love cannot exist together. They are like light and darkness: when light comes, darkness disappears. If you love yourself you will be surprised—<u>self-love means the self disappears</u>. In self-love there is no self ever found. That is the paradox: Self-love is utterly selfless. It is not selfish—because whenever there is light there is no darkness, and whenever there is love there is no self. Love melts the frozen self. The self is like an ice cube, love is like the morning sun. The warmth of love . . . and the self starts melting. The more you love yourself the less you will find of the self in you, and then it becomes a great meditation, a great leap into godliness.

And you know it! You may not know it as far as self-love is concerned, because you have not loved yourself. But you have loved other people; glimpses of it must have happened to you. There must have been rare moments when, for a moment, suddenly you were not there and only love was there. Only love energy flowing, from no center, from nowhere to nowhere. When two lovers are sitting together there are two nothingnesses sitting together, two zeros sitting together—and that is the beauty of love, that it makes you utterly empty of the self.

So remember, egoistic pride is never love for oneself. Egoistic pride is just the opposite. The person who has not been able to love himself becomes egoistic. Egoistic pride is what psychoanalysts call the narcissistic pattern of life, narcissism.

You must have heard the parable of Narcissus. He had fallen in love with himself. Looking into a silent pool of water, he fell in love with his own reflection.

Now see the difference: The man who loves himself does not love his reflection, he simply loves *himself*. No mirror is needed; he knows himself from within. Don't you know yourself, that you are? Do you need a proof that you are? Do you need a mirror to prove that you exist? If there were no mirror, would you become suspicious of your existence?

Narcissus fell in love with his own reflection—not with himself. That is not true self-love. He fell in love with the reflection; the reflection is the other. He had become two, he had become divided. Narcissus was split. He was in a kind of schizophrenia. He had become two—the lover and the loved. He had become his own object of love—and that's what happens to so many people who think they are in love.

When you fall in love with a woman, watch, be alert—it may be nothing but narcissism. The woman's face, and her eyes, and her words, may be simply functioning as a lake in which you are seeing your reflection. My own observation is this: Out of a hundred loves, ninety-nine are narcissistic. People don't love the woman that is there. They love the appreciation that the woman is giving to them, the attention that the woman is giving to them, the flattery that the woman is showering on the man. The woman flatters the man, the man flatters the woman—it is a mutual flattery. The woman says, "There is nobody as beautiful as you are. You are a miracle! You are the greatest that God has ever made. Even Alexander the Great was nothing compared to you." And you are puffed up, and your chest becomes doubled, and your head starts swelling—there is nothing but straw, but it starts swelling. And you say to the woman, "You are the greatest creation of God. Even Cleopatra was nothing compared to you. I can't believe that God will ever be able to improve upon you. There will never again be another woman so beautiful."

This is what you call love! This is narcissism—the man becomes the pool of water and reflects the woman, and the woman becomes the pool of water and reflects the man. In fact, the pool not only reflects the truth but decorates it, in a thousand and one ways makes it look more and more beautiful. This is what people call love. This is not love; this is mutual ego-satisfaction.

The real love knows nothing of the ego. The real love starts first as self-love.

Naturally, you have this body, this being, you are rooted in it— enjoy it, cherish it, celebrate it! And there is no question of pride or ego because you are not comparing yourself with anybody. Ego comes only with comparison. Self-love knows no comparison—you are you, that's all. You are not saying that somebody else is inferior to you; you are not comparing at all. Whenever comparison comes, know well it is not love; it is a trick somewhere, a subtle strategy of the ego.

Ego lives through comparison. When you say to a woman, "I love you," it is one thing; when you say to a woman, "Cleopatra was nothing compared to you," it is another—totally another, just the opposite. Why bring Cleopatra in? Can't you love this woman without bringing Cleopatra in? Cleopatra is brought in to puff the ego. Love *this* man—why bring in Alexander the Great?

Love knows no comparison; love simply loves without comparing.

So whenever there is comparison, remember, it is egoistic pride. It is narcissism. And whenever there is no comparison, remember, it is love, whether of oneself or the other.

In real love there is no division. The lovers melt into each other. In egoistic love there is great division, the division of the lover and the loved. In real love there is no relationship. Let me repeat it: In real love there is no relationship, because there are not two persons to be related to. In real love there is only love, a flowering, a fragrance, a melting, a merging. Only in egoistic love are there two persons, the lover and the loved. And whenever there is the lover and the loved, love disappears. Whenever there is love, the lover and the beloved both disappear into love.

Love is such a great phenomenon; you cannot survive in it.

Real love is always in the present. Egoistic love is always either in the past or in the future. In real love there is a passionate coolness. It will look paradoxical, but all greater realities of life are paradoxical; hence I call it passionate coolness. There is warmth, but there is no heat in it. Warmth certainly is there, but there is also coolness in it, a very collected, calm, cool state. Love makes one less feverish. But if it is not real love but egoistic love, then there is great heat. Then the passion is there like fever, there is no coolness at all.

If you can remember these things you will have the criterion for judging. But one has to start with oneself, there is no other way. One has to start from where one is.

Love yourself, love immensely, and in that very love your pride, your ego and all that nonsense, will disappear. And when it has disappeared your love will start reaching to other people. And it will not be a relationship but a sharing. It will not be an object/subject relationship but a melting, a togetherness. It will not be feverish, it will be a cool passion. It will be warm and cool together. It will give you the first taste of the paradox-icalness of life.

■ *Why is love so painful?*

Love is painful because it creates the way for bliss. Love is painful because it transforms; love is mutation. Each transformation is going to be painful because the old has to be left for the new. The old is familiar, secure, safe, the new is absolutely unknown. You will be moving in an uncharted ocean. You cannot use your mind with the new; with the old, the mind is skillful.

The mind can function only with the old; with the new, the mind is utterly useless.

Hence, fear arises. And leaving the old, comfortable, safe world, the world of convenience, pain arises. It is the same pain that the child feels when he comes out of the womb of the mother. It is the same pain that the bird feels when he comes out of the egg. It is the same pain that the bird will feel when he will try for the first time to be on the wing. The fear of the unknown, and the security of the known, the insecurity of the unknown, the unpredictability of the unknown, makes one very much frightened.

And because the transformation is going to be from the self toward a state of no-self, agony is very deep. But you cannot have ecstasy without going through agony. If the gold wants to be purified, it has to pass through fire.

Love is fire.

It is because of the pain of love that millions of people live a loveless life. They, too, suffer, and their suffering is futile. To suffer in love is not to suffer in vain. To suffer in love is creative; it takes you to higher levels of consciousness. To suffer without love is utterly a waste; it leads you nowhere, it keeps you moving in the same vicious circle.

The man who is without love is narcissistic, he is closed. He knows only himself. And how much can he know himself if he has not known the other? because only the other can function as a mirror. You will never know yourself without knowing the other. Love is very fundamental for self-knowledge, too. The person who has not known the other in deep love, in intense passion, in utter ecstasy, will not be able to know who he is, because he will not have the mirror to see his own reflection.

Relationship is a mirror, and the purer the love is, the higher the love is, the better the mirror, the cleaner the mirror. But the higher love needs you to be open. The higher love needs you to be vulnerable. You have to drop your armor; that is painful. You have not to be constantly on guard. You have to drop the calculating mind. You have to risk. You have to live dangerously. The other can hurt you; that is the fear in being vulnerable. The other can reject you; that is the fear in being in love.

The reflection that you will find in the other of your own self may be ugly—that is the anxiety; avoid the mirror! But by avoiding the mirror you are not going to become beautiful. By avoiding the situation you are not going to grow, either. The challenge has to be taken.

One has to go into love. That is the first step toward God, and it cannot be bypassed. Those who try to bypass the step of love will never reach God. That is absolutely necessary, because you become aware of your totality only when you are provoked by the presence of the other, when your presence is enhanced by the presence of the other, when you are brought out of your narcissistic, closed world under the open sky.

Love is an open sky. To be in love is to be on the wing. But certainly, the unbounded sky creates fear.

And to drop the ego is very painful because we have been taught to cultivate the ego. We think the ego is our only treasure. We have been protecting it, we have been decorating it, we have been continuously polishing it. And when love knocks on the door, all that is needed to fall in love is to put aside the ego. Certainly it is painful. It is your whole life's work, it is all that you have created—this ugly ego, this idea that "I am separate from existence."

This idea is ugly because it is untrue. This idea is illusory, but our society exists, is based on this idea that each person is a person, not a presence.

The truth is that there is no person at all in the world; there is only presence. You are not—not as an ego, separate from the whole. You are part of the whole. The whole penetrates you, the whole breathes in you, pulsates in you, the whole is your life.

Love gives you the first experience of being in tune with something that is not your ego. Love gives you the first lesson that you can fall into harmony with someone who has never been part of your ego. If you can be in harmony with a woman, if you can be in harmony with a friend, with a man, if you can be in harmony with your child or with your mother, why can't you be in harmony with all human beings? And if to be in harmony with a single person gives such joy, what will be the outcome if you are in harmony with all human beings? And if you can be in harmony with all human beings, why can't you be in harmony with animals and birds and trees? Then one step leads to another.

Love is a ladder. It starts with one person, it ends with the totality. Love is the beginning, God is the end. To be afraid of love, to be afraid of the growing pains of love, is to remain enclosed in a dark cell. Modern man is living in a dark cell. It is narcissistic—narcissism is the greatest obsession of the modern mind. And then there are problems, which are meaningless. There are problems that are creative because they lead you to higher awareness. There are problems that lead you nowhere; they simply keep you tethered, they simply keep you in your old mess. Love creates problems. You can avoid those problems by avoiding love— but those are very essential problems! They have to be faced, encountered; they have to be lived and gone through and gone beyond. And to go beyond, the way is through. Love is the only real thing worth doing. All else is secondary. If it helps love, it is good. All else is just a means, love is the end. So whatsoever the pain, go into love.

If you don't go into love, as many people have decided, then you are stuck with yourself. Then your life is not a pilgrimage, then your life is not a river going to the ocean; your life is a stagnant pool, dirty, and soon there will be nothing but dirt and mud. To keep clean, one needs to keep flowing. A river remains clean because it goes on flowing. Flow is the process of remaining continuously virgin.

A lover remains a virgin—all lovers are virgin. The people who don't love cannot remain virgin; they become dormant, stagnant; they start stinking sooner or later—and sooner rather than later— because they have nowhere to go. Their life is dead.

That's where modern man finds himself, and because of this, all kinds of neuroses, all kinds of madnesses have become rampant. Psychological illness has taken epidemic proportions. It is no longer that a few individuals are psychologically ill; the reality is the whole earth has become a madhouse. The whole of humanity is suffering from a kind of neurosis, and that neurosis is coming from your narcissistic stagnancy. Everyone is stuck with their own illusion of having a separate self; then people go mad. And this madness is meaningless, unproductive, uncreative. Or people start committing suicide. Those suicides are also unproductive, uncreative.

You may not commit suicide by taking poison or jumping from a cliff or by shooting yourself, but you can commit a suicide which is a very slow process, and that's what happens. Very few people commit suicide suddenly. Others have decided for a slow suicide; gradually, slowly, slowly they die. But the tendency to be suicidal has become almost universal.

This is no way to live. And the reason, the fundamental reason, is that we have forgotten the language of love. We are no longer courageous enough to go into that adventure called love.

Hence people are interested in sex, because sex is not risky. It is momentary, you don't get involved. Love is involvement; it is commitment. It is not momentary. Once it takes roots, it can be forever. It can be a lifelong involvement. Love needs intimacy, and only when you are intimate does the other become a mirror. When you meet sexually with a woman or a man, you have not met at all; in fact, you avoided the soul of the other person. You just used the body and escaped, and the other used your body and escaped. You never became intimate enough to reveal each other's original faces.

Love is the greatest Zen koan.

It is painful, but don't avoid it. If you avoid it you have avoided the greatest opportunity to grow. Go into it, suffer love, because through the suffering comes great ecstasy. Yes, there is agony, but out of the agony, ecstasy is born. Yes, you will have to die as an ego, but if you can die as an ego, you will be born as God, as a buddha.

And love will give you the first tongue-tip-taste of Tao, of Sufism, of Zen. Love will give you the first proof that life is not meaningless. The people who say life is meaningless are the people who have not known love. All that they are saying is that their life has missed love.

Let there be pain, let there be suffering. Go through the dark night, and you will reach a beautiful sunrise. It is only in the womb of the dark night that the sun evolves. It is only through the dark night that the morning comes.

My whole approach is that of love. I teach love and only love and nothing else. You can forget about God; that is just an empty word. You can forget about prayers because they are only rituals imposed by others on you. Love is the natural prayer, not imposed by anybody. You are born with it. Love is the true God—not the God of theologians, but the God of Buddha, Jesus, Mohammed, the God of the Sufis. Love is a device, a method to kill you as a separate individual and to help you become the infinite. Disappear as a dewdrop and become the ocean—but you will have to pass through the door of love.

And certainly when one starts disappearing like a dewdrop, and one has lived long as a dewdrop, it hurts, because one has been thinking, "I am this, and now this is going. I am dying." You are not dying, but only an illusion is dying. You have become identified with the illusion, true, but the illusion is still an illusion. And only when the illusion is gone will you be able to see who you are. And that revelation brings you to the ultimate peak of joy, bliss, celebration.

■ *How is it that the inscription on the Greek temple of Delphi says "Know Thyself" and not "Love Thyself"?*

The Greek mind has an obsession with knowledge. The Greek mind thinks in terms of knowledge, *how to know*. That's why Greeks produced the greatest tradition of philosophers, thinkers, logicians—great rational minds, but the passion is to know.

In the world, as I see it, there are only two types of minds: the

Greek and the Hindu. The Greek mind has a passion to know, and the Hindu mind has a passion to be. The Hindu passion is not too concerned about knowing, but about being. *Sat*, being, is the very search—who am I? Not to know it in a logical way, but to drown in one's own existence so one can taste it, so one can be it—because there is no other way to know, really. If you ask Hindus, they will say there is no other way to know than to be. How can you know love? The only way is to become a lover. Be a lover and you will know. And if you are trying to stand outside the experience and just be an observer, then you may know *about* love, but you will never know love.

The Greek mind has produced the whole scientific growth. Modern science is a by-product of the Greek mind. Modern science insists on being dispassionate, standing outside, watching, unprejudiced. Be objective, be impersonal—these are the basic requirements if you want to become a scientist. Be impersonal, don't allow your emotions to color anything; be dispassionate, almost not interested in any hypothesis in any way. Just watch the fact—don't get involved in it, remain outside. Don't be a participant. This is the Greek passion: a dispassionate search for knowledge.

It has helped, but it has helped only in one direction, the direction of matter. That is the way to know matter. You can never come to know mind that way, only matter. You can never come to know consciousness that way. You can know the outside, you can never know the inside—because in the inside you are already involved. There is no way to stand outside of it, you are already there. The inside is you—how can you get out of it? I can watch a stone, a rock, a river, dispassionately because I am separate. How can I watch myself dispassionately? I am involved in it. I cannot be outside it. I cannot reduce myself to being an object. I will remain the subject, and I will remain the subject—whatsoever I do, I am the knower, I'm not the known.

So the Greek mind shifted, by and by, toward matter. The motto, the inscription at Delphi's temple, *Know Thyself*, became the source of the whole scientific progress. But by and by, the very idea of dispassionate knowledge led the Western mind away from its own being.

The Hindu mind, the other type of mind in the world, has another direction. The direction is of being. In the Upanishads, the great master Udallak says to his son and his disciple Swetketu, "That art thou"—*Tatwamasi*, Swetketu. That art thou—there is no distinction between *that* and *thou*. *That* is your reality; *thou* is the reality—there is no distinction. There is no possibility to know it as you know a rock. There is no possibility to know it as you know other things; you can only *be* it.

On the temple of Delphi, of course it was written *Know Thyself.* It is expressive of the Greek mind. Because the temple is in Greece, the inscription is Greek. If the temple had been in India then the inscription would have been *Be Thyself*—because that art thou. The Hindu mind moved closer and closer to one's own being— that's why it became nonscientific. It became religious, but non-scientific. It became introvert, but then it lost all moorings in the outside world. The Hindu mind became very rich inside, but the outside became very poor.

A great synthesis is needed, a great synthesis between the Hindu and the Greek mind. It can be the greatest blessing for the earth. Up to now it has not been possible, but now the basic require-ments are there and a synthesis is possible. The East and West are meeting in a very subtle way. The Eastern people are going to the West to learn science, to become scientists, and the Western seekers are moving toward the East to learn what religion is. A great min-gling and merging is happening.

In the future, the East is not going to be East and the West is not going to be West. The earth is going to become a global village—a small place where all distinctions will disappear. And then for the first time the great synthesis will arise, the greatest ever—which will not think in extremes, which will not think that if you go outside, if you are a searcher after knowledge then you lose your roots in being; or if you search in your being you lose your roots in the world, in the scientific realm. Both can be together, and whenever this happens a man has both wings and he can fly to the highest sky possible. Otherwise you have only one wing.

As I see it, Hindus are lopsided as much as the Greek mind is lopsided. Both are half of the reality. Religion is half; science is half. Something has to happen to bring religion and science together in a greater whole, where science does not deny religion and where religion does not condemn science.

"How is it that the inscription on the Greek temple to Delphi says *Know Thyself,* and not *Love Thyself?" Love thyself* is possible only if you become thyself, if you *be thyself.* Otherwise it is not possible. Otherwise the only possibility is to go on trying to know who you are, and that too from the outside; watching from the outside who you are, and that too in an objective way, not in an intuitive way.

The Greek mind developed a tremendous logical capacity. Aristotle became the father of all logic and all philosophy. The Eastern mind looks illogical—it is. The very insistence on meditation is illogical because meditation says that you can know only when the mind is dropped, when thinking is dropped and you merge yourself into your being so totally that not even a single thought is there to distract you. Only then can you know. And the Greek mind says you can know only when thinking is clear, logical, rational, systematic. The Hindu mind says, When thinking disappears completely, only then is there any possibility to know. They are totally different, moving in diametrically opposite directions; but there is a possibility to synthesize both.

A person can use his mind when working on matter; then logic is a great instrument. And the same person can put aside the mind when he moves into his meditation chamber and moves into the no-mind. Because mind is not you—it is an instrument just like my hand, just like my legs. If I want to walk I use my legs, if I don't want to walk I don't use my legs. Exactly in the same way you can use the mind logically if you are trying to know about matter. It is perfectly right, it fits there. And when you are moving inward, put it aside. Now legs are not needed; thinking is not needed. Now you need a deep, silent state of no-thought.

And both these things can happen in one person—when I say it, I say it from my own experience. I have been doing both. When it is needed, I can become as logical as any Greek. When it is not needed, I can become as absurd, illogical as any Hindu. So when I say it I mean it, and it is not a hypothesis. I have experienced it that way.

The mind can be used and can be put aside. It is an instrument, a very beautiful instrument; no need to be so obsessed with it. No need to be so fixed, fixated with it. Then it becomes a disease. Just think of a man who wants to sit but cannot sit because he says, "I have legs—how can I sit?" Or, think of a man who wants to keep quiet and silent and cannot keep quiet and silent because he says, "I have a mind." It is the same.

One should become so capable that even the closest instrument of mind can be put aside and can be put off. It can be done, it has been done, but it has not been done on a great scale. But more and more it will be done—this is what I am trying to do here with you. I talk to you, I discuss problems with you—that's logical, that is using the mind. And then I say to you, "Drop the mind and move into deep meditation. If you dance, dance so totally that there is not a single thought inside; your whole energy becomes dance. Or sing, then just sing. Or sit, then just sit—be in Zazen, don't do anything else. Don't allow a single thought to pass through. Just be quiet, absolutely quiet." These are contradictory things.

Every morning you meditate and every morning you come and listen to me. Every morning you listen to me and then you go and meditate. This is contradictory. If I were just Greek, I would talk to you, I would make a logical communication with you, but then I would not say to meditate. That is foolish. If I were just Hindu, there would be no need to talk to you. I can say, "Just go and meditate, because what is the point of talking? One has to become silent." I am both. And this is my hope: that you will also become both—because then life is very enriched, tremendously enriched. Then you don't lose anything. Then everything is absorbed; then you become a great orchestra. Then all polarities meet in you.

For the Greeks, the very idea of "love thyself" would have been absurd, because they would say—and they would say logically—that love is possible only between two persons. You can love somebody else, you can even love your enemy, but how can you love yourself? Only you are there, alone. Love can exist between a duality, a polarity; how can you love yourself? For the Greek mind, the very idea of loving oneself is absurd: For love, the other is needed.

For the Hindu mind, in the Upanishads they say that you love your wife not for your wife's sake; you love your wife just for your own sake. You love yourself through her. Because she gives you pleasure, that's why you love her—but deep down, you love your own pleasure. You love your son, you love your friend, not because of them but because of you. Deep down your son makes you happy, your friend gives you solace. That's what you are hankering for. So the Upanishads say that you love yourself, really. Even if you say that you love others, that is just a *via media* to love yourself, a long, roundabout way to love yourself.

Hindus say that there is no other possibility; you can love only yourself. And Greeks say there is no possibility to love oneself because at least two are needed.

If you ask me, I'm both Hindu and Greek. If you ask me I will say love is a paradox. It is a very paradoxical phenomenon. Don't try to reduce it to one pole; both polarities are needed. The other is needed, but in deep love the other disappears. If you watch two lovers, they are two and one together. That's the paradox of love, and that's the beauty of it—they are two, yes, they are two; and yet they are not two, they are one. If this oneness has not happened then love is not possible. They may be doing something else in the name of love. If they are still two and not one also, then love has not happened. And if you are just alone and there is nobody else, then too love is not possible.

Love is a paradoxical phenomenon. It needs two in the first place, and in the last place it needs two to exist as one. It is the greatest enigma; it is the greatest puzzle.

■ *How can I love better?*

Love is enough unto itself. It needs no betterment. It is perfect as it is; it is not in any way meant to be more perfect. The very desire shows a misunderstanding about love and its nature. Can you have a perfect circle? All circles are perfect; if they are not perfect, they are not circles. Perfection is intrinsic to a circle and the same is the law about love. You cannot love less, and you cannot love more—because it is not a quantity. It is a quality, which is immeasurable.

Your very question shows that you have never tasted what love is, and you are trying to hide your lovelessness in the desire of knowing "how to love better." No one who knows love can ask this question.

Love has to be understood, not as a biological infatuation—that is lust. That exists in all the animals; there is nothing special about it; it exists even in trees. It is nature's way of reproduction. There is nothing spiritual in it and nothing especially human. So the first thing is to make a clear-cut distinction between lust and love. Lust is a blind passion; love is the fragrance of a silent, peaceful, meditative heart. Love has nothing to do with biology or chemistry or hormones.

Love is the flight of your consciousness to higher realms, beyond matter and beyond body. The moment you understand love as something transcendental, then love is no longer a fundamental question. The fundamental question is how to transcend the body, how to know something within you that is beyond—beyond all that is measurable. That is the meaning of the word *matter.* It comes from a Sanskrit root, *matra,* which means measurement; it means that which can be measured. The word *meter* comes from the same root. The fundamental question is how to go beyond the measurable and enter into the immeasurable. In other words, how to go beyond matter and open your eyes toward more consciousness. And there is no limit to consciousness—the more you become conscious, the more you realize how much more is possible ahead. As you reach one peak, another peak arises in front of you. It is an eternal pilgrimage.

Love is a by-product of a rising consciousness. It is just like the fragrance of a flower. Don't search for it in the roots; it is not there. Your biology is your roots; your consciousness is your flowering. As you become more and more an open lotus of consciousness, you will be surprised—taken aback—with a tremendous experience, which can only be called love. You are so full of joy, so full of bliss, each fiber of your being is dancing with ecstasy. You are just like a rain cloud that wants to rain and shower.

The moment you are overflowing with bliss, a tremendous longing arises in you to share it. That sharing is love.

Love is not something that you can get from someone who has not attained to blissfulness—and this is the misery of the whole world. Everybody is asking to be loved, and pretending to love. You cannot love because you don't know what consciousness is. You don't know the *satyam*, the *shivam*, the *sundram*; you don't know truth, you don't know the experience of the divine, and you don't know the fragrance of beauty. What have you got to give? You are so empty, you are so hollow . . . Nothing grows in your being, nothing is green. There are no flowers within you; your spring has not come yet.

Love is a by-product. When the spring comes and you suddenly start flowering, blossoming, and you release your potential fragrance—sharing that fragrance, sharing that grace, sharing that beauty is love.

I don't want to hurt you but I am helpless, I have to say the truth to you: You don't know what love is. You can't know because you have not yet gone deeper in your consciousness. You have not experienced yourself, you know nothing of who you are. In this blindness, in this ignorance, in this unconsciousness, love does not grow. This is a desert in which you are living. In this darkness, in this desert, there is no possibility of love blossoming.

First you have to be full of light, and full of delight—so full that you start overflowing. That overflowing energy is love. Then love is known as the greatest perfection in the world. It is never less, and never more.

But our very upbringing is so neurotic, so psychologically sick that it destroys all possibilities of inner growth. You are being taught from the very beginning to be a perfectionist, and then naturally you go on applying your perfectionist ideas to everything, even to love.

Just the other day I came across a statement: *A perfectionist is a person who takes great pains, and gives even greater pains to others.* And the outcome is just a miserable world!

Everybody is trying to be perfect. And the moment somebody starts trying to be perfect, he starts expecting everybody else to be perfect. He starts condemning people, he starts humiliating people. That's what all your so-called saints have been doing down the ages. That's what your religions have done to you—poisoned your being with an idea of perfection.

Because you cannot be perfect, you start feeling guilty, you lose respect for yourself. And the man who has lost respect for himself has lost all the dignity of being human. Your pride has been crushed, your humanity has been destroyed by beautiful words like perfection.

Man cannot be perfect. Yes, there is something that man can experience, but which is beyond the ordinary conception of man. Unless man also experiences something of the divine, he cannot know perfection.

Perfection is not something like a discipline; it is not something that you can practice. It is not something for which you have to go through rehearsals. But that is what is being taught to everybody, and the result is a world full of hypocrites, who know perfectly well that they are hollow and empty, but they go on pretending all kinds of qualities that are nothing but empty words.

When you say to someone, "I love you," have you ever thought what you mean? Is it just biological infatuation between the two sexes? Then once you have satisfied your animal appetite all so-called love will disappear. It was just a hunger and you have fulfilled your hunger and you are finished. The same woman who was looking the most beautiful in the world, the same man who was looking like Alexander the Great—you start thinking how to get rid of this fellow!

It will be very enlightening to understand this letter written by Paddy to his beloved Maureen:

My Darling Maureen,
   I would climb the highest mountain for your sake, and swim the wildest sea. I would endure any hardships to spend a moment by your side.
Your ever-loving, Paddy.
P.S. I'll be over to see you on Friday night if it is not raining.

The moment you say to someone "I love you," you don't know what you are saying. You don't know that it is just lust hiding behind a beautiful word, love. It will disappear. It is very momentary.

Love is something eternal. It is the experience of the buddhas, not the unconscious people the whole world is full of. Only very few people have known what love is, and these same people are the most awakened, the most enlightened, the highest peaks of human consciousness.

If you really want to know love, forget about love and remember meditation. If you want to bring roses into your garden, forget about roses and take care of the rosebush. Give nourishment to it, water it, take care that it gets the right amount of sun, water. If everything is taken care of, in the right time the roses are destined to come. You cannot bring them earlier, you cannot force them to open up sooner. And you cannot ask a rose to be more perfect.

Have you ever seen a rose that is not perfect? What more do you want? Every rose in its uniqueness is perfect. Dancing in the wind, in the rain, in the sun . . . can't you see the tremendous beauty, the absolute joy? A small ordinary rose radiates the hidden splendor of existence.

Love is a rose in your being. But prepare your being—dispel the darkness and the unconsciousness. Become more and more alert and aware, and love will come on its own accord, in its own time. You need not worry about it. And whenever it comes it is always perfect.

Love is a spiritual experience—nothing to do with sexes and nothing to do with bodies, but something to do with the innermost being. But you have not even entered into your own temple. You don't know at all who you are, and you are trying to find out how to love better. First, be thyself; first, know thyself, and love will come as a reward. It is a reward from the beyond. It showers on you like flowers . . . fills your being. And it goes on showering on you, and it brings with it a tremendous longing to share.

In human language that sharing can only be indicated by the word *love*. It does not say much, but it indicates the right direction.

Love is a shadow of alertness, of consciousness. Be more conscious, and love will come as you become more conscious. It is a guest that comes, that comes inevitably to those who are ready and prepared to receive it. You are not even ready to recognize it! If love comes to your door, you will not recognize it. If love knocks on your doors, you may find a thousand and one excuses; you may think perhaps it is some strong wind, or some other excuse; you will not open the doors. And even if you open the doors you will not recognize love because you have never seen love before; how can you recognize it?

You can recognize only something that you know. When love

comes for the first time and fills your being you are absolutely overwhelmed and mystified. You don't know what is happening. You know your heart is dancing, you know you are surrounded by celestial music, you know fragrances that you have never known before. But it takes a little time to put all these experiences together and to remember that perhaps this is what love is. Slowly, slowly it sinks into your being.

Only mystics know love. Other than mystics there is no category of human beings that has ever experienced love. Love is absolutely the monopoly of the mystic. If you want to know love you will have to enter into the world of the mystic.

Jesus says "God is love." He has been part of a mystery school, the Essenes, an ancient school of mystics. But perhaps he did not graduate from the mystery school, because what he is saying is just not right. God is not love, love is God—and the difference is tremendous; it is not just a change of words. The moment you say God is love you are simply saying that love is only an attribute of God. He is also wisdom, he is also compassion, he is also forgiveness, he can be millions of things besides love; love is only one of the attributes of God.

And in fact, even to make it a small attribute of God is very irrational and illogical, because if God is love then he cannot be "just." If God is love then he cannot be cruel enough to throw sinners into eternal hell. If God is love then God cannot be the law. One great Sufi mystic, Omar Khayyam, shows more understanding than Jesus when he says, "I will go on just being myself. I am not going to take any notice of the priests and the preachers because I trust that God's love is great enough; I cannot commit a sin that can be greater than his love. So why be worried? Our hands are small and our sins are small. Our reach is small; how can we commit sins which God's love cannot forgive? If God is love then he cannot be present on the last judgment day to sort out the saints and throw the remaining millions and millions of people into hell for eternity."

The teachings of the Essenes were just the opposite; Jesus quotes them wrongly. Perhaps he was not very deeply rooted in their teachings. Their teaching was, "Love is God." That is such a tremendous difference. Now God becomes only an attribute of love; now God becomes only a quality of the tremendous experience of love. Now God is no longer a person but only an experience of those who have known love. Now God becomes secondary to love. And I say unto you, the Essenes were right. Love is the ultimate value, the final flowering. There is nothing beyond it; hence, you cannot perfect it.

In fact, before you attain to it you will have to disappear. When love will be there you will not be there.

A great Eastern mystic, Kabir, has a very significant statement— a statement that can be made only by one who has experienced, who has realized, who has entered the inner sanctum of ultimate reality. The statement is, "I had been searching for truth, but it is strange to say that as long as the searcher was there, truth was not found. And when the truth was found, I looked all around . . . I was absent. When the truth was found, the seeker was no more; and when the seeker was, truth was nowhere."

Truth and the seeker cannot exist together. You and love cannot exist together. There is no coexistence possible: Either you or love, you can choose. If you are ready to disappear, melt and merge, leaving only a pure consciousness behind, love will blossom. You cannot perfect it because you will not be present. And it does not need perfection in the first place; it comes always as perfect.

But love is one of those words that everybody uses and nobody understands. Parents are telling their children, "We love you"— and they are the people who destroy their children. They are the people who give their children all kinds of prejudices, all kinds of dead superstitions. They are the people who burden their children with the whole load of rubbish that generations have been carrying and each generation goes on transferring it to another generation. The madness goes on . . . becoming mountainous.

Yet all parents think they love their children. If they really loved their children, they would not like their children to be their images, because they are just miserable and nothing else. What is their experience of life? Pure misery, suffering . . . life has been not a blessing to them, but a curse. And still they want their children to be just like themselves.

I was a guest in a family. I was sitting in their garden in the evening. The sun was setting and it was a beautiful, silent evening. The birds were returning back to the trees, and the small child of the family was sitting by my side. I just asked him, "Do you know who you are?" And children are clearer, more perceptive than the grownups, because the grownups are already spoiled, corrupted, polluted with all kinds of ideologies, religions. That small child looked at me and he said, "You are asking me a very difficult question."

I said, "What is the difficulty in it?"

He said, "The difficulty is that I am the only child of my parents, and as long as I can remember, whenever some guests come, somebody says my eyes look like my father's, somebody says my nose looks like my mother's, somebody says my face looks like my uncle's. So I don't know who I am, because nobody says anything looks like me."

But this is what is being done to every child. You don't leave the child alone to experience himself, and you don't leave the child to become himself. You go on loading on the child your own unfulfilled ambitions. Every parent wants his child to be his image.

But a child has a destiny of his own; if he becomes your image he will never become himself. And without becoming yourself, you will never feel contentment; you will never feel at ease with existence. You will always be in a condition of missing something.

Your parents love you, and they also tell you that you have to love them because they are your fathers, they are your mothers. It is a strange phenomenon and nobody seems to be aware of it. Just because you are a mother does not mean that the child has to love you. You have to be lovable; your being a mother is not enough. You may be a father, but that does not mean that automatically you become lovable. Just because you are a father does not create a tremendous feeling of love in the child. But it is expected . . . and the poor child does not know what to do. He starts pretending; that's the only possible way. He starts smiling when there is no smile in his heart; he starts showing love, respect, gratitude—and all are just false. He becomes an actor, a hypocrite from the very beginning, a politician.

We are all living in this world where parents, teachers, priests—everybody has corrupted you, displaced you, has taken away from yourself. My effort is to give your center back to you. I call this centering "meditation." I want you simply to be yourself, with a great self-respect, with the dignity of knowing that existence needed you—and then you can start searching for yourself. First come to the center, and then start searching for who you are.

Knowing one's original face is the beginning of a life of love, of a life of celebration. You will be able to give so much love—because it is not something that is exhaustible. It is immeasurable, it cannot be exhausted. And the more you give it, the more you become capable of giving it.

The greatest experience in life is when you simply give without any conditions, without any expectations of even a simple thank-you. On the contrary, a real, authentic love feels obliged to the person who has accepted his love. He could have rejected it.

When you start giving love with a deep sense of gratitude to all those who accept it, you will be surprised that you have become an emperor—no longer a beggar asking for love with a begging bowl, knocking on every door. And those people on whose doors you are knocking cannot give you love; they are themselves beggars. Beggars are asking each other for love and feeling frustrated, angry, because the love is not coming. But this is bound to happen. Love belongs to the world of emperors, not of beggars. And a man is an emperor when he is so full of love that he can give it without any conditions.

Then comes an even greater surprise: When you start giving your love to anybody, even to strangers, the question is not to whom you are giving it—the very joy of giving is so much that who cares who is on the receiving end? When this space comes into your being, you go on giving to each and everybody—not only to human beings but to animals, to the trees, to the faraway stars, because love is something that can be transferred even to the farthest star just by your loving look. Just by your touch, love can be transferred to a tree. Without saying a single word . . . it can be conveyed in absolute silence. It need not be said, it declares itself. It has its own ways of reaching into the very depths, into your being.

First be full of love, then the sharing happens. And then the great surprise . . . that as you give, you start receiving from unknown sources, from unknown corners, from unknown people, from trees, from rivers, from mountains. From all nooks and corners of existence love starts showering on you. The more you give, the more you get. Life becomes a sheer dance of love.

PART TWO

From Relationship to Relating

The moment you feel you are <u>no longer dependent</u> on any-one, a deep coolness and a deep silence settles inside, <u>a re-laxed let-go</u>. <u>It does not mean you stop loving</u>. On the contrary, for the first time you know a new quality, a new dimension of love—a love that is no longer biological, a love that is closer to friendliness than any relationship. That's why I am not even using the word friendship, because that "ship" has drowned so many people.

CHAPTER FIVE

The Honeymoon that Never Ends

Love is not a relationship. Love relates, but it is not a relationship. A relationship is something finished. A relationship is a noun; the full stop has come, the honeymoon is over. Now there is no joy, no enthusiasm, now all is finished. You can carry it on, just to keep your promises. You can carry it on because it is comfortable, convenient, cozy. You can carry it on because there is nothing else to do. You can carry it on because if you disrupt it, it is going to create much trouble for you . . . Relationship means something complete, finished, closed.

Love is never a relationship; <u>love is relating</u>. It is always a river, flowing, unending. Love knows no full stop; the honeymoon begins but never ends. It is not like a novel that starts at a certain point and ends at a certain point. It is an ongoing phenomenon. Lovers end, love continues—it is a continuum. It is a verb, not a noun.

And why do we reduce the beauty of relating to relationship? Why are we in such a hurry? Because to relate is insecure, and relationship is a security. Relationship has a certainty; relating is just a meeting of two strangers, maybe just an overnight stay and in the morning we say good-bye. Who knows what is going to happen tomorrow? And we are so afraid that we want to make it certain, we want to make it predictable. We would like tomorrow to be according to our ideas; we don't allow it freedom to have its own say. So we immediately reduce every verb to a noun.

You are in love with a woman or a man and immediately you start thinking of getting married. Make it a legal contract. Why? How does the law come into love? The law comes into love because love is not there. It is only a fantasy, and you know the fantasy will disappear. Before it disappears settle down, before it disappears do something so it becomes impossible to separate.

In a better world, with more meditative people, with a little more enlightenment spread over the earth, people will love, love immensely, but their love will remain a relating, not a relationship. And I am not saying that their love will be only momentary. There is every possibility their love may go deeper than your love, may have a higher quality of intimacy, may have something more of poetry and more of godliness in it. And there is every possibility their love may last longer than your so-called relationship ever lasts. But it will not be guaranteed by the law, by the court, by the policeman. The guarantee will be inner. It will be a commitment from the heart, it will be a silent communion.

If you enjoy being with somebody, you would like to enjoy it more and more. If you enjoy the intimacy, you would like to explore the intimacy more and more. And there are a few flowers of love that bloom only after long intimacies. There are seasonal flowers, too; within six weeks they are there, in the sun, but within six weeks again they are gone forever. There are flowers that take years to come, and there are flowers that take *many* years to come. The longer it takes, the deeper it goes. But it has to be a commitment from one heart to another heart. It has not even to be verbalized, because to verbalize it is to profane it. It has to be a silent commitment; eye to eye, heart to heart, being to being. It has to be understood, not said.

Forget relationships and learn how to relate.

Once you are in a relationship you start taking each other for granted—that's what destroys all love affairs. The woman thinks she knows the man, the man thinks he knows the woman. Nobody knows either! It is impossible to know the other, the other remains a mystery. And to take the other for granted is insulting, disrespectful.

To think that you know your wife is very, very ungrateful. How can you know the woman? How can you know the man? They are processes, they are not things. The woman that you knew yesterday is not there today. So much water has gone down the Ganges; she is somebody else, totally different. Relate again, start again, don't take it for granted.

And the man that you slept with last night, look at his face again in the morning. He is no more the same person, so much has changed. So much, incalculably much has changed. That is the difference between a thing and a person. The furniture in the room is the same, but the man and the woman, they are no more the same. Explore again, start again. That's what I mean by relating.

Relating means you are always starting, you are continuously trying to become acquainted. Again and again, you are introducing yourself to each other. You are trying to see the many facets of the other's personality. You are trying to penetrate deeper and deeper into his realm of inner feelings, into the deep recesses of his being. You are trying to unravel a mystery that cannot be unraveled. That is the joy of love: the exploration of consciousness.

And if you relate, and don't reduce it to a relationship, then the other will become a mirror to you. Exploring him, unawares you will be exploring yourself, too. Getting deeper into the other, knowing his feelings, his thoughts, his deeper stirrings, you will be knowing your own deeper stirrings, too. Lovers become mirrors to each other, and then love becomes a meditation.

Relationship is ugly, relating is beautiful.

In relationship both persons become blind to each other. Just think, how long has it been since you saw your wife eye to eye? How long has it been since you looked at your husband? Maybe years. Who looks at one's own wife? You have already taken it for granted that you know her; what more is there to look at? You are more interested in strangers than in the people you know—you know the whole topography of their bodies, you know how they respond, you know everything that has happened is going to happen again and again. It is a repetitive circle.

It is not so, it is not really so. Nothing ever repeats; everything is new every day. Just your eyes become old, your assumptions become old, your mirror gathers dust and you become incapable of reflecting the other.

Hence I say relate. By saying relate, I mean remain continuously on a honeymoon. Go on searching and seeking each other, finding new ways of loving each other, finding new ways of being with each other. And each person is such an infinite mystery, inexhaustible, unfathomable, that it is not possible that you can ever say, "I have known her," or, "I have known him." At the most you can say, "I have tried my best, but the mystery remains a mystery."

In fact the more you know, the more mysterious the other becomes. Then love is a constant adventure.

CHAPTER SIX

From Lust to Love to Loving

Love is almost impossible in the ordinary state of the human mind. Love is possible only when one has attained to being, not before. Before that it is always something else. We go on calling it love but sometimes it is almost stupid to call it love.

A person falls in love with a woman because he likes the way she walks, or her voice, or the way she says "hello" or her eyes. Just the other day I was reading that some woman said about a man, "He has the most beautiful eyebrows in the world." Nothing is wrong in it—eyebrows can be beautiful—but if you fall in love with eyebrows then sooner or later you will be disappointed, because eyebrows are a very nonessential part of the person.

And for such nonessential things people fall in love! The shape, the eyes . . . these are nonessential things. Because when you live with a person, you are not living with a proportion of the body; you are not living with the eyebrows or the color of the hair. When you live with a person, a person is a very great and vast thing . . . almost indefinable, and these small things on the periphery sooner or later become meaningless. But then suddenly one is surprised: What to do?

Every love starts in a romantic way. By the time the honeymoon is finished, the whole thing is finished because one cannot live with romance. One has to live with reality—and the reality is totally different. When you see a person, you don't see the person's totality; you just see the surface. It is as if you have fallen in love with a car because of its color. You have not even looked under the bonnet; there may be no engine at all, or maybe something is defective. The color is not going to help, finally.

When two persons come together, their inside realities clash and the outer things become meaningless. What to do with eyebrows, and with hair and the hairstyle? You almost start forgetting them. They no longer attract you because they are there. And the more you know the person, the more you become afraid because then you come to know the madness of the person, and the other person comes to know your madness. Then both feel cheated and both become angry. Both start taking revenge on the other, as if the other has been deceiving or cheating. Nobody is cheating anybody, although everybody is cheated.

One of the most basic things to realize is that when you love a person, you love because the person is not available. Now the person is available, so how can the love exist?

You wanted to become rich because you were poor—the whole desire to become rich was because of your poverty. Now you are rich, you don't care. Or think of it in another way. You are hungry, so you are obsessed with food. But when you are feeling well and your stomach is full, who bothers? Who thinks about food?

The same happens with your so-called love. You are chasing a woman and the woman goes on withdrawing herself, escaping from you. You become more and more heated up, and then you chase her more. And that's part of the game. Every woman knows intrinsically that she has to escape, so the chase is continued. Of course she is not to escape so much that you forget all about her—she has to remain in view, alluring, fascinating, calling, inviting and yet escaping.

So first the man runs after the woman and the woman tries to escape. Once the man has caught the woman, immediately the whole tide turns. Then the man starts escaping and the woman starts chasing—"Where are you going? With whom were you talking? Why are you late? With whom have you been?"

And the whole problem is that both were attracted to each other because they were unknown to each other. The unknown was the attraction, the unfamiliar was the attraction. Now both know each other well. They have made love to each other many times and now it has become almost a repetition—at the most it is a habit, a relaxation, but the romance is gone. Then they feel bored. The man becomes a habit, the woman becomes a habit. They cannot live without each other because of the habit, and they cannot live together because there is no romance.

This is the real point where one has to understand whether it was love or not. And one should not deceive oneself; one should be clear. If it was love, or if even a fragment of it was love, these things will pass. Then one should understand that these are natural things. There is nothing to be angry about. And you still love the person. Even if you know the person, you still love him or her.

In fact if love is there, you love the person more because you know. If love is there, it survives. If it is not there it disappears. Both are good.

To an ordinary state of mind, what I call love is not possible. It happens only when you have a very integrated being. Love is a function of the integrated being. It is not romance, it has nothing to do with these foolish things. It goes directly to the person and looks into the soul. Love then is a sort of affinity with the innermost being of the other person—but then it is totally different. Every love can grow into it, should grow into it, but ninety-nine out of a hundred loves never grow to that point. The turmoils and troubles are so great that they can destroy everything.

But I am not saying that one has to cling. One has to be alert and aware. If your love consists of just these foolish things, it will disappear. It is not worth bothering about. But if it is real, then through all turmoils it will survive. So just watch . . .

Love is not the question. Your awareness is the question. This may be just a situation in which your awareness will grow and you will become more alert about yourself. Maybe this love disappears but the next love will be better; you will choose with a better consciousness. Or maybe this love, with a better consciousness, will change its quality. So whatsoever happens, one should remain open.

Love has three dimensions. One is animal-like; it is only lust, a physical phenomenon. The other is manlike; it is higher than lust, than sexuality, than sensuality. It is not just exploitation of the other as a means. The first is only an exploitation; the other is used as a means in the first. In the second the other is not used as a means, the other is equal to you. The other is as much an end unto herself or himself as you are, and love is not an exploitation but a mutual sharing of your being, of your joys, of your music, of your pure poetry of life. It is sharing and mutual.

The first is possessive, the second is nonpossessive. The first creates a bondage, the second gives freedom. And the third dimension of love is godly, godlike: when there is no object to love, when love is not a relationship at all, when love becomes a state of your being. You are simply loving—not in love with somebody in particular, but simply a state of love, so whatsoever you do, you do it lovingly; whomsoever you meet, you meet lovingly. Even if you touch a rock, you touch the rock as if you are touching your beloved; even if you look at the trees, your eyes are full of love.

The first uses the other as a means; in the second, the other is no longer a means; in the third the other has completely disappeared. The first creates bondage, the second gives freedom, the third goes beyond both; it is transcendence of all duality. There is no lover and no beloved, there is only love.

That's the ultimate state of love, and that's the goal of life to be attained. The majority of people remain confined to the first. Only very rare people enter into the second, and rarest is the phenomenon I am calling the third. Only a Buddha, a Jesus . . . There are a few people here and there, they can be counted on one's fingers, who have entered the third dimension of love. But if you keep your eyes fixed on the faraway star, it is possible. And when it becomes possible, you are fulfilled. Then life lacks nothing, and in that fulfillment is joy, eternal joy. Even death cannot destroy it.

CHAPTER SEVEN

Let There Be Spaces...

In Kahlil Gibran's *The Prophet*, Almustafa says:

Let there be spaces in your togetherness.
And let the winds of heavens dance between you.
Love one another, but make not a bond of love:
Let it rather be a moving sea between the shores of your souls.

If your togetherness is not out of lust, your love is going to deepen every day. Lust lessens everything, because biology is not interested in whether you remain together or not. Its interest is reproduction; for that, love is not needed. You can go on producing children without any love.

I have been observing all kinds of animals. I have lived in forests, in mountains, and I was always puzzled—whenever they are making love they look very sad. I have never seen animals making love joyfully; it is as if some unknown force is pressuring them to do it. It is not out of their own choice; it is not their freedom but their bondage. That makes them sad.

The same I have observed in man. Have you seen a husband and wife on the road? You may not know whether they are husband and wife, but if they are both sad you can be certain they are.

I was traveling from Delhi to Srinagar. In my air-conditioned compartment there were only two seats, and one was reserved for me. A couple came, a beautiful woman and a young, beautiful man. Both could not be accommodated in that small coupe, so he left the woman and he went into another compartment. But he was coming at every station, bringing sweets, fruits, flowers.

I was watching the whole scene. I asked the woman, "How long have you been married?"

She said, "It must have been seven years."

I said, "Don't lie to me! You can deceive anybody else, but you cannot deceive me. You are not married."

She was shocked. From a stranger, who had not spoken . . . who had simply been watching. She said, "How did you come to know?"

I said, "There is nothing in it, it is simple. If he were your husband, then once he had disappeared, if he had come back at the station where you were going to get off, you would be fortunate!"

She said, "You don't know me, I don't know you. But what you are saying is right. He's my lover. He's my husband's friend."

I said, "Then everything makes sense . . ."

What goes wrong between husbands and wives? It is not love, and everybody has accepted it as if he knows what love is. It is pure lust. Soon you are fed up with each other. Biology has tricked you for reproduction and soon there is nothing new—the same face, the same geography, the same topography. How many times have you explored it? The whole world is sad because of marriage, and the world still remains unaware of the cause.

Love is one of the most mysterious phenomena. About that love, Almustafa is speaking. You cannot be bored, because it is not lust.

Almustafa says, *Let there be spaces in your togetherness.*

Be together but do not try to dominate, do not try to possess and do not destroy the individuality of the other.

When you live together, *let there be spaces* . . . The husband comes home late; there is no need, no necessity for the wife to inquire where he has been, why he's late. He has his own space, he's a free individual. Two free individuals are living together and nobody encroaches on each other's spaces. If the wife comes late, there is no need to ask "Where have you been?" Who are you?—she has her own space, her own freedom.

But this is happening every day, in every home. Over small matters they are fighting, but deep down the point is that they are not ready to allow the other to have his own space.

Likings are different. Your husband may like something, you may not like it. That does not mean that it is the beginning of a fight, that because you are husband and wife, your likings should also be the same. And all these questions . . . every husband returning home goes on in his mind, "What is she going to ask? How am I going to answer?" And the woman knows what she's going to ask and what he's going to answer, and all those answers are fake, fictitious. He's cheating her.

What kind of love is this, that is always suspicious, always afraid of jealousies? If the wife sees you with some other woman—just laughing, talking—that's enough to destroy your whole night. You will repent; this is too much just for a little laughter. If the husband sees the wife with another man and she seems to be more joyous, more happy, this is enough to create turmoil.

People are unaware that they don't know what love is. Love never suspects, love is never jealous. Love never interferes in the other's freedom. Love never imposes on the other. Love gives freedom, and the freedom is possible only if there is space in your togetherness.

This is the beauty of Kahlil Gibran . . . tremendous insight. Love should be happy to see that his woman is happy with someone, because love wants his woman to be happy. Love wants the husband to be joyous. If he's just talking to some woman and feels joyous, the wife should be happy, there is no question of quarrel. They are together to make their lives happier, but just the opposite goes on happening. It seems as if wives and husbands are together just to make each other's lives miserable, ruined. The reason is, they don't understand even the meaning of love.

But *let there be spaces in your togetherness* . . . It is not contradictory. The more space you give to each other, the more you are together. The more you allow freedom to each other, the more intimate you are. Not intimate enemies, but intimate friends.

And let the winds of heavens dance between you.

It is a fundamental law of existence that being together too much, leaving no space for freedom, destroys the flower of love. You have crushed it, you have not allowed it space to grow.

Scientists have discovered that animals have a territorial imperative. You must have seen dogs pissing on this pillar, pissing on that pillar—you think it is useless? It is not. They are drawing the boundary—"This is my territory." The smell of their urine will prevent another dog from entering in. If another dog comes just close to the boundary, the dog whose territory it is will not take any note. But just one step more and there is going to be a fight.

All the animals in the wild do the same. Even a lion, if you don't cross his boundary, is not going to attack you—you are a gentleman. But if you cross his boundary then whoever you are, he's going to kill you.

We have still to discover human beings' territorial imperative. You must have felt it, but it has not yet been scientifically established. Going in a local train in a city like Bombay, the train is so overcrowded . . . people are all standing, very few have found seats. But watch the people who are standing—although they are very close, they are trying in every way not to touch each other.

As the world becomes more overcrowded, more and more people are going insane, committing suicide, murders, for the simple reason that they don't have any space for themselves. At least lovers should be sensitive, that the wife needs her own space just as you need your own space.

One of my most-loved books is by Rabindranath Tagore—*Akhari Kavita*, "The Last Poem." It is not a book of poetry, it is a novel—but a very strange novel, very insightful.

A young woman and a man fall in love and as it happens, immediately they want to get married. The woman says, "Only on one condition . . ." She is very cultured, very sophisticated, very rich.

The man says, "Any condition is acceptable, but I cannot live without you."

She said, "First listen to the condition; then think it over. It is not an ordinary condition. The condition is that we will not live in the same house. I have a vast land, a beautiful lake surrounded by trees and gardens and lawns. I will make you a house on one side, just the opposite from where I live."

He said, "Then what is the point of marriage?"

She said, "Marriage is not destroying each other. I am giving you your space, I have my own space. Once in a while, walking in the garden we may meet. Once in a while, boating in the lake we may meet—accidentally. Or sometimes I can invite you to have tea with me, or you can invite me."

The man said, "This idea is simply absurd."

The woman said, "Then forget all about marriage. This is the only right idea—only then can our love go on growing, because we always remain fresh and new. We never take each other for granted. I have every right to refuse your invitation just as you have every right to refuse my invitation; in no way are our freedoms disturbed. Between these two freedoms grows the beautiful phenomenon of love."

Of course the man could not understand, and dropped the idea. But Rabindranath has the same insight as Kahlil Gibran . . . and they were writing at almost the same time.

If this is possible—to have space and togetherness both—then *the winds of heaven dance between you.*

Love one another, but make not a bond of love. It should be a free gift, given or taken, but there should be no demand. Otherwise, very soon you are together but you are as apart as faraway stars. No understanding bridges you; you have not left the space even for the bridge.

Let it rather be a moving sea between the shores of your souls.

Don't make it something static. Don't make it a routine. *Let it rather be a moving sea between the shores of your souls.*

If freedom and love together can be yours, you don't need anything more. You have got it—that for which life is given to you.

CHAPTER EIGHT

The Koan of Relationship

The best koan there is, is love, is relationship. That's how it is being used here. A relationship is a puzzle with no clue to it. Howsoever you try to manage it, you will never be able to manage it. Nobody has ever been able to manage it. It is made in such a way that it simply remains puzzling. The more you try to demystify it, the more mysterious it becomes. The more you try to understand it, the more elusive it is.

It is a greater koan than any koan that Zen masters give to their disciples, because their koans are meditative—one is alone. When you are given the koan of relationship it is far more complicated, because you are two—differently made, differently conditioned, polar opposites to each other, pulling in different directions, manipulating each other, trying to possess, dominate . . . there are a thousand and one problems.

While meditating, the only problem is how to be silent, how not to be caught in thoughts. In relationship there are a thousand and one problems. If you are silent, there is a problem. Just sit silently by the side of your wife and you will see—she will immediately jump upon you: "Why are you silent? What do you mean?" Or speak, and you will be in trouble—whatsoever you say, you are always misunderstood.

No relationship can ever come to a point where it is not a problem. Or if sometimes you see a relationship coming to a point where it is no longer a problem, that simply means it is not a relationship anymore.

The relationship has disappeared—the fighters are tired, they have started accepting things as they are. They are bored; they don't want to fight any more. They have accepted it, they don't want to improve upon it.

Or, in the past, people tried to create a kind of harmony forcibly. That's why, down the ages, women were repressed—that was one way of sorting things out. Just force the woman to follow the man, then there is no problem. But it is not a relationship, either. When the woman is no longer an independent person the problem disappears—but the woman has also disappeared. Then she is just a thing to be used; then there is no joy, and the man starts looking for some other woman.

If you ever come across a happy marriage, don't trust it on the surface. Just go a little deeper and you will be surprised. I have heard about one happy marriage . . .

A hillbilly farmer decided it was time to get married, so he saddled his mule and set off for the city to find a wife. In time, he met a woman and they were married. So they both climbed up on the mule and started back for the farm. After a while, the mule balked and refused to move. The farmer got down, found a big stick, and beat the mule until it again began to move.

"That's once," the farmer said.

A few miles later, the mule balked again, and the entire scene was repeated. After the beating, when the mule was moving again, the farmer said, "That's twice."

A few miles later, the mule balked for a third time. The farmer got down, got his wife down, and then took out a pistol and shot the mule in the eye, killing it instantly.

"That was a stupid thing to do!" the wife shouted. "That was a valuable animal and just because he annoyed you, you killed him! That was stupid, criminal . . ." and she went on like this for some time. As she stopped for breath, the farmer said, "That's once."

And it is said, after that they lived forever in married happiness! That is one way of solving things, that's how it has been done in the past. In the future, the reverse is going to be tried—the husband has to follow the wife. But it is the same thing.

A relationship is a koan. And unless you have solved a more fundamental thing about yourself, you cannot solve it. The problem of love can be solved only when the problem of meditation has been solved, not before it. Because it is really two nonmeditative persons who are creating the problem. Two persons who are in confusion, who don't know who they are—naturally they multiply each other's confusion, they magnify it.

Unless meditation is achieved, love remains a misery. Once you have learned how to live alone, once you have learned how to enjoy your simple existence, for no reason at all, then there is a possibility of solving the second, more complicated problem of two persons being together. Only two meditators can live in love—and then love will not be a koan. But then it will not be a relationship, either, in the sense that you understand it. It will be simply a state of love, not a state of relationship.

So I understand the trouble of relationship. But I encourage people to go into these troubles because these troubles will make you aware of the fundamental problem—that you, deep inside your being, are a riddle. And the other simply is a mirror. It is difficult to know your own troubles directly, it is very easy to know them in a relationship. A mirror becomes available; you can see your face in the mirror, and the other can see his face in your mirror. And both are angry, because both see ugly faces. And naturally both shout at each other, because their natural logic is, "It is *you*, this mirror, which is making me look so ugly. Otherwise I am such a beautiful person."

That's the problem that lovers go on trying to solve, and cannot solve. What they are saying again and again is this: "I am such a beautiful person, but you make me look so ugly."

Nobody is making you look ugly—you *are* ugly. Sorry, but that's how it is. Be thankful to the other, be grateful to the other, because he helps you to see your face. Don't be angry. And go deeper into yourself, go deeper into meditation.

But what happens is that whenever a person is in love he forgets all about meditation. I go on looking around me—whenever I see a few persons missing, I know what has happened to them. Love has happened to them. Now they don't think that they are needed here. They will come only when love creates much trouble and it becomes impossible for them to solve it. Then they will come and ask, "Osho, what to do?"

When you are in love, don't forget meditation. Love is not going to solve anything. Love is only going to show you who you are, where you are. And it is good that love makes you alert—alert of the whole confusion and the chaos within you. Now is the time to meditate! If love and meditation go together, you will have both the wings, you will have a balance.

And the opposite also happens. Whenever a person starts moving deep in meditation, he starts avoiding love, because he thinks if he goes into love his meditation will be disturbed—that, too, is wrong. Meditation will not be disturbed, meditation will be helped. Why will it be helped? Because love will go on showing you where there are still problems, where they are. Without love, you will become unconscious of your problems. But becoming unconscious does not mean that you have solved them. If there is no mirror, that does not mean that you don't have any face.

Love and meditation should go hand in hand. That is one of the most essential messages that I would like to share with you: Love and meditation should go hand in hand. Love and meditate, meditate and love—and slowly slowly you will see a new harmony arising in you. Only that harmony will make you contented.

QUESTIONS

▪ *How can I know that a woman has fallen in love in reality, and not playing games?*

This is difficult! Nobody has ever been able to know it because, in fact, love *is* a game. That is its reality! So if you are waiting and watching and thinking and analyzing whether this woman who is in love with you is just playing a game or is in reality in love, you will never be able to love any woman—because love is a game, the supreme game.

There is no need to ask for it to be real. Play the game, that's its reality. And if you are too much a seeker for reality, then love is not for you. It is a dream, it is a fantasy, it is a fiction—it is romance, it is poetry. If you are too much a seeker after reality, obsessed with reality, then love is not for you. Then meditate.

And I know the questioner is not that type—no meditation is possible for him, at least in this life! He has many karmas to fulfill with women. So he continuously thinks about meditation and continuously goes on moving with this woman or that. Now the women he moves with, they also come to me and they say, "Is he really in love with us? What to do?" And here he comes with a question!

But this problem comes to everybody sometime or other, because there is no way to judge. We are such strangers—we *are* strangers, and our meeting is just accidental. Just on the road suddenly we have come across each other, not knowing who we are, not knowing who the other is. Two strangers meeting on a road, feeling alone, hold each other's hands—and think they are in love.

They are in need of the other, certainly, but how to be certain that there is love?

I was reading a beautiful joke; listen to it carefully:

A woman arrived at a small Midwestern town late at night, only to find there wasn't a single hotel room available. "I'm sorry," said the desk clerk, "but the last room we had was just taken by an Italian."

"What number is it?" said the woman in desperation. "Maybe I can work out something with him."

The clerk told her the room and the woman went up and knocked on the door. The Italian let her in.

"Look, mister," she said, "I don't know you and you don't know me, but I need some place to sleep desperately. I won't be any bother, I promise, if you just let me use that little couch over there."

The Italian thought for a minute and then said, "Okay." The woman curled up on the couch and the Italian went back to bed. But the couch was very uncomfortable and after a few minutes the woman tiptoed over to the bed and tapped the Italian's arm. "Look, mister," she said, "I don't know you and you don't know me, but that couch is impossible to sleep on. Could I just sleep here, at the edge of the bed?"

"Okay," said the Italian, "use the edge of the bed."

The woman lay down on the bed, but after a few minutes she felt very cold. Again she tapped the Italian.

"Look, mister," she said, "I don't know you and you don't know me, but it's very cold out here. Could I just get under the cover with you."

"Okay," said the Italian, "get under the cover."

The woman snuggled under, but the closeness of a male body stirred her and she started to feel a little horny. Again she tapped the Italian.

"Look, mister," she said, "I don't know you and you don't know me, but how about having a little party?"

Exasperated, the Italian bolted up in the bed. "Look, lady," he hollered, "I don't know you and you don't know me. In the middle of the night, who we gonna invite to a party?"

But this is how it goes: "You don't know me, I don't know you." It is just accidental. Needs are there; people feel lonely; they need somebody to fill their loneliness. They call it love. They show love because that is the only way to hook the other. The other also calls it love because that is the only way to hook you. But who knows whether there is love or not? In fact, love is just a game.

Yes, there is a possibility of a real love, but that happens only when you don't need anybody—that's the difficulty. It is the same way banks function. If you go to a bank and you need money, they will not give you any. If you don't need money, you have enough, they will come to you and they will always be ready to give you some. When you don't need, they are ready to give you; when you need, they are not ready to give you.

When you don't need a person at all, when you are totally sufficient unto yourself, when you can be alone and tremendously happy and ecstatic, then love is possible. But then, too, you cannot be certain whether the *other's* love is real or not—you can be certain about only one thing: whether your love is real. How can you be certain about the other? But then there is no need.

This continuous anxiety about whether the other's love is real or not simply shows one thing: that your love is not real. Otherwise, who bothers? Why be worried about it? Enjoy it while it lasts, be together while you can be together! It is a fiction, but you need fiction.

Nietzsche used to say that man is such that he cannot live without lies. He cannot live with truth; truth will be too much to bear. You need lies—lies, in a subtle way, lubricate your system. They are lubricants—you see a woman, you, say, "How beautiful! I have never come across such a beautiful person." These are just lubricating lies—you know it! You have said the same thing to other women before, and you know you will say the same thing again to other women in the future. And the woman also says that you are the only person who has ever attracted her. These are lies. Behind these lies there is nothing but need. You want the woman to be with you to fill your inner hole; you want to stuff that inner emptiness with her presence. She also wants that. You are trying to use each other as means.

That's why lovers, so-called lovers, are always in conflict—because nobody wants to be used, because when you use a person the person becomes a thing, you have reduced him to a commodity. And every woman feels, after making love to a man, a little sad, deceived, cheated, because the man turns over and goes to sleep—finished is finished!

Many women have told me that they cry and weep after the man has made love to them—because after making love he is no longer interested. His interest was only for a particular need; then he turns over and goes to sleep and he is not even bothered about what has happened to the woman. And men also feel cheated. They, by and by, start suspecting that the woman loves them for something else—for money, power, security. The interest may be economical, but it is not love.

But it is true. This is how it can be; *only* this is how it can be! The way you are, living almost asleep, moving in a stupor, somnambulistic, this is the only way it is possible. But don't be worried about it, whether the woman loves you really or not. While you are asleep you will need somebody's love—even if it is false, you will need it. Enjoy it! Don't create anxiety. And try to become more and more awake.

One day when you are really awake you will be able to love—but then you will be certain about *your* love only. But that's enough! Who bothers? Because right now you want to use others; when you are really blissful on your own, you don't want to use anybody. You simply want to share. You have so much, so much is overflowing, and you would like somebody to share it. And you will feel thankful that somebody was ready to receive. Finished, that is the end of it!

Right now, you are worried too much whether the other loves you, really, because you are not certain about your own love. That's one thing. And you are not certain about your own worth. You cannot believe that somebody can really love you; you don't see anything in yourself. You cannot love yourself, how can somebody else love you? It seems unreal, it seems impossible.

Do you love yourself? You have not even asked the question. People hate themselves, people condemn themselves—they go on condemning; they go on thinking that they are rotten. How can the other love you, such a rotten person. No, nobody can love you really—the other must be befooling, cheating; there must be some other reason. She must be after something else; he must be after something else.

You know your rottenness, worthlessness—love seems to be out of the question. And when some woman comes and says she adores you, you cannot trust. When you go to a woman and you say you adore her, and she hates herself, how can she believe you? It is self-hatred that is creating the anxiety.

There is no way to be certain about the other. First be certain about yourself. And a person who is certain about himself is certain about the whole world. A certainty achieved at your innermost core becomes a certainty about everything that you do and everything that happens to you. Settled, centered, grounded, in yourself, you never worry about such things. You accept.

If somebody loves you, you accept it because you love yourself. You are happy with yourself; somebody else is happy—good! It does not get in your head, it does not make you madly egoistic. You simply enjoy yourself; somebody else also finds you enjoyable—good! While it lasts, live the fiction as beautifully as possible—it will not last forever.

That, too, creates a problem. When a love is finished, you start thinking it was false—that's why it has come to an end. No, not necessarily—not necessarily. It may have had some glimmer of truth in it, but you were both unable to keep and hold that truth. You killed it. It was there and you murdered it. You were not capable of love. You needed love, but you were not capable of it. So you meet a woman or a man; things go very well, very smoothly, fantastically beautifully—in the beginning. The moment you have settled, things start getting sour, bitter. The more you have settled, the more conflict arises. That kills love.

As I see it, every love has in the beginning a ray of light in it, but the lovers destroy that. They jump on that ray of light with all their darknesses within. They jump on it and they destroy it. When it is destroyed they think it was false. They have killed it! It was not false—they are false. The ray was real, true.

So don't be worried about the other; don't be worried whether the love is real or not. While it is there, enjoy it. Even if it is a dream, it's good to dream about it. And become more and more alert and aware so sleep is dropped.

When you are aware, a totally different kind of love will arise in your heart—which is absolutely true, which is part of eternity. But that is not a need, it is a luxury.

▪ *If the jealousies, the possessiveness, the attachment, the needs and expectations and desires and illusions drop, will anything be left of my love? Has all my poetry and passion been a lie? Have my love pains had more to do with pain than with love? Will I ever learn to love?*

Love cannot be learned, it cannot be cultivated. The cultivated love will not be love at all. It will not be a real rose, it will be a plastic flower. When you learn something, it means something comes from the outside; it is not an inner growth. And love has to be your inner growth if it is to be authentic and real.

Love is not a learning but a growth. All that is needed on your part is not to learn the ways of love, but to unlearn the ways of unlove. The hindrances have to be removed, the obstacles have to be destroyed—then love is your natural, spontaneous being. Once the obstacles are removed, the rocks thrown away, the flow starts. It is already there—hidden behind many rocks, but the spring is already there. It is your very being.

It is a gift, but not something that is going to happen in the future; it is a gift that has already happened with your birth. To *be* is to be love. To be able to breathe is enough to be able to love. Love is like breathing. What breathing is to the physical body, love is to the spiritual being. Without breathing the body dies; without love the soul dies.

So the first thing to remember: It is not something that you can learn. And if you learn you will miss the whole point; you will learn something else in the name of love. It will be pseudo, false. And the false coin can look like the real coin; if you don't know the real, the false can go on deceiving you. Only by knowing the real, will you be able to see the distinction between the false and the real.

And these are the obstacles: jealousies, possessiveness, attachment, expectations, desires . . . And your fear is right: "If all these disappear, will anything be left of my love?" Nothing will be left of your love. *Love* will be left . . . but love has nothing to do with "I" or "you." In fact, when all possessiveness, all jealousies, all expectations disappear, <u>love does not disappear—*you* disappear, the ego disappears.</u> These are the shadows of the ego.

It is not love that is jealous. Watch, look, observe again. When you feel jealous, it is not love that feels jealous; love has never known anything of jealousy. Just as the sun has never known anything of darkness, love has never known anything of jealousy. It is the ego that feels hurt, it is the ego that feels competitive, in a constant struggle. It is the ego that is ambitious and wants to be higher than others, wants to be somebody special. It is the ego that starts feeling jealous, possessive—because the ego can exist only with possessions.

The more you possess, the more the ego is strengthened; without possessions the ego cannot exist. It leans on possessions, it depends on possessions. So if you have more money, more power, more prestige, a beautiful woman, a beautiful man, beautiful children, the ego feels immensely nourished. When possessions disappear, when you don't possess anything at all, you will not find the ego inside. There will be nobody who can say "I."

And if you think *this* is your love, then certainly your love will also disappear. Your love is not really love. It is jealousy, possessiveness, hatred, anger, violence; it is a thousand and one things except love. It masquerades as love—because all these things are so ugly they cannot exist without a mask.

<u>An ancient parable:</u>

The world was created, and God was sending every day new things to the world. One day he sent Beauty and Ugliness to the world. It is a long journey from paradise to the earth—the moment they arrived it was early morning, the sun was just rising. They landed near a lake and both decided to have a bath because their whole bodies, their clothes, were so full of dust.

Not knowing the ways of the world—they are so new—they take their clothes off; utterly naked, they jump into the cool water of the lake. The sun is rising, people start coming. Ugliness plays a trick—when Beauty goes swimming far away into the lake, Ugliness comes up on the bank, puts on the garments of Beauty, and escapes. By the time Beauty becomes aware that "People are arriving and I am naked," and she looks around . . . her clothes are gone! Ugliness is gone and Beauty is standing naked in the sun, and the crowd is coming closer. Finding no other way, she puts on the clothes of Ugliness and goes in search of Ugliness so that the clothes can be changed.

The story says she is still looking . . . but Ugliness is cunning and goes on escaping. Ugliness is still in the clothes of Beauty, masked as Beauty, and Beauty is moving in the clothes of Ugliness.

It is a tremendously beautiful parable.

All these things are so ugly that you cannot tolerate to be with them even for a single moment if you see their reality. So they don't allow you to see the reality. Jealousy pretends to be love, possessiveness creates a mask of love . . . and then you are at ease.

You are not fooling anybody else but yourself. These things are not love. So what you know as love, what you have known up to now as love, will disappear. It has nothing of poetry in it. Yes, passion is there—but passion is a feverish state, passion is an unconscious state. Passion is not poetry. The poetry is known only by the buddhas—the poetry of life, the poetry of existence.

Excitement, fever, are not ecstasies. They look alike, that is the problem. In life many things look alike and the distinctions are very delicate and fine and subtle. Excitement can look like ecstasy—it is not, because ecstasy is basically cool. Passion is hot. Love is cool, not cold but cool. Hatred is cold. Passion, lust, is hot. Love is exactly in the middle. It is cool—neither cold nor hot. It is a state of tremendous tranquility, calmness, serenity, silence. And out of that silence is poetry, out of that silence is song, out of that silence arises a dance of your being.

What you call poetry and passion are nothing but lies—with beautiful facades. Out of your hundred poets, ninety-nine are not really poets but only people in a state of turmoil, emotion, passion, heat, lust, sexuality, sensuality. Only one out of your hundred poets is a real poet.

And the real poet may never compose any poetry, because his whole being is poetry. The way he walks, the way he sits, the way he eats, the way he sleeps—it is all poetry. He exists as poetry. He may create poetry, he may not create poetry, that is irrelevant.

But what you call poetry is nothing but the expression of your fever, of your heated state of consciousness. It is a state of insanity. Passion is insane, blind, unconscious—because it gives you the feeling as if it is love.

Love is possible only when meditation has happened. If you don't know how to be centered in your being, if you don't know how to rest and relax in your being, if you don't know how to be utterly alone and blissful, you will never know what love is.

Love appears as relationship, but begins in deep solitude. Love expresses as relating, but the source of love is not in relating; the source of love is in meditating. When you are absolutely happy in your aloneness—when you don't need the other at all, when the other is not a need—then you are capable of love. If the other is your need you can only exploit, manipulate, dominate, but you cannot love.

Because you depend on the other, possessiveness arises—out of fear. "Who knows? The other is with me today; tomorrow he may not be with me. Who knows about the next moment?" Your woman may have left you, your children may have grown up and left, your husband can desert you. Who knows about the next moment? Out of that fear of the future you become very possessive. You create a bondage around the person you think you love.

But love cannot create a prison—and if love creates a prison, then nothing is left for hatred to do. Love brings freedom, love gives freedom. It is nonpossessiveness. But that is possible only if you have known a totally different quality of love, not of need but of sharing.

Love is a sharing of overflowing joy. You are too full of joy; you cannot contain it, you have to share it. Then there is poetry and then there is something tremendously beautiful that is not of this world, that is something that comes from the beyond. This love cannot be learned, but obstacles can be removed.

Many times I say learn the art of love, but what I really mean is: Learn the art of removing all that hinders love. It is a negative process. It is like digging a well: You go on removing many layers of earth, stones, rocks, and then suddenly there is water. The water was always there; it was an undercurrent. Now you have removed all the barriers, the water is available. So is love: Love is the undercurrent of your being. It is already flowing, but there are many rocks, many layers of earth to be removed.

That's what I mean when I say learn the art of love. It is really not learning love but unlearning the ways of unlove.

■ *What is the difference between liking and loving, to like and to love? And also, what is the difference between ordinary love and spiritual love?*

There is a great difference between liking and loving. Liking has no commitment in it, loving is commitment. That's why people don't talk much about love. In fact people have started talking about love in such contexts where no commitment is needed. For example, somebody says, "I love ice cream." Now how can you love ice cream? You can like, you cannot love. And somebody says "I love my dog, I love my car, I love this and that."

In fact people are very very afraid of saying to a person, "I love you."

I have heard: A man was dating a girl, for months together. And the girl was of course waiting, waiting—they were even making love but the man had not said to her, "I love you."

Just see the difference—in the ancient days, people used to "fall in love." Now people "make love." You see the difference? Falling in love is being overwhelmed by love; it is passive. Making love is almost profane, almost destroying its beauty. It is active, as if you are *doing* something; you are manipulating and controlling. Now people have changed the language—rather than using "falling in love" they use "making love."

And the man was making love to the woman, but he had not said a single time, "I love you." And the woman was waiting and waiting and waiting.

One day he phoned and he said, "I have been thinking and thinking to say it to you. It seems now the time for it has come. I have to say it; now I cannot contain it anymore." And the woman was thrilled, and she became all ears—for this she was waiting. And she said, "Say it! Say it!" And the man said, "I have to say it, now I cannot contain it anymore: I really like you so much."

People are saying to each other, "I like you." Why don't they say, "I love you"? Because love is commitment, involvement, risk, responsibility. Liking is just momentary—I can like you, and I may not like you tomorrow; there is no risk in it. When you say to a person, "I love you," you take a risk. You are saying "I love you: I will remain loving you, I will love you tomorrow, too. You can depend on me, this is a promise."

Love is a promise, liking has nothing to do with any promise. When you say to a man, "I like you," you say something about *you*, not about the man. You say, "This is how I am, I like you. I like ice cream, too, and I like my car, too. In the same way, I like you." You are saying something about you.

When you say to a person, "I love you," you are saying something about the person, not about you. You are saying, "You are lovely." The arrow is pointing to the other person. And then there is danger—you are giving a promise. Love has the quality of promise in it, and commitment, and involvement. And love has something of eternity in it. Liking is momentary; liking is nonrisky, nonresponsible.

You ask me: *What is the difference between liking and loving? And also, what is the difference between ordinary love and spiritual love?*

Liking and loving are different, but there is no difference between ordinary love and spiritual love. Love *is* spiritual. I have never come across ordinary love; the ordinary thing is liking. Love is never ordinary—it can't be, it is intrinsically extraordinary. It is not of this world.

When you say to a woman or a man, "I love you," you are simply saying, "I cannot be deceived by your body, I have seen you. Your body may become old but I have seen you, the bodiless you. I have seen your innermost core, the core that is divine." Liking is superficial. Love penetrates and goes to the very core of the person, touches the very soul of the person.

No love is ordinary. Love cannot be ordinary, otherwise it is not love. To call love ordinary is to misunderstand the whole phenomenon of love. Love is never ordinary, love is always extraordinary, always spiritual. That is the difference between liking and love: Liking is material, love is spiritual.

■ *You confused me when you talked about the differences between love and liking. You said love is committed, but I thought commitment was another kind of attachment. There are many people I love but I don't feel committed to. How can I predict if I will love them tomorrow?*

The question is significant. You will have to be very, very understanding, because it is subtle and complex, too.

When I said that love is commitment, what do I mean by it? I don't mean that you have to promise for tomorrow, but the promise is there. You don't have to promise, but the promise is there. This is the complexity and the subtleness of it. You don't say, "I will love you tomorrow, too"—but in the moment of love that promise is there, utterly present. It needs no expression.

When you love a person you can't imagine otherwise; you can't think that you will not love this person some day; that is impossible, that is not part of love. And I am not saying that you will not be able to get out of this love affair. You may be, you may not be; that is not the point. But when you are in the love moment, when the energy is flowing between two persons, there is a bridge, a golden bridge, and they are bridged through it. It simply does not happen: The mind cannot conceive and comprehend that there will be a time when you will not be with this person and this person will not be with you. This is commitment. Not that you say as much, not that you go to a court and make a formal statement: "I will remain forever with you." In fact, to make that formal statement simply shows there is no love; you need a legal arrangement. If the commitment is there, there is no need for any legal arrangement.

Marriage is needed because love is missing. If love is there profoundly, marriage will not be needed. What is the point of marriage? That is like putting legs on a snake, or painting a red rose red. It is unnecessary. Why go to the court? There must be some fear inside you that the love is not total.

Even while in deep love you are thinking of the possibility that tomorrow you may desert this woman. The woman is thinking, "Who knows? Tomorrow this man may desert me. It is better to go to the court. First let it become legal, then one can be certain." But what does it show? It simply shows that love is not total. Otherwise, total love has that quality of commitment on its own accord. Commitment does not have to be brought to it, it is its intrinsic quality.

And when you are in love it comes naturally to you, not that you plan. This feeling comes naturally and sometimes in words, too: "I will love you forever." This is *this* moment's depth. It doesn't say anything about tomorrow, remember. It is not a promise. It is just that the depth and the totality of love is such that it comes automatically to you to say, "I will love you forever and ever. Even death will not be able to part us." This is the feeling of total love.

And let me repeat again—that does not mean that tomorrow you will be together. Who knows? That is not the point at all. Tomorrow will take care of itself. Tomorrow never enters into the mind that is in love. Tomorrow is not conceived at all; future disappears, this moment becomes eternity. This is commitment.

And when tomorrow . . . it is possible you may not be together, but you are not betraying. You are not deceiving, you are not cheating. You will feel sad about it, you will feel sorry about it, but you have to part. And I'm not saying that it has to happen—it may not happen. It depends on a thousand and one things.

Life does not depend only on your love. If it were to depend only on your love then you would live forever and ever. But life depends on a thousand and one things. Love has the feeling that "We will live together forever," but love is not the whole of life. When it is there it is so intense, one is drunk with it. But then there are again a thousand and one things, sometimes small things.

You may fall in love with a man, and in that moment you are ready to go to hell with him—and you can say so, and you are not cheating. You are utterly true and honest and you say, "If I have to go to hell with you I will go!"—and I say again, you are true, you are not saying anything false.

But tomorrow, living with that man, small things—a dirty bathroom may disturb your affair. Hell is too far away, there is no need to go that far—a dirty bathroom! Or just a small habit: the man snores in the night and drives you crazy. And you were ready to go to hell, and that was true, it was authentic in that moment. It was not false, you had no other idea—but the man snores in the night, or his perspiration smells like hell, or he has bad breath and when he kisses you, you feel you are tortured.

Just small things, very small things; one never thinks of them when one is in love. Who bothers about a bathroom, and who thinks about snoring? But when you live together with a person a thousand and one things are involved, and any small thing can become a rock and can destroy the flower of love.

So I'm not saying that the commitment has any promise in it. I'm simply saying that the *moment of love* is a moment of commitment. You are utterly in it, it is so decisive. And naturally, out of this moment will come the next, so there is every possibility that you may be together. Out of today, tomorrow will be born. It will not be coming from the blue, it will grow out of today. If today has been of great love, tomorrow will also carry the same love. It will be a continuity. So there is every possibility that you may love—but it is always a perhaps. And love understands that.

And if one day you leave your woman or your woman leaves you, you will not start shouting at her, "What do you mean now? You had told me one day that 'I will live always and always with you.' Now what? Why are you going?" If you loved, if you had known love, you will understand. Love has that quality of commitment.

Love is a mystery. When it is there, everything looks heavenly. When it is gone, everything looks simply stale, meaningless. You could not have lived without this woman, and now you cannot live with this woman. And both are authentic states.

You ask, *"You confused me when you talked about the differences between love and liking. You said love is committed, but I thought commitments were another kind of attachment."*

My meaning of commitment and your meaning of commitment are different. Your meaning is legal, my meaning is not legal. I was simply describing to you the quality of love, what happens when you are encompassed in it: The commitment happens. Commitment does not create love, love creates it. Love is first, commitment follows it. If one day love disappears, that commitment will also disappear; it was the shadow.

When love is gone, don't talk about commitment; then you are being foolish. It was a shadow of love. It always comes with love. And if love is no more, it goes—it disappears. You don't go on harping on that commitment: "What about the commitment?" There is no more commitment if love is not there. Love is commitment! Love gone, all commitment is gone. This is my meaning.

And I understand your meaning. Your meaning is: When love is gone, what about the commitment? That is your meaning. You want the commitment to continue when the love is gone and love is no more. Your meaning of commitment is legal.

Always remember, when you are listening to me, try to follow my meaning. It is difficult, but you have to try. In that very trying you will get out of your meanings. Slowly, slowly a window will open and you will be able to see what I mean. Otherwise, there is going to be confusion: I say something, you hear something else.

■ *Even if sometimes lovelike feelings arise in my heart, immediately the next moment I start feeling this is not love, this is not love at all. It is all my hidden cravings for sex and all that.*

So what is wrong in it? Love has to arise out of lust. If you avoid lust, you will be avoiding the whole possibility of love itself. Love is not lust, true; but love is not without lust—that, too, is true. Love is higher than lust, yes, but if you destroy lust completely, you destroy the very possibility of the flower arising out of the mud. Love is the lotus, lust is the mud the lotus arises out of.

Remember it; otherwise you will never attain to love. At the most, you can pretend that you have transcended lust. Because without love, nobody can transcend lust; you can repress it. Repressed, it becomes more poisonous. It spreads into your whole system, it becomes toxic, it destroys you. Lust transformed into love gives you a glow, a radiance. You start feeling light, as if you can fly. You start gaining wings. With lust repressed you become heavy, as if you are carrying a weight, as if a big rock is hanging around your neck. With lust repressed, you lose all opportunities to fly in the sky. With lust transformed into love, you have passed the test of existence.

You have been given a raw material to work with, to be creative. Lust is raw material.

I have heard. . . .

Berkowitz and Michaelson, who were not only business partners but lifelong friends, made a pact: Whichever one died first would come back and tell the other what it was like in heaven.

Six months later, Berkowitz died. He was a very moral man, almost saintlike, a puritan who had never done anything wrong, who had always remained afraid of lust and sex.

And Michaelson waited for his dear departed holy friend to show some sign that he had returned to earth. Michaelson passed the time impatiently hoping for and eagerly awaiting a message from Berkowitz.

Then one year after the day of his death, Berkowitz spoke to Michaelson. It was late at night; Michaelson was in bed.

"Michaelson, Michaelson," echoed the voice.

"Is that you, Berkowitz?"

"Yes."

"What is it like where you are?"

"We have breakfast and then we make love, then we eat lunch and we make love, we have dinner and then we make love."

"Is that what heaven is like?" asked Michaelson.

"Who said anything about heaven?" said Berkowitz. "I am in Wisconsin, and I am a bull."

Remember, this happens to people who repress sex. Nothing else can happen because that whole energy repressed becomes a load and pulls you down. You move toward lower stages of being.

If love arises out of lust, you start rising toward higher being. So remember—what you want to become, a buddha or a bull, depends on you. If you want to become a buddha, then don't be afraid of sex. Move into it, know it well, become more and more alert about it. Be careful; it is tremendously valuable energy. Make it a meditation and transform it, by and by, into love. It is raw material, like a raw diamond. You have to cut it, polish it; then it becomes of tremendous value. If somebody gives you an unpolished, raw, uncut diamond, you may not even recognize that it is a diamond. Even the Kohinoor in its raw state is worthless.

Lust is a Kohinoor; it has to be polished, it has to be understood.

The questioner seems to be afraid and antagonistic: "It is all my hidden cravings for sex and all that." There is a condemnation in it. Nothing is wrong; man is a sexual animal. That's how we are. That's the way life means us to be. That's how we have found ourselves here. Go into it. Without going, you will never be able to transform it. I'm not speaking for mere indulgence. I'm saying move into it with deep, meditative energy to understand what it is. It must be something tremendously valuable because you have come out of it, because the whole existence enjoys it, because the whole existence is sexual.

Sex is the way God has chosen to be in the world, notwithstanding what Christians go on saying, that Jesus was born out of a virgin woman—all foolishness. They pretend that sex was not involved in Jesus' birth. They are so afraid of sex that they create foolish stories like this, that Jesus is born out of a virgin Mary. Mary must have been very pure, that's true; she must have been spiritually virgin, that is true—but there is no way to enter into life without passing through the energy that sex is. The body knows no other law. And nature is all-inclusive. It believes in no exceptions, it allows no exceptions. You are born out of sex, you are full of sex energy, but this is not the end. This may be the beginning. Sex is the beginning, but not the end.

There are three types of people. One thinks that sex is the end, also. They are the people who live a life of indulgence. They miss, because sex is the beginning but not the end. Then there are people who are against indulgence. They take the other, the opposite extreme. They don't want sex even to be the beginning, so they start cutting it. Cutting it, they cut themselves. Destroying it, they destroy themselves, they wither away. Both are foolish attitudes.

There is the third possibility, the possibility of the wise, who looks at life. Who has no theories to enforce on life, who just tries to understand. He comes to see that sex is the beginning but not the end. Sex is just an opportunity to grow beyond it—but one has to pass through it.

■ *In the East, it has been stressed that one should stay with a person, one person, in a love relationship. In the West, now people float from one relationship to another. Which are you in favor of?*

I am in favor of love.

Let me explain it to you: Be true to love, and don't bother about partners. Whether one partner or many partners is not the question. The question is whether you are true to love. If you live with a woman or with a man and you don't love him, you live in sin. If you are married to somebody and you don't love that person and you still go on living with him, making love to him or her, you are committing a sin against love.

You are deciding against love for social comforts, conveniences, formalities. It is as wrong as if you go and rape a woman. You go and rape a woman; it is a crime—because you don't love the woman and the woman does not love you. But the same happens if you live with a woman and you don't love her. Then it is a rape—socially accepted, of course, but it is a rape—and you are going against love.

So, like in the East, people have decided to live with one partner for their whole lives; nothing is wrong. If you remain true to love, it is one of the most beautiful things to remain with one person, because intimacy grows. But, ninety-nine percent are the possibilities that there is no love; you only live together. And by living together a certain relationship grows that is only of living together, not of love. And don't mistake it for love.

But if it is possible, if you love a person and live the whole life with him or with her, a great intimacy will grow and love will have deeper and deeper revelations to make to you. It is not possible if you go on changing partners very often. It is as if you go on changing a tree from one place to another, then another; then it never grows roots anywhere. To grow roots, a tree needs to remain in one place. Then it goes deeper; then it becomes stronger.

Intimacy is good, and to remain in one commitment is beautiful, but the basic necessity is love. If a tree is rooted in a place where there are only rocks and they are killing the tree, then it is better to remove it. Then don't insist that it should remain in the one place. Remain true to life—remove the tree, because now it is going against life.

In the West, people are changing—too many relationships. Love is killed in both ways. In the East it is killed because people are afraid to change. In the West it is killed because people are afraid to remain with one partner for a longer time—afraid because it becomes a commitment. Before it becomes a commitment, change, so you remain floating and free. So a certain licentiousness is growing, and in the name of freedom, love is almost crushed, starved to death. Love has suffered both ways. In the East people cling to security, comfort, formality; in the West they cling to their ego's freedom, noncommitment. But love is suffering both ways.

I am in favor of love. I am neither Eastern nor Western, and I don't bother to which society you belong. I belong to no society, I am in favor of love.

Always remember: if it is a love relationship, good. While love lasts remain in it, and remain in it as deeply committed as possible. Remain in it as totally as possible; be absorbed by the relationship. Then love will be able to transform you. If there is no love, it is better to change. But then, don't become an addict of change. Don't make it a habit. Don't let it become a mechanical habit that you have to change after each two or three years, as one has to change one's car after each two or three years, or after each year. A new model comes, so what to do?—you have to change your car. Suddenly, you come across a new woman—it is not much different.

A woman is a woman, as a man is a man. The differences are only secondary, because it is a question of energy. The female energy is female energy. In each woman all women are represented, and in each man all men are represented. The differences are very superficial. The nose is a little longer, or it is not a little longer; the hair is blond or brunette—small differences, just on the surface. Deep down, the question is of female and male energy. So if love is there, stick to it. Give it a chance to grow. But if it is not there, change before you become addicted to a relationship without love.

A young wife in the confessional box asked the priest about contraceptives. "You must not use them," said the priest. "They are against God's law. Take a glass of water."

"Before, or after?" asked the wife.

"Instead!" replied the priest.

You ask me whether to follow the Eastern way or the Western way. Neither; you follow the divine way. And what is the divine way? Remain true to love. If love is there, everything is permitted. If love is not there, nothing is permitted. If you don't love your wife, don't touch her, because that is trespassing. If you don't love a woman, don't sleep with her; that is going against the law of love, and that is the ultimate law. Only when you love is everything permitted.

Somebody asked Augustine of Hippo, "I am a very uneducated man and I cannot read scriptures and great theology books. You just give me a small message. I'm very foolish and my memory is also not good, so you just give me the gist, so I can remember it and follow it." Augustine was a great philosopher, a great saint, and he had delivered great sermons, but nobody had asked for just the gist. He closed his eyes, he meditated for hours, it is said. And the man said, "Please, if you have found, just tell me so I can go, because I have been waiting for hours." Augustine said, "I cannot find anything else except this: Love, and everything else is permitted to you. Just love."

Jesus says, "God is love." I would like to say to you, love is God. Forget all about God; love will do. Remain courageous enough to move with love; no other consideration should be made. If you consider love, everything will become possible to you.

First, don't move with a woman or man you don't love. Don't move just out of whim; don't move just out of lust. Find out whether the desire to be committed to a person has arisen in you.

Are you ripe enough to make a deep contact? Because that contact is going to change your whole life.

And when you make the contact, make it truthfully. Don't hide from your beloved or your lover—be true. Drop all false faces that you have learned to wear. Drop all masks. Be true. Reveal your whole heart; be nude. Between two lovers there should not be any secrets, otherwise love is not. Drop all secrecy. It is politics; secrecy is politics. It should not be in love. You should not hide anything. Whatsoever arises in your heart should remain transparent to your beloved, and whatsoever arises in her heart should remain transparent to you. You should become two transparent beings to each other. By and by, you will see that through each other you are growing to a higher unity.

By meeting the woman outside, by really meeting, loving her—committing yourself to her being, dissolving into her, melting into her—you will, by and by, start meeting the woman that is within you; you will start meeting the man that is within you. The outer woman is just a path to the inner woman; and the outer man is also just a path to the inner man.

The real orgasm happens inside you when your inner man and woman meet. That is the meaning of the Hindu symbolism of *Ardhanarishwar*. You must have seen statues of Shiva as half man, half woman—each man is half man, half woman; each woman is half woman, half man. It has to be so, because half of your being comes from your father and half of your being comes from your mother—you are both. An inner orgasm, an inner meeting, an inner union is needed. But to reach to that inner union you will have to find a woman outside who responds to the inner woman, who vibrates your inner being, and your inner woman, who is lying fast asleep, awakes. Through the outer woman, you have to meet the inner woman; and the same for the man.

So if the relationship continues for a long period, it will be better, because that inner woman needs time to be awakened. As it is happening in the West—hit-and-run affairs—the inner woman has no time, the inner man has no time to rise and become awake. By the time there is a stirring, the woman is gone . . . another woman, with another vibration. And of course, if you go on changing your woman and your man you will become neurotic, because so many things, so many sounds will enter into your being, and so many different qualities of vibrations that you will be at a loss to find your inner woman. It will be difficult. And the possibility is that you may become an addict to change. You will just start enjoying change. Then you are lost.

The outer woman is just a way to the inner woman, and the outer man is the way to the inner man. And the ultimate yoga, the ultimate mystic union happens inside you. When that happens, then you are free of all women and all men. Then you are free of man- and womanhood. Then suddenly, you go beyond; then you are neither. This is what transcendence is; this is what *brahmacharya* is. Then you attain again your pure virginity; your original nature is again claimed.

■ *Lately, I have begun to realize how even my lover is a stranger to me. Still, there is an intense longing to overcome the separation between us. It almost feels as if we are lines running parallel to each other but destined never to meet. Is the world of consciousness like the world of geometry— or is there a chance that parallels can meet?*

It is one of the great miseries that every lover has to face. There is no way for lovers to drop their strangeness, unfamiliarity, separation. In fact, the whole functioning of love is that lovers should be polar opposites. The further away they are, the more attractive. Their separation is their attraction. They come close, they come very close, but they never become one. They come so close that it almost feels like just one step more and they will become one. But that step has never been taken, cannot be taken out of sheer necessity, out of a natural law.

On the contrary, when they are very close, immediately they start becoming separate again, going further away. Because when they are very close, their attraction is lost; they start fighting, nagging, being bitchy. These are ways to create the distance again. And as the distance is there, immediately they start feeling attracted. So this goes on like a rhythm: coming closer, going away; coming closer, going away.

There is a longing to be one—but on the level of biology, on the level of the body, becoming one is not possible. Even while making love you are not one; the separation on the physical level is inevitable.

You are saying, "Lately, I have begun to realize how even my lover is a stranger to me." This is good. This is part of a growing understanding. Only childish people think that they know each other. You don't know even yourself, how can you conceive that you know your lover?

Neither the lover knows himself nor do you know yourself. Two unknown beings, two strangers who don't know anything about themselves are trying to know each other—it is an exercise in futility. It is bound to be a frustration, a failure. And that's why all lovers are angry at each other. They think perhaps the other is not allowing an entry into his private world: "He is keeping me separate, he is keeping me a little far away." And both go on thinking in the same way. But it is not true, all complaints are false. It is simply that they don't understand the law of nature.

On the level of body, you can come close but you cannot become one. Only on the level of the heart, can you become one— but only momentarily, not permanently.

At the level of being, you *are* one. There is no need to become one; it has only to be discovered.

You are saying, "Still there is an intense longing to overcome the separation between us." If you go on trying on the physical level, you will go on failing. The longing simply shows that love needs to go beyond the body, that love wants something higher than the body, something greater than the body, something deeper than the body. Even the heart-to-heart meeting—although sweet, although immensely joyful—is still insufficient, because it happens only for a moment and then again strangers are strangers. Unless you discover the world of being, you will not be able to fulfill your longing of becoming one. And the strange fact is, the day you become one with your lover, you will become one with the whole existence, too.

You are saying, "It almost feels as if we are lines running parallel to each other but destined never to meet." Perhaps you don't know non-Euclidean geometry because it is still not taught in our educational institutes. We are still taught Euclidean geometry, which is two thousand years old. In Euclidean geometry, parallel lines never meet. But it has been found that if you go on and on and on they do meet. The latest finding is that there are no parallel lines; that's why they meet. You cannot create two parallel lines.

New findings are very strange—you cannot even create a line, a straight line, because the earth is round. If you create a straight line here, if you go on drawing it from both the ends and go on and go on, finally you will find it has become a circle. And if a straight line drawn to the ultimate becomes a circle, it was not a straight line in the first place; it was only part of a very big circle, and a part of a big circle is an arc, not a line. Lines have disappeared in non-Euclidean geometry and when there are no lines, what to say about parallel lines? There are no parallel lines, either.

So if it were a question of parallel lines, there is a chance that lovers could meet somewhere—perhaps in old age when they cannot fight, they don't have any energy left. Or they have become so accustomed . . . what is the point—the same arguments they have had, the same problems, the same conflicts; they are bored with each other.

In the long run, lovers stop even speaking to each other. What is the point? Because to start speaking means to start an argument, and it is the same argument; it is not going to change. And they have argued it so many times and it comes to the same end. But even then, parallel lines as far as lovers are concerned . . . in geometry they may start meeting, but in love there is no hope; they cannot meet.

And it is good that they cannot meet because if lovers could satisfy their longing of becoming one at the level of physical body, they would never look upward. They would never try to find that there was much more hidden in the physical body—the consciousness, the soul, the God.

It is good that love fails, because the failure of love is bound to take you on a new pilgrimage. The longing will haunt you until it brings you to the temple where the meeting happens—but the meeting always happens with the whole . . . in which your lover will be, but in which the trees will also be, and the rivers and the mountains and the stars.

In that meeting, only two things will not be there: Your ego will not be there, and your lover's ego will not be there. Other than these two things, the whole existence will be there. And these two egos were really the problem, were what was making them two parallel lines.

It is not love that is creating the trouble, it is the ego. But the longing will not be satisfied. Birth after birth, life after life, the longing will remain there unless you discover the right door to go beyond the body and to enter the temple.

An old couple of ninety-three and ninety-five go to their lawyer and say that they want a divorce. "A divorce!" exclaims the lawyer. "At your age? But surely you need each other more than ever now, and anyway, you have been married so long, what is the point?"

"Well," says the husband, "We have been wanting a divorce for years now but we thought we would wait until the children were dead."

They really waited! Now there is no problem, they can have the divorce—still no meeting, but divorce.

Just keep your longing burning, aflame; don't lose heart. Your longing is the seed of your spirituality. Your longing is the beginning of the ultimate union with existence. Your lover is just an excuse.

Don't be sad, be happy. Rejoice that there is no possibility of meeting on the physical level. Otherwise, lovers will not have any way of transformation. They will get stuck with each other, they will destroy each other.

And there is no harm in loving a stranger. In fact, it is more exciting to love a stranger. When you were not together, there was great attraction. The more you have been together, the more the attraction has become dull. The more you have become known to each other, superficially, the less is the excitement. Life becomes very soon a routine.

People go on repeating the same thing, again and again. If you look at the faces of people in the world, you will be surprised: Why do all these people look so sad? Why do their eyes look as if they have lost all hope? The reason is simple; the reason is repetition. Man is intelligent; repetition creates boredom. Boredom brings a sadness because one knows what is going to happen tomorrow, and the day after tomorrow . . . until one goes into the grave, it will be the same, the same story.

Finkelstein and Kowalski are sitting in a bar watching the news on television. On the news, they are showing a woman standing on a ledge, threatening to jump. Finkelstein says to Kowalski, "I will tell you what. I will make a bet with you: If she jumps, I get twenty dollars. If she does not, you get twenty dollars. Okay?"

"Fair enough," says Kowalski.

A few minutes later the woman jumps off the ledge and kills herself.

Kowalski gets out his wallet and hands twenty dollars to Finkelstein.

A few minutes later Finkelstein turns to Kowalski and says, "Look here, I can't take this twenty dollars from you. I have a confession to make: I saw this on the news earlier this afternoon. This was a repeat."

"No, no," says Kowalski. "You keep the money, you won

it fair and square. You see, I saw this on TV earlier in the day, too."

"You did?" says Finkelstein. "Well, then why did you bet that the woman would not jump?"

"Well," says Kowalski. "I didn't think she would be stupid enough to do it twice!"

But life is such . . .

This sadness in the world, this boredom and this misery can be changed if people know that they are asking for the impossible.

Don't ask for the impossible.

Find the law of existence and follow it.

Your longing to be one is your spiritual desire, is your very essential, religious nature. It is just that you are focusing yourself on the wrong spot.

Your lover is only an excuse. Let your lover be just an experience of a greater love—the love for the whole existence.

Let your longing be a search of your own inner being; there, the meeting is already happening, there, we are already one.

There, nobody has ever separated.

The longing is perfectly right; only the object of longing is not right. That is creating the suffering and the hell. Just change the object and your life becomes a paradise.

PART THREE

Freedom

Man has reduced woman into a slave and the woman has reduced man into a slave. And of course both hate the slavery, both resist it. They are constantly fighting; any small excuse and the fight starts.

But the real fight is somewhere else deep down; the real fight is that they are asking for freedom. They cannot say it so clearly, they may have forgotten completely. For thousands of years this is the way people have lived. They have seen that their father and their mother have lived the same way, they have seen that their grandparents have lived in the same way. This is the way people live—they have accepted it. Their freedom is destroyed.

It is as if we are trying to fly in the sky with one wing. A few people have the wing of love and a few people have the wing of freedom—both are incapable of flying. Both wings are needed.

CHAPTER NINE

Tabula Rasa

Philosophers have always believed that essence precedes existence, that man is born with what he is going to be already determined. Just like a seed, he contains the whole program; now the question is only of unfoldment. There is no freedom—that has been the attitude of all the philosophers of the past, that man has a certain fate, a destiny. One is going to become a certain entity that is fixed, the script is already written. You are not aware of it, that's another matter, but whatsoever you are doing, *you* are not doing it. It is being done through you by natural, unconscious forces, or by God.

This is the attitude of the determinist, the fatalist. The whole of humanity has suffered from it immensely, because this kind of approach means there is no possibility of any radical change. Nothing can be done at all about man's transformation; everything is going to happen the way it is going to happen. The East has suffered most because of this attitude. When nothing can be done, then one starts accepting everything— slavery, poverty, ugliness; one has to accept it. This is not understanding, it is not awareness; it is not what Gautama the Buddha calls suchness, *tathata*. It is just despair, hopelessness hiding itself in beautiful words.

But the consequence is going to be disastrous. You can see it in its most developed form in India: the poverty, the beggars, the illness, the crippled people, the blind people. And nobody takes any note of it because this is how life is, this is how life has always been and this is how life is always going to be. A kind of lethargy seeps into the very soul.

But the whole approach is basically false. It is a consolation, not a discovery that comes from looking into the reality. It is somehow to hide one's wounds—it is a rationalization. And whenever rationalizations start hiding your reality you are bound to fall into darker and darker realms.

Essence does not precede existence; on the contrary, existence precedes essence. Man is the only being on the earth who has freedom. A dog is born a dog, will live like a dog, will die like a dog; there is no freedom. A rose will remain a rose, there is no possibility of any transformation; it cannot become a lotus. There is no question of choice, there is no freedom at all. This is where man is totally different. This is the dignity of man, his specialness in existence, his uniqueness.

That's why I say Charles Darwin is not right, because he starts categorizing man with other animals; this basic difference he has not even taken note of. The basic difference is that all animals are born with a program, only man is born without a program. Man is born as a *tabula rasa*, a clean slate; nothing is written on it. You have to write everything that you want to write on it; it is going to be your creation.

Man is not only free, man is *freedom*. That is his essential core, that's his very soul. The moment you deny freedom to man you have denied him his most precious treasure, his very kingdom. Then he is a beggar, and in a far more ugly situation than other animals because at least they have a certain program. Then man is simply lost.

Once this is understood, that man is born *as freedom*, then all the dimensions open up to grow. Then it is up to you what to become and what not to become; it is going to be your own creation. Then life becomes an adventure—not an unfoldment but an adventure, an exploration, a discovery. The truth is not already given to you; you have to create it. In a way, each moment you are creating yourself.

Even if you accept the theory of fate, that is also an act of deciding about your life. By accepting fatalism you have chosen the life of a slave—it is your choice! You have chosen to enter into a prison, you have chosen to be chained, but it is still your choice. You can come out of the prison.

Of course people are afraid to be free, because freedom is risky. One never knows what one is doing, where one is going, what the ultimate result of it all is going to be. If you are not ready-made then the whole responsibility is yours. You cannot throw the responsibility on somebody else's shoulders. Ultimately, you will be standing before existence totally responsible for yourself. Whatsoever you are, whosoever you are, you cannot shirk it; you cannot escape from it—this is the fear. Out of this fear people have chosen all kinds of determinist attitudes.

And it is a strange thing; the religious and the irreligious are agreed only on one point—that there is no freedom. On every other point they disagree, but on one point their agreement is strange. The communists say they are atheists, irreligious, but they say that man is determined by the social, economic, political situations. Man is not free; man's consciousness is determined by outside forces. It is the same logic! You can call the outside force the economic structure. Hegel calls it "History"—with a capital H, remember—and the religious people call it "God"; again the word is with a capital G. God, History, Economics, Politics, Society—all outside forces, but they are all agreed upon one thing, that you are not free.

I say to you, you are absolutely free, unconditionally free. Don't avoid the responsibility; avoiding is not going to help. The sooner you accept it the better, because immediately you can start creating yourself. And the moment you create yourself great joy arises, and when you have completed yourself, the way *you* wanted to, there is immense contentment, just as when a painter finishes his painting, the last touch, and a great contentment arises in his heart. A job well done brings great peace. One feels that one has participated with the whole.

The only prayer is to be creative, because it is only through creativity that you participate in the whole; there is no other way to participate. God has not to be thought about, you have to participate in some way. You cannot be an observer, you can only be a participant; only then will you taste the mystery of it. Creating a painting is nothing. Creating a poem is nothing, creating music is nothing compared to creating yourself, creating your consciousness, creating your very being.

But people have been afraid, and there are reasons to be afraid. The first is that it is risky, because only you are responsible. Secondly, the freedom can be misused—because you can choose the wrong thing to be. Freedom means you can choose the right or the wrong; if you are only free to choose the right, it is not freedom. Then it will be like when Ford made his first cars—they were all black. And he would take his customers into the showroom and tell them, "You can choose any color, provided it is black!"

But what kind of freedom is this?—*provided* it is right. Provided it follows the Ten Commandments, provided it is according to the Bhagavad-Gita or the Koran, provided it is according to Buddha, Mahavira, Zarathustra. Then it is not freedom at all! Freedom basically means, intrinsically means that you are capable of both: either choosing the right or the wrong.

And the danger is—hence the fear—that the wrong is always easier to do. The wrong is a downhill task and the right is an uphill task. Going uphill is difficult, arduous; and the higher you go the more arduous it becomes. But going downhill is very easy. You need not do anything, gravitation does everything for you. You can just roll like a rock from the hilltop and the rock will reach to the very bottom; nothing has to be done. But if you want to rise in consciousness, if you want to rise in the world of beauty, truth, bliss, then you are longing for the highest peaks possible and that certainly is difficult.

Secondly, the higher you reach the more there is a danger of falling, because the path becomes narrow and you are surrounded on all sides by dark valleys. A single wrong step and you will simply be gone into the abyss, you will disappear. It is more comfortable, convenient to walk on the plain ground, not to bother about the heights.

Freedom gives you the opportunity either to fall below the animals or to rise above the angels. Freedom is a ladder. One end of the ladder reaches hell, the other end touches heaven. It is the *same* ladder; the choice is yours, the direction has to be chosen by you.

And to me, if you are *not* free you cannot misuse your unfreedom. Unfreedom cannot be misused. The prisoner cannot misuse his situation—he is chained, he is not free to do anything. And that is the situation of all other animals except man—they are not free; they are born to be a certain kind of animal and they will fulfill it. In fact, nature itself fulfills it; they are not required to do anything. There is no challenge in their life. It is only man who has to face the challenge, the great challenge. And very few people have chosen to risk, to go to the heights, to discover their ultimate peaks. Only a few—the Buddha, the Christ— only very few, they can be counted on the fingers.

Why hasn't the whole of humanity chosen to reach the same state of bliss as Buddha, the same state of love as Christ, the same state of celebration as Krishna? Why?—for the simple reason that it is dangerous even to aspire to those heights. It is better not to think about it, and the best way not to think about it is to accept that there is no freedom— you are already determined beforehand. There is a certain script handed over to you before your birth and you have just to fulfill it.

Only freedom can be misused, slavery cannot be misused. That's why you see so much chaos in the world today. It has never been there before, for the simple reason that man was not so free. You see more chaos in America for the simple reason that they are enjoying the greatest freedom that has ever been enjoyed anywhere in the world, at any time in history. Whenever there is freedom, chaos erupts. But that chaos is worth it, because only out of that chaos are stars born.

I am not giving you any discipline, because every discipline is a subtle kind of slavery. I am not giving you any commandments, because any commandments given by anybody else coming from the outside are going to imprison you, to enslave you. I am only teaching you how to be free and then leaving you to yourself, to do what you want to do with your freedom. If you want to fall below the animals that is your decision, and you are perfectly allowed to do it because it is your life. If you decide it that way, then it is your prerogative. But if you understand freedom and its value you will not start falling; you will not go below the animals, you will start rising above the angels.

Man is not an entity, he is a bridge, a bridge between two eternities—the animal and the god, the unconscious and the conscious. Grow in consciousness, grow in freedom. Take each step out of your own choice. Create yourself and take the whole responsibility for it.

CHAPTER TEN

The Fundamental Slavery

Sex is the most powerful instinct in man. The politician and the priest have understood from the very beginning that sex is the most driving energy in man. It has to be curtailed, it has to be cut. If man is allowed total freedom in sex, then there will be no possibility to dominate him. To make a slave out of him will be impossible.

Have you not seen it being done? When you want a bull to be yoked to a cart, what do you do? You castrate him, you destroy his sex energy. And have you seen the difference between a bull and an ox? What a difference! An ox is a poor phenomenon, a slave. A bull is a beauty; a bull is a glorious phenomenon, a great splendor. See a bull walking, how he walks like an emperor! And see an ox pulling a cart.

The same has been done to man. The sex instinct has been curtailed, cut, crippled. Man does not exist as the bull now, he exists like the ox, and each man is pulling a thousand and one carts. Look and you will find behind you a thousand and one carts, and you are yoked to them.

Why can't you yoke a bull? The bull is too powerful. If he sees a cow passing by, he will throw both you and the cart, and he will move to the cow! He will not bother a bit about who you are, and he will not listen. It will be impossible to control the bull. Sex energy is life energy; it is uncontrollable. And the politician and the priest are not interested in you, they are interested in channeling your energy into other directions. So there is a certain mechanism behind it—it has to be understood.

Sex repression, tabooing sex, is the very foundation of human slavery. Man cannot be free unless sex is free. Man cannot be really free unless his sex energy is allowed natural growth.

These are the five tricks through which man has been turned into a slave, into an ugly phenomenon, a cripple.

The first is:

Keep man as weak as possible if you want to dominate him. If the priest wants to dominate you or the politician wants to dominate you, you have to be kept as weak as possible. And the best way to keep a man weak is not to give love total freedom. Love is nourishment. Now the psychologists have discovered that if a child is not given love, he shrivels up into himself and becomes weak. You can give him milk, you can give him medicine, you can give him everything else, but just don't give love. Don't hug him, don't kiss him, don't hold him close to the warmth of your body, and the child will start becoming weaker and weaker and weaker. There are more chances of his dying than surviving.

What happens? Why? Just hugging, kissing, giving warmth, and somehow the child feels nourished, accepted, loved, needed. The child starts feeling worthy; the child starts feeling a certain meaning in his life.

Now, from the very childhood we starve them; we don't give love as much as is needed. Then we try to force the young men and young women not to fall in love unless they get married. By the age of fourteen they become sexually mature. But their education may take more time, ten years more, until they are twenty-four, twenty-five years old—then they will be getting their M.A.s, or Ph.D.s, or M.D.s. So we try to force them not to love.

Sexual energy comes to its climax near the age of eighteen. Never again will a man be so potent, and never again will a woman be able to have a greater orgasm than she will be able to near the age of eighteen. But we force them not to make love—girls and boys are kept separate, and just between them stands the whole mechanism of police, magistrates, vice-chancellors, principals, headmasters. They are all standing there, just in between, just holding the boys back from moving to the girls, holding the girls back from moving to the boys. Why? Why is so much care taken'? They are trying to kill the bull and create an ox.

By the time you are eighteen you are at the peak of your sexual energy, your love energy. By the time you get married at twenty-five, twenty-six, twenty-seven . . . and the age has been going up and up. The more cultured a country the longer you wait, because more has to be learned, the job has to be found, this and that. By the time you get married you are almost declining in your powers. Then you love, but the love never becomes really hot; it never comes to the point where people evaporate, it remains lukewarm. And when you have not been able to love totally, you cannot love your children because you don't know how. When you have not been able to know the peaks of it, how can you teach your children? How can you help your children to have the peaks of it?

So down the ages man has been denied love so that he should remain weak.

Second:

Keep man as ignorant and deluded as possible so that he can easily be deceived. And if you want to create a sort of idiocy—which is a must for the priest and the politician and their conspiracy—then the best thing is not to allow man to move into love freely. Without love a man's intelligence falls low. Have you not watched it? When you fall in love, suddenly all your capacities are at their peak, at their crescendo. Just a moment ago you were looking dull and then you meet your woman and suddenly a great joy has erupted in your being; you are aflame. While people are in love they perform at their maximum. When love disappears or when love is not there, they perform at their minimum.

The most intelligent people are the most sexual people. This has to be understood, because love energy is basically intelligence. If you cannot love you are somehow closed, cold; you cannot flow. While in love one flows. While in love one feels so confident that one can touch the stars. That's why a woman becomes a great inspiration, a man becomes a great inspiration. When a woman is loved she becomes more beautiful *immediately*, instantly! Just a moment ago she was just an ordinary woman, and now love has showered upon her—she is bathed in a totally new energy, a new aura arises around her. She walks more gracefully, a dance has come to her step. Her eyes have tremendous beauty now; her face glows, she is luminous. And the same happens to the man.

When people are in love they perform at the optimum. Don't allow love and they will remain at the minimum. When they remain at the minimum they are stupid, they are ignorant, they don't bother to know. And when people are ignorant and stupid and deluded, they can be easily deceived.

When people are sexually repressed, lovewise repressed, they start hankering for the other life. They think about heaven, paradise, but they don't think to create the paradise here, now. When you are in love, paradise is here now. Then you don't bother; then who goes to the priest? Then who bothers that there should be a paradise? You are already there! You are no longer interested. But when your love energy is repressed, you start thinking, "Here is nothing, now is empty. Then there must be somewhere some goal . . ." You go to the priest and ask about heaven and he paints beautiful pictures of heaven. Sex has been repressed so that you can become interested in the other life. And when people are interested in the other life, naturally they are not interested in *this* life.

This life is the only life. The other life is hidden in this life! It is not against it, it is not away from it; it is *in* it. Go into it—this is it! Go into it and you will find the other, too. God is hidden in the world, God is hidden here now. If you love, you will be able to feel it.

The third secret:

Keep man as frightened as possible. And the sure way is not to allow him love, because love destroys fear—"love casteth out fear." When you are in love you are not afraid. When you are in love you can fight against the whole world. When you are in love you feel infinitely capable of anything. But when you are not in love, you are afraid of small things. When you are not in love you become more interested in security, in safety. When you are in love you are more interested in adventure, in exploration. People have not been allowed to love because that is the only way to make them afraid. And when they are afraid and trembling they are always on their knees, bowing to the priest and bowing to the politician.

It is a great conspiracy against humanity. It is a great conspiracy against *you!* Your politician and your priest are your enemies, but they pretend that they are public servants. They say, "We are here to serve you, to help you attain a better life. We are here to create a good life for you." And they are the destroyers of life itself.

The fourth:

Keep man as miserable as possible—because a miserable man is confused, a miserable man has no self-worth, a miserable man is self-condemnatory, a miserable man feels that he must have done something wrong. A miserable man has no grounding—you can push him from here and there, he can be turned into driftwood very easily. And a miserable man is always ready to be commanded, to be ordered, to be disciplined, because he knows: "On my own I am simply miserable. Maybe somebody else can discipline my life." He is a ready victim.

And the fifth:

Keep men as alienated from each other as possible, so that they cannot band together for some purpose of which the priest and the politician may not approve. Keep people separate from each other. Don't allow them too much intimacy. When people are separate, lonely, alienated from each other, they cannot band together. And there are a thousand and one tricks to keep them apart.

For example, if you are holding the hand of a man—you are a man and you are holding the hand of a man and walking down the road, singing—you will feel guilty because people will start looking at you. Are you gay, homosexual or something? Two men are not allowed to be happy together. They are not allowed to hold hands, they are not allowed to hug each other. They are condemned as homosexuals. Fear arises. If your friend comes and takes your hand in his hand, you look around: "Is somebody looking or not?" And you are just in a hurry to drop the hand.

You shake hands in such a hurry. Have you watched it? You just touch each other's hand and shake and you are finished. You don't hold hands, you don't hug each other; you are afraid. Do you remember your father hugging you, ever? Do you remember your mother hugging you after you became sexually mature? Why not? Fear has been created. A young man and his mother hugging?—maybe some sex will arise between them, some idea, some fantasy. Fear has been created: the father and the son, no; the father and the daughter, no. The brother and the sister no; the brother and the brother—no!

People are kept in separate boxes with great walls around them. Everybody is classified, and there are a thousand and one barriers. Yes, one day, after twenty-five years of all this training, you are allowed to make love to your wife. But now the training has gone too deep into you, and suddenly you don't know what to do. How to love? You have not learned the language. It is as if a person has not been allowed to speak for twenty-five years. Just listen: For twenty-five years he has not been allowed to speak a single word and then suddenly you put him on a stage and tell him, "Give us a great lecture." What will happen? He will fall down, then and there. He may faint, he may die . . . twenty-five years of silence and now suddenly he is expected to deliver a great lecture? It is not possible.

This is what is happening! Twenty-five years of antilove, of fear, and then suddenly you are legally allowed—a license is issued and now you can love this woman. "This is your wife, you are her husband, and you are allowed to love." But where are those twenty-five years of wrong training going to go? They will be there.

Yes, you will "love" . . . you will make a gesture. It is not going to be explosive, it is not going to be orgasmic; it will be very tiny. That's why you are frustrated after making love—ninety-nine percent of people are frustrated after making love, more frustrated than they have ever been before. And they feel, "What is this? There is nothing! It is not true!"

First, the priest and the politician have managed that you should not be able to love, and then they come and they preach that there is nothing significant in love. And certainly their preaching looks right, their preaching looks exactly in tune with your experience. First they create the experience of futility, of frustration—then, their teaching. And both look logical together, of a piece. This is a great trick, the greatest that has ever been played upon man.

These five things can be managed through a single thing, and that is the taboo against love. It is possible to accomplish all these objectives by somehow preventing people from loving each other. And the taboo has been managed in such a scientific way. This taboo is a great work of art—great skill and great cunningness have gone into it. It is really a masterpiece! This taboo has to be understood.

First, it is indirect, it is hidden. It is not apparent, because whenever a taboo is too obvious, it will not work. The taboo has to be very hidden, so you don't know how it works. The taboo has to be so hidden that you cannot even imagine that thing against it is possible. The taboo has to go into the unconscious, not into the conscious. How to make it so subtle and so indirect?

The trick is: First go on teaching that love is great, so people never think that the priests and the politicians are against love. Go on teaching that love is great, that love is the right thing, and then don't allow any situation where love can happen. Don't allow the opportunity. Don't give any opportunity, and go on teaching that food is great, that eating is a great joy; "Eat as well as you can"—but don't supply anything to eat. Keep people hungry and go on talking about love. So all the priests go on talking about love. Love is praised as highly as anything, just next to God, and denied every possibility of happening. Directly they encourage it; indirectly they cut its roots. This is the masterpiece.

No priests talk about how they have done the harm. It is as if you go on saying to a tree, "Be green, bloom, enjoy," and you go on cutting the roots so that the tree cannot be green. And when the tree is not green you can jump upon the tree and say, "Listen! You don't listen. You don't follow us. We all go on saying 'Be green, bloom, enjoy dance' . . ." and meanwhile you go on cutting the roots.

Love is denied so much—and love is the rarest thing in the world; it should not be denied. If a man can love five persons, he should love five. If a man can love fifty, he should love fifty. If a man can love five hundred, he should love five hundred. Love is so rare that the more you can spread it the better. But there are great tricks—you are forced into a narrow, very narrow, corner. You can love only your wife, you can love only your husband, you can love only this, you can love only that—the conditions are too much. It is as if there was a law that you can breathe only when you are with your wife, you can breathe only when you are with your husband. Then breathing will become impossible! Then you will die, and you will not even be able to breathe while you are with your wife or with your husband. You have to breathe twenty-four hours a day.

Be loving.

Then there is another trick. They talk about "higher love" and they destroy the lower. They say that the lower has to be denied; bodily love is bad, spiritual love is good.

Have you ever seen any spirit without a body? Have you ever seen a house without a foundation? The lower is the foundation of the higher. The body is your abode; the spirit lives in the body, with the body. You are an embodied spirit and an ensouled body—you are together. The lower and the higher are not separate, they are one—rungs of the same ladder. The lower has not to be denied, the lower has to be transformed into the higher. The lower is good—if you are stuck with the lower the fault is with you, not with the lower. Nothing is wrong with the lower rung of a ladder. If you are stuck with it, *you* are stuck; it is something in you.

Move.

Sex is not wrong. *You* are wrong if you are stuck there. Move higher. The higher is not against the lower; the lower makes it possible for the higher to exist.

And these tricks have created many other problems. Each time you are in love somehow you feel guilty; a guilt has arisen. When there is guilt you cannot move totally into love—the guilt prevents you, it keeps you holding on. Even while making love to your wife or your husband, there is guilt. You know this is sin, you know you are doing something wrong. "Saints don't do it"—you are a sinner. So you cannot move totally even when you are allowed, superficially, to love your wife. The priest is hidden behind you in your guilt; he is pulling you from there, pulling your strings.

When guilt arises, you start feeling that you are wrong; you lose self-worth, you lose self-respect. And another problem arises: When there is guilt you start pretending. Mothers and fathers don't allow their children to know that they make love, they pretend. They pretend that sex does not exist. Their pretension will be known by the children sooner or later. When the children come to know about the pretension, they lose all trust. They feel betrayed, they feel cheated.

And fathers and mothers say that their children don't respect them— you are the cause of it, how can they respect you? You have been deceiving them in every way, you have been dishonest, you have been mean. You were telling them not to fall in love—"Beware!" and you were making love all the time. And the day will come, sooner or later, when they will realize that even their father, even their mother was not true with them. How can they respect you?

First, guilt creates pretension. Then pretension creates alienation from people. Even the child, your own child, will not feel in tune with you. There is a barrier—your pretension. One day you will come to know that you are just pretending and so are others. When everybody is pretending, how can you relate? When everybody is false, how can you relate? How can you be friendly when everywhere there is deception and deceit? You become very, very sore about reality, you become very bitter. You see it only as a devil's workshop.

And everybody has a false face, nobody is authentic. Everybody is carrying masks, nobody shows his original face. You feel guilty, you feel that you are pretending and you know that everybody else is pretending. Everybody is feeling guilty and everybody has become just like an ugly wound. Now it is very easy to make these people slaves—to turn them into clerks, stationmasters, schoolmasters, deputy collectors, ministers, governors, presidents. Now it is very easy to distract them. You have distracted them from their roots.

Sex is the root; hence the name *muladhar* in the language of tantra and yoga. *Muladhar* means the root energy.

I have heard . . .

It was her wedding night and the haughty Lady Jane was performing her marital duties for the first time.

"My lord," she asked her bridegroom, "is this what the common people call lovemaking?"

"Yes, it is, my lady," replied Lord Reginald, and proceeded as before.

After a while Lady Jane exclaimed indignantly, "It is too good for the common people!"

The common people have not really been allowed lovemaking: "It is too good for them." But the problem is that when you poison the whole common world, you are also poisoned. If you poison the air that the common people breathe, the air that the king breathes will also be poisoned. It cannot be separate—it is all one. When the priest poisons the common people, finally he also is poisoned. When the politician poisons the common people's air, finally he also breathes the same air— there is no other air.

A curate and a bishop were in opposite corners of a railway carriage on a long journey. As the bishop entered, the curate put away his copy of *Playboy*, and started reading *The Church Times*. The bishop ignored him and went on doing the *Times* crossword. Silence prevailed.

After a while the curate tried to make conversation. And when the bishop began to do a lot of head-scratching and "tut-tut-tutting" the curate tried again. "Can I help you sir?"

"Perhaps. I am only beaten by one word. What is it that has four letters, the last three are U-N-T, and the clue is *'essentially feminine'*?"

"Why, sir," said the curate after a slight pause, "that would be *aunt*."

"Of course, of course!" said the bishop. "I say, young man, can you lend me an eraser?"

When you repress things on the surface, they all go deep inside, into the unconscious. It is there. Sex has not been destroyed—fortunately. It has not been destroyed, it has only been poisoned. It *cannot* be destroyed; it is life energy. It has become polluted, and it can be purified.

Your life problems can basically be reduced to your sex problem. You can go on solving your other problems but you will never be able to solve them because they are not true problems. And if you solve your sex problem, all problems will disappear because you have solved the basic one. But you are so afraid even to look into it.

It is simple. If you can put aside your conditioning, it is very simple. It is as simple as this story.

A frustrated spinster was a pest to the police. She kept ringing up saying there was a man under her bed. She was finally sent to a mental hospital, where they gave her the latest drugs and after some weeks a doctor came to interview her and determine whether she had been cured.

"Miss Rustifan," the doctor asked, "do you see a man under the bed now?"

"No, I don't," she said. But just as the doctor was ready to sign her release she said, "Now I can see two."

The doctor told the hospital staff that there was only really one sort of injection that would cure her complaint, which he called "malignant virginity"—he suggested they set her up in her bedroom with Big Dan, the hospital carpenter.

Big Dan was fetched, told what the woman's complaint was, and that he would be locked in with her for an hour. He said it would not take that long, and an anxious group gathered on the landing . . . they heard, "No, stop it, Dan. Mother would never forgive me!"

"Shut up your yelling, it's got to be done some time. It should have been done years ago!"

"Have your way by force then, you brute!"

"It's only what your husband would have done, had you had one."

The medics could not wait, they burst in.

"I have cured her," said the carpenter.

"He has cured me!" said Miss Rustifan.

He had sawed the legs off the bed.

Sometimes the cure is very simple. And you go on doing a thousand and one things . . . And the carpenter did well—just cutting the legs off the bed and it was finished! Now where could the man hide?

Sex is the root of almost all your problems. It has to be so because of thousands of years of poisoning. A great purification is needed. Reclaim your freedom. Reclaim your freedom to love. Reclaim your freedom to be and then life is no longer a problem. It is a mystery, it is an ecstasy, it is a benediction.

CHAPTER ELEVEN

Beware of the Popes

I have heard that the pope, addressing the youth in Latin America, said, "My dear ones, beware of the devil. The devil will tempt you with drugs, alcohol, and most particularly premarital sex." Now, who is this devil? I have never met him, he has never tempted me. I don't think any of you have ever met the devil, or that he has tempted you.

Desires come from your own nature, it is not some devil who is tempting you. But it is a strategy of religions to throw the responsibility on an imaginary figure, the devil, so you don't feel you are being condemned. You *are* being condemned but indirectly. The pope is saying to you that *you* are the devil—but he has not the guts to say that, so he is saying that the devil is something else, a separate agency, whose only function is to tempt people.

But it is very strange . . . millions of years have passed and the devil is not tired, he goes on tempting. And what does he gain out of it? In no scripture have I found what is his reward for all this arduous work for millions of years. Who is paying him? By whom is he employed? That is one thing . . .

And the second: Is not your God omnipotent? That's what your scriptures say, that God is all-powerful. If he is all-powerful, can't he do a simple thing?—just stop this devil from tempting people! Rather than going to every person and telling every person, "Don't be tempted by the devil," why not finish this one devil? Or, whatsoever he wants, give it to him.

This is something to be decided between God and the devil. What business is it of ours to be unnecessarily trampled between these two? God has not been able in millions of years to convince the devil or to change the devil or to finish the devil. And if God is so powerless before the devil, what about his poor people, to whom these representatives of God go on saying, "Don't be tempted by the devil"? If God is so powerless and impotent before the devil, what can ordinary human beings do?

For centuries these people have been telling these lies, and not even once have they themselves tried to be responsible. This is irresponsibility—telling young people, "Be aware, the devil is going to tempt you." In fact this man has put the temptation already in the minds of these people. They may not have been thinking right then of drugs, alcohol, premarital sex. They had come to listen to the pope, to some spiritual sermon. They will go back home thinking of premarital sex, how to get tempted by the devil, where to find the drug dealers.

But alcohol is certainly not a temptation of the devil, because Jesus Christ was drinking alcohol—not only drinking it but making it available to his apostles. Alcohol is not against Christianity—Christianity accepts alcohol perfectly, because to deny alcohol would be putting Jesus in jeopardy. Jesus was not a member of Alcoholics Anonymous. He enjoyed drinking, and he has never said that drinking is a sin—how could he say it? Now the pope seems to be far more religious than Jesus Christ.

And I can certainly visualize that if the only begotten son drinks, the Father must be a drunkard and the Holy Ghost, too. These people may be the cause, because from where did Jesus learn? Certainly the devil could not tempt *him*. We know that the devil used to try to tempt him and he said to the devil, "Get behind me, I am not to be tempted by you."

But these people seem to be mentally sick. You never come across the devil, and you don't talk with the devil this way: "Get behind me, and let me go on my way. Don't prevent me, don't try to tempt me."

And if you do say these things and somebody hears, he is going to inform the nearest police station, "Here comes a man who is talking to the devil, and we don't see any devil anywhere."

Jesus is also contaminated by the rabbis and the priests. It is the same company, just with different labels and different trademarks. But the business is the same, the company is the same, their work is the same—they corrupt human beings, they destroy your innocence. This pope is worried about premarital sex—it must be on his mind, otherwise how can this warning come out of it? And that is his most emphatic point!

But what is wrong with premarital sex? It was a problem in the past, but have you entered into the twentieth century or not? It was a problem in the past because sex can lead to pregnancy, to children, and then the problem will arise of who is going to bring up those children. Then who is going to marry that girl who has a child? So there will be complications and difficulties. There need not be—it is just in the mind.

In fact, most marital difficulties arise because premarital sex is denied. It is as if you are told that until you are twenty-one you cannot swim: Don't be tempted by the devil; pre-adult swimming is a sin. Okay, one day you become twenty-one—but you don't know how to swim. And thinking that now you are twenty-one you are allowed to swim, you jump into the river. You are jumping to your death! Because just by becoming twenty-one there is no necessity, there is no intrinsic law that you will be able to swim. And when are you going to learn? What actually are these people saying? They are saying that before entering the river you should learn to swim; if you enter the river you are committing a sin. But where are you going to learn to swim?—in your bedroom, on your mattress? For swimming you will need to go to the river.

There are aboriginal tribes that are far more human, natural, where premarital sex is supported by the society, encouraged, because that is the time to learn. At fourteen years of age the girl becomes sexually mature; at eighteen years of age the boy becomes sexually mature. And the age is going down—as human societies become more scientific, technological, the food is sufficient and health is taken care of and the age goes on falling. In America girls become mature earlier than in India.

And of course in Ethiopia, how can you become sexually mature? You will die long before. In America the age has fallen from fourteen to thirteen to twelve, because physically people are more energetic, have better food, a more comfortable life. They become sexually mature early, and they will also be able to function longer than in poor countries.

In India people simply cannot believe when they read in the newspapers that some American at the age of ninety is going to get married. The Indians cannot believe it—what is happening to these Americans? By the time an Indian is ninety he has been in the grave almost twenty years; only his ghost can get married, not he. And even if they are in their bodies, a ninety-year-old person marrying a woman who is eighty-seven . . . just great! Simply unbelievable! And they go on a honeymoon. They are really very practiced, they have done this all their lives, many times—getting married, going on a honeymoon—and they have been fortunate enough so that in one life they have lived at least five, six, seven lives.

Premarital sex is one of the most important things to be decided by human society.

The girl will never be more alive sexually than she is at the age of fourteen, and the boy will never be so sexually alive as he is at the age of eighteen. When nature is at its peak, you prevent them. By the time the boy is thirty you allow him to get married. He is already declining in his sexuality. In his life energy he is already on the decline, he is losing interest. Biologically he is already fourteen or sixteen years late— he has missed the train long ago.

It is because of this that so many marital problems arise, and so many marital counselors thrive, because both partners have passed their peak hours and those peak hours were the time when they could have known what orgasm is. Now they read about it in books and they dream of it, fantasize about it—and it doesn't happen. They are too late. The popes are standing in between.

I would like to say to you: Don't be tempted by the popes. These are the real evil ones. They will spoil your whole life. They have spoiled the lives of millions of people.

When you are thirty you cannot have that quality, that intensity, that fire that you had when you were eighteen. But that was the time to be celibate, not to be tempted by the devil. Whenever the devil tempts you, just start praying to God, repeating a mantra, *om mani padme hum*. That's what the Tibetans do.

Whenever you see a Tibetan quickly doing "Om mani padme hum" you can be certain he is tempted by the devil, because that mantra is used to make the devil afraid. And the faster you do it, the faster the devil will run away.

In India there exists a small book, *Hanuman Chalisa*. It is a prayer to the monkey god, Hanuman, who is thought to be a celibate and a protector of all those who want to remain celibate. So all the people who want to remain celibate are worshippers of Hanuman. And this small book you can memorize very easily. They go on repeating this prayer, so Hanuman goes on protecting their celibacy, goes on protecting them from the devil who is always around, waiting for the chance to get hold of them and tempt them.

Nobody is tempting you. It is simply nature, not the devil. And nature is not against you, it is all for you.

In a better human society, premarital sex should be appreciated just the way it is appreciated in a few aboriginal tribes. The reasoning is very simple. First, nature has prepared you for something; you should not be denied your natural right. If the society is not ready for you to get married, that is society's problem, not yours. The society should find some way. The aboriginals have found the way. It is very rare that a girl gets pregnant. If a girl gets pregnant, the boy and the girl get married. There is no shame about it, there is no scandal about it, there is no condemnation about it. On the contrary, the elders bless the young couple because they have proved that they are vigorous; nature is powerful in them, their biology is more alive than anybody else's. But it rarely happens.

What happens is that every boy and every girl become trained. In aboriginal societies I have visited, it is a rule that after the fourteenth year the girl, and after the eighteenth, the boy, are not allowed to sleep in their houses. They have a common hall in the middle of the village where all the girls and all the boys go and sleep. Now there is no need for them to hide behind the car, in the car porch. This is ugly—this is society forcing people to be thieves, deceivers, liars. And their first experiences of love have happened in such ugly situations—hiding, afraid, guilty, knowing that it is a temptation of the devil. They cannot enjoy it when they are capable of enjoying it to its fullest, and experiencing it at its peak.

What I am saying is that if they had experienced it at its peak, its grip over them would have been lost. Then their whole life they would not be looking at *Playboy* magazines; there would be no need. And they would not be dreaming about sex, having sexual fantasies. They would not be reading third-rate novels and looking at Hollywood movies. All this is possible because they have been denied their birthright.

In the aboriginal society they live together in the night. One rule only is told to them: "Don't be with one girl more than three days, because she is not your property, you are not her property. You have to become acquainted with all the girls, and she has to become acquainted with all the boys before you choose your life partner."

Now, this seems to be absolutely sane. Before choosing a life partner you should be given a chance to be acquainted with all available women, all available men. You can see all over the world that neither arranged marriage has been successful, nor what you call love marriage. Both have failed, and the basic reason is that in both cases the couple is inexperienced; the couple has not been given enough freedom to find the right person.

There is no other way than through experience to find the right person. Very small things can be disturbing. Somebody's body smell may be enough to spoil your whole marriage. It is not a great thing, but it is enough: every day . . . how long can you tolerate it? But to somebody else that smell may be very fitting, may be the smell that he likes.

Just let people have experience—and particularly now, when problems of pregnancy are no longer there. Those aboriginals were courageous to do it for thousands of years—and then, too, there have not been many problems. Once in a while the girl may get pregnant, then they get married; otherwise there is no problem.

In those tribes there are no divorces because, of course, once you have looked at all the women, have been with all the women of the tribe and then you choose, now what else are you going to change? You have chosen out of experience, so in those societies there is no need, there is no question of divorce. The question has not arisen. It is not that divorce is not allowed; the very question of divorce has not arisen in those tribes. They have not thought about it, it has never been a problem. Nobody has said that they want to separate.

All civilized societies suffer from marital problems because the husband and wife are almost enemies. You can call them "intimate enemies" but that does not make any difference—it is better that the enemies are far away and not too intimate! If they are intimate, that means that it is a twenty-four-hour-a-day war, continuously—day in, day out. And the simple reason is the stupid idea of these religious teachers: "Beware of premarital sex."

If you want to beware, beware of marital sex, because that is where the problem is. Premarital sex is not a problem, and particularly now when all sorts of birth control methods are available.

Every college, every university, every school, should make it a point that every child, girl or boy, goes through all kinds of experiences, all types of people, and finally chooses. This choice will be based and rooted in knowing, in understanding.

But the problem for the pope is not that the whole of humanity is suffering from marriage, that all couples are suffering from marriage and that because of their suffering their children start learning the ways of suffering—he is not concerned. His whole concern is that birth control methods should not be used. In fact the pope is not saying, "Beware of the devil," he is saying, "Beware of birth control methods."

Real problems are not being dealt with, only unreal, bogus ones. And he goes on advising the whole world . . .

CHAPTER TWELVE

Is There Life After Sex?

At a certain age, sex becomes important—not that you make it important, it is not something that you make happen; it *happens*. At the age of fourteen, somewhere near there, suddenly your energy is flooded with sex. It happens as if the floodgates have been opened in you. Subtle sources of energy, which were not yet open, have become open, and your whole energy becomes sexual, colored with sex. You think sex, you sing sex, you walk sex—everything becomes sexual. Every act is colored. This happens; you have not done anything about it. It is natural.

Transcendence is also natural. If sex is lived totally, with no condemnation, with no idea of getting rid of it, then at the age of forty-two—just as at the age of fourteen sex gets opened and the whole energy becomes sexual, at the age of forty-two or near about—those floodgates close again. And that, too, is as natural as sex becoming alive; it starts disappearing.

Sex is transcended not by any effort on your part. If you make any effort, that will be repressive, because it has nothing to do with you. It is in-built in your body, in your biology. You are born as sexual beings; nothing is wrong with it. That is the only way to be born. To be human is to be sexual. When you were conceived, your mother and your father were not praying, they were not listening to a priest's sermon. They were not in the church, they were making love. Even to think that your mother and father were making love when you were conceived seems to be difficult. They were making love; their sexual energies were meeting and merging into each other. Then you were conceived; in a deep sexual act you were conceived. The first cell was a sex cell, and then out of that cell other cells have arisen. But each cell remains sexual, basically. Your whole body is sexual, made of sex cells. Now they are millions.

Remember it: You exist as a sexual being. Once you accept it, the conflict that has been created down through the centuries dissolves. Once you accept it deeply, with no ideas in between, when sex is thought of as simply natural, you live it. You don't ask me how to transcend eating, you don't ask me how to transcend breathing—because no religion has taught you to transcend breathing, that's why. Otherwise, you would be asking, "How to transcend breathing?" You breathe! You are a breathing animal; you are a sexual animal, also. But there is a difference. Fourteen years of your life, in the beginning, are almost nonsexual, or at the most, just rudimentary sexual play that is not really sexual—just preparing, rehearsing, that's all. At the age of fourteen, suddenly the energy is ripe.

Watch . . . a child is born—immediately, within three seconds the child has to breathe, otherwise he will die. Then breathing is to continue the whole of his life, because it has come at the first step of life. It cannot be transcended. Maybe before you die then, just three seconds before, it will stop, but not before it. Always remember: Both ends of life, the beginning and end, are exactly similar, symmetrical. The child is born, he starts breathing in three seconds. When the child is old and dying, the moment he stops breathing, within three seconds he will be dead.

Sex enters at a very late stage. For fourteen years the child has lived without sex. And if the society is not too repressed and hence obsessed with sex, a child can live completely oblivious to the fact that sex, or that anything like sex, exists. The child can remain absolutely innocent. That innocence is also not possible, because people are so repressed. When repression happens, then side by side, obsession also happens.

So priests go on repressing; and there are antipriests, Hugh Hefners and others—they go on creating more and more pornography. So on one side there are priests who go on repressing, and then there are others, antipriests, who go on making sexuality more and more glamorous. They both exist together—aspects of the same coin. When churches disappear, only then will *Playboy* magazines disappear, not before it. They are partners in the business. They look like enemies, but don't be deceived by that. They talk against each other, but that's how things work.

I have heard about two men who were out of business, had gone broke, so they decided to create a very simple new business. They started journeying, touring from one town to another town. First one would enter, and in the night he would throw coal tar on people's windows and doors. After two or three days the other would come to clean. He would advise that he could clean even coal tar from their houses, and he would clean the windows. During that time the other would be doing his half of the business in the next town. This way, they started earning much money.

This is what is happening between the church and the Hugh Hefners and other people who are creating pornography. It is together; they are partners in a conspiracy. Whenever you are too repressed, you start finding a perverse interest. A perverted interest is the problem, not sex.

So never carry a single idea against sex in your mind, otherwise you will never be able to transcend it. People who transcend sex are people who accept it very naturally. It is difficult, I know, because you are born in a society that is neurotic about sex. Either this way or that, but it is neurotic all the same. It is very difficult to get out of this neurosis but if you are a little alert, you can get out of it. So the real thing is not how to transcend sex but how to transcend this perverted ideology of the society: this fear of sex, this repression of sex, this obsession with sex.

Sex is beautiful. Sex in itself is a natural, rhythmic phenomenon. It happens when the child is ready to be conceived, and it is good that it happens—otherwise life would not exist. Life exists through sex; sex is its medium. If you understand life, if you love life, you will know sex is sacred, holy. Then you live it, then you delight in it, and as naturally as it has come it goes of its own accord. By the age of forty-two, or somewhere near there, sex starts disappearing as naturally as it had come into being. But it doesn't happen that way.

You will be surprised when I say near about forty-two. You know people who are seventy, eighty, and yet they have not gone beyond. You know "dirty old people." They are victims of the society. Because they could not be natural, it is a hangover—because they repressed when they should have enjoyed and delighted. In those moments of delight they were not totally in it. They were not orgasmic, they were halfhearted.

So whenever you are halfhearted in anything, it lingers longer. If you are sitting at your table and eating, and if you eat only halfheartedly and your hunger remains, then you will continue to think about food for the whole day. You can try fasting and you will see: You will continuously think about food. But if you have eaten well—and when I say eaten well, I don't mean only that you have stuffed your stomach. Then it is not necessarily so that you have eaten well; you could have stuffed yourself. But eating well is an art, it is not just stuffing. It is great art to taste the food, to smell the food, to touch the food, to chew the food, to digest the food, and to digest it as divine. It is divine; it is God's gift.

Hindus say, *Anam Brahma*, food is divine. So with deep respect you eat and while eating you forget everything, because it is prayer. It is existential prayer. You are eating God, and God is going to give you nourishment. It is a gift to be accepted with deep love and gratitude. And you don't stuff the body, because stuffing the body is going against the body. It is the other pole. There are people who are obsessed with fasting and there are people who are obsessed with stuffing themselves. Both are wrong because in both ways the body loses balance.

A real lover of the body eats only to the point where the body feels perfectly quiet, balanced, tranquil; where the body feels to be neither leaning to the left nor to the right but just in the middle. It is an art to understand the language of the body, to understand the language of your stomach, to understand what is needed, to give only what is needed and to give that in an artistic way, in an aesthetic way.

Animals eat, man eats. Then what is the difference? Man makes a great aesthetic experience out of eating. What is the point of having a beautiful dining table? What is the point of having candles burning there? What is the point of incense? What is the point of asking friends to come and participate? It is to make it an art, not just stuffing. But these are outward signs of the art; the inward signs are to understand the language of your body, to listen to it, to be sensitive to its needs. And *then* you eat, and then the whole day you will not remember food at all. Only when the body is hungry again will the remembrance come. Then it is natural.

With sex the same happens. If you have no "anti" attitude about it, you take it as a natural, divine gift, with great gratitude. You enjoy it; with prayer you enjoy it. Tantra says that before you make love to a woman or to a man, first pray—because it is going to be a divine meeting of energies. God will surround you—wherever two lovers are, there is God. Wherever two lovers' energies are meeting and mingling, there is life, alive, at its best; God surrounds you. Churches are empty; love-chambers are full of God. If you have tasted love the way Tantra says to taste it, if you have known love the way Tao says to know it, then by the time you reach forty-two, sex starts disappearing of its own accord. And you say goodbye to it with deep gratitude because you are fulfilled. It has been delightful, it has been a blessing; you say goodbye to it.

And forty-two is the age for meditation, the right age. Sex disappears; that overflowing energy is no longer there. One becomes more tranquil. Passion has gone, compassion arises. Now there is no more fever; one is not interested in the other. With sex disappearing, the other is no longer the focus. One starts returning toward one's own source—the return journey starts.

Sex is transcended not by your effort. It happens if you have lived it totally. So my suggestion is, drop all "anti" attitudes, antilife attitudes, and accept the facticity: sex *is*, so who are you to drop it? And who is trying to drop it? It is just the ego. Remember, sex creates the greatest problem for the ego.

So there are two types of people: Very egoistic people are always against sex; humble people are never against sex. But who listens to humble people? In fact, humble people don't go preaching, only egoists.

Why is there a conflict between sex and ego?—because sex is something in your life where you cannot be egoistic, where the other becomes more important than you. Your woman, your man, becomes more important than you. In every other case, you remain the most important. In a love relationship the other becomes very, very important, tremendously important. You become a satellite and the other becomes the nucleus, and the same is happening for the other: You become the nucleus and he becomes a satellite. It is a reciprocal surrender. Both are surrendering to love, and both become humble.

Sex is the only energy that gives you hints that there is something that you cannot control. Money you can control, politics you can control, the market you can control, knowledge you can control, science you can control, morality you can control. Somewhere, sex brings in a totally different world; you cannot control it. And the ego is the great controller. It is happy if it can control; it is unhappy if it cannot control. So there starts a conflict between ego and sex. Remember, it is a losing battle. The ego cannot win it because ego is just superficial. Sex is very deep-rooted. Sex is your life; ego is just your mind, your head. Sex has roots all over you; ego has roots only in your ideas—very superficial, just in the head.

So who will try to transcend sex?—the head will try to transcend sex. If you are too much in the head then you want to transcend sex, because sex brings you down to the guts. It does not allow you to remain hanging in the head. Everything else you can manage from there; sex you cannot manage from there. You cannot make love with your heads. You have to come down, you have to descend from your heights, you have to come closer to earth.

Sex is humiliating to the ego, so egoistic people are always against sex. They go on finding ways and means to transcend it—they can never transcend it. They can, at the most, become perverted. Their whole effort from the very beginning is doomed to failure. You may pretend that you have won over sex, but an undercurrent . . . You may rationalize, you may find reasons, you may pretend, you may create a very hard shell around yourself but deep down the real reason, the reality, will stand untouched. And the real cause will explode; you cannot hide it, it is not possible.

So you can try to control sex, but an undercurrent of sexuality will run and it will show itself in many ways. Out of all your rationalizations, it will again and again raise its head.

I will not suggest that you make any effort to transcend it. What I suggest is just the contrary: Forget about transcending it. Move into it as deeply as you can. While the energy is there, move as deeply as you can, love as deeply as you can, and make an art of it. It is not just to be "done"—that is the whole meaning of making an art of lovemaking. There are subtle nuances, which only people who enter with a great aesthetic sense will be able to know. Otherwise, you can make love for your whole life and still remain unsatisfied because you don't know that satisfaction is something very aesthetic. It is like a subtle music arising in your soul.

If through sex you fall into harmony, if through love you become relaxed—if love is not just throwing energy because you don't know what to do with it, if it is not just a relief but a relaxation, if you relax into your woman and your woman relaxes into you—if for a few seconds, for a few moments or a few hours you forget who you are, and you are completely lost in oblivion, you will come out of it purer, more innocent, more virgin. And you will have a different type of being—at ease, centered, rooted.

If this happens, one day suddenly you will see that the flood has gone and it has left you very, very rich. You will not be sorry that it has gone. You will be thankful, because now richer worlds open. When sex leaves you, the doors of meditation open. When sex leaves you, then you are not trying to lose yourself in the other. You become capable of losing yourself in yourself. Now another world of orgasm, the inner orgasm of being with oneself, arises. But that arises only through being with the other.

One grows, matures through the other; then a moment comes when you can be alone, tremendously happy. There is no need for any other, the need has disappeared but you have learned much through it—you have learned much about yourself. The other became the mirror. And you have not broken the mirror—you have learned so much about yourself, now there is no need to look into the mirror. You can close your eyes and you can see your face there. But you would not be able to see that face if there had been no mirror from the very beginning.

Let your woman be your mirror, let your man be your mirror. Look into her eyes and see your face, move into her to know yourself. Then one day the mirror will not be needed. But you will not be against the mirror—you will be so grateful to it, how can you be against it? You will be so thankful, how can you be against it? Then, transcendence.

Transcendence is not repression. Transcendence is a natural outgrowing—you grow above, you go beyond, just as a seed breaks and a sprout starts rising above the ground. When sex disappears, the seed disappears. In sex, you were able to give birth to somebody else, a child. When sex disappears, the whole energy starts giving birth to *you*. This is what Hindus have called *dwija*, the twice-born. One birth has been given to you by your parents, the other birth is waiting. It has to be given to you by yourself. You have to father and mother yourself.

Then your whole energy is turning in—it becomes an inner circle. Right now it will be difficult for you to make an inner circle. It will be easier to connect it with another pole—a woman or a man—and then the circle becomes complete. Then you can enjoy the blessings of the circle. But by and by you will be able to make the inner circle alone, because inside of you also, you are man and woman, woman and man.

Nobody is just a man, and nobody is just a woman—because you come from a man and a woman's communion. Both have participated; your mother has given something to you, your father has given something to you. Fifty-fifty, they have contributed to you; both are there. There is a possibility that both can meet inside you; again your father and mother can love—inside you. Then your reality will be born. Once they met when your body was born; now, if they can meet inside you, your soul will be born. That's what transcendence of sex is. It is a higher sex.

When you transcend sex, you reach to a higher sex. Ordinary sex is gross, higher sex is not gross at all. Ordinary sex is outward-moving, higher sex is inward-moving. In ordinary sex, two bodies meet, and the meeting happens on the outside. In higher sex, your own inner energies meet. It is not physical, it is spiritual—it is transcendence.

CHAPTER THIRTEEN

It Takes a Village . . .

Man has outgrown the family. The utility of the family is finished; it has lived too long. It is one of the most ancient institutions, so only very perceptive people can see that it is dead already. It will take time for others to recognize the fact that the family is dead.

It has done its work. It is no longer relevant in the new context of things; it is no longer relevant for the new humanity that is just being born.

The family has been good and bad. It has been a help—man has survived through it—and it has been very harmful because it has corrupted the human mind. But there was no alternative in the past, there was no way to choose anything else. It was a necessary evil. That need not be so in the future. The future can have alternative styles.

My idea is that the future is not going to be one fixed pattern; it will have many, many alternative styles. If a few people still choose to have a family, they should have the freedom to have it. It will be a very small percentage. There are families on the earth—very rare, not more than one percent—that are really beautiful, that are really beneficial, in which growth happens. In which there is no authority, no power trip, no possessiveness; in which children are not destroyed. In which the wife is not trying to destroy the husband and the husband is not trying to destroy the wife; where love is and freedom is; where people have gathered together just out of joy, not for other motives; where there is no politics. Yes, these kinds of families have existed on earth; they are still there. For these people there is no need to change. In the future they can continue to live in families.

But for the greater majority, the family is an ugly thing. You can ask the psychoanalysts and they will say that all kinds of mental diseases arise out of the family. All kinds of psychoses, neuroses, arise out of the family. The family creates a very, very ill human being.

There is no need; alternative styles should be possible. For me, one alternative style is the commune—it is the best.

A commune means people living in a liquid family. Children belong to the commune—they belong to all. There is no personal property, no personal ego. A man lives with a woman because they feel like living together, because they cherish it, they enjoy it. The moment they feel that love is no longer happening, they don't go on clinging to each other. They say goodbye with all gratitude, with all friendship. They start moving with other people.

The only problem in the past was what to do with the children. In a commune, children can belong to the commune and that will be far better. They will have more opportunities to grow with many more kinds of people. Otherwise a child grows up with the mother—for years the mother and the father are the only two images of human beings for him. Naturally he starts imitating them. Children turn out to be imitators of their fathers, and they perpetuate the same kind of illness in the world as their parents did. They become carbon copies. It is very destructive. And there is no way for the children to do something else; they don't have any other source of information.

If a hundred people live together in a commune there will be many male members, many female members; the child need not get fixed and obsessed with one pattern of life. He can learn from his father, he can learn from his uncles, he can learn from all the men in the community. He will have a bigger soul.

Families crush people and give them very little souls. In the community, the child will have a bigger soul; he will have more possibilities, he will be far more enriched in his being. He will see many women; he will not have one idea of a woman. It is very destructive to have only one single idea of a woman—because throughout your whole life you will be searching and searching for your mother. Whenever you fall in love with a woman, watch! There is every possibility that you have found someone that is similar to your mother, and that may be the thing that you should have avoided.

Each child is angry with his mother. The mother has to prohibit many things, the mother has to say no—it cannot be avoided. Even a good mother sometimes has to say no, and restrict, and deny. The child feels rage, anger. He hates the mother and loves the mother, also, because she is his survival, his source of life and energy. So he hates the mother and loves the mother together. And that becomes the pattern. You will love the woman and you will hate the same woman. And you don't have any other kind of choice. You will always go on searching, unconsciously, for your mother. And that happens to women, also, they go on searching for their father. Their whole life is a search to find Dad as a husband.

Now your dad is not the only person in the world; the world is far richer. And in fact, if you can find the dad you will not be happy. You can be happy with a beloved, with a lover, not with your daddy. If you can find your mother you will not be happy with her. You know her already, there is nothing else to explore. That is familiar already, and familiarity breeds contempt. You should search for something new, but you don't have any image.

In a commune a child will have a richer soul. He will know many women, he will know many men; he will not be addicted to one or two persons.

The family creates an obsession in you, and the obsession is against humanity. If your father is fighting with somebody and you see he is wrong, that doesn't matter—you have to be with the father and on his side. Just as people say, "Wrong or right, my country is my country!" so they say, "My father is my father, wrong or right. My mother is my mother, I have to be with her, otherwise it will be a betrayal." This situation teaches you to be unjust. You can see your mother is wrong and she is fighting with the neighbor and the neighbor is right—but you have to be with the mother. This is the learning of an unjust life.

In a commune you will not be attached too much to one family—
there will be no family to be attached to. You will be more free, less
obsessed. You will be more just. And you will have love from many
sources. You will feel that life is loving.

The family teaches you a kind of conflict with society, with other
families. The family demands monopoly—it asks you to be for it and
against all others. You have to be in the service of the family, you have
to go on fighting for the name and the fame of the family. The family
teaches you ambition, conflict, aggression. In a commune you will be
less aggressive, you will be more at ease with the world because you
have known so many people.

So instead of the family I would like to see a commune, where all
will be friends. Even husbands and wives should not be more than
friends. Their marriage should be just an agreement between the two—
they have decided to be together because they are happy together. The
moment even one of them decides that unhappiness is settling, then
they separate. There is no need for any divorce—because there is no
marriage, there is no divorce. One lives spontaneously.

When you live miserably, by and by you become habituated to misery. Never for a single moment should one tolerate any misery. It may
have been good to live with a man in the past, and joyful, but if it is
no longer joyful then you have to get out of it. And there is no need
to get angry and destructive, and there is no need to carry a grudge—
because nothing can be done about love. Love is like a breeze. You
see . . . it just comes. If it is there, it is there. Then it is gone. And when
it is gone, it is gone. Love is a mystery, you cannot manipulate it. Love
should not be manipulated, love should not be legalized, love should
not be forced—for no reason at all.

In a commune, people will be living together just out of the sheer
joy of being together, for no other reason. And when the joy has disappeared, they part. Maybe it feels sad, but they have to part. Maybe
the nostalgia of the past still lingers in the mind, but they have to part.
They owe it to each other that they should not live in misery; otherwise
misery becomes a habit. They part with heavy hearts but with no
grudge. They will seek other partners.

In the future there will be no marriage as it has been in the past, and no divorce as it has been in the past. Life will be more liquid, more trusting. There will be more trust in the mysteries of life than in the clarities of the law, more trust in life itself than in anything—the court, the police, the priest, the church. And the children should belong to all—they should not carry the badges of their family. They will belong to the commune; the commune will take care of them.

This will be the most revolutionary step in human history—for people to start living in communes and to start being truthful, honest, trusting, and to go on dropping the law more and more.

In a family, love disappears sooner or later. In the first place it may not have been there at all, from the very beginning. It may have been an arranged marriage—for other motives, for money, power, prestige. There may not have been any love from the very beginning. Then children are born out of a wedlock that is more like a deadlock—children are born out of no love. From the very beginning they become deserts. And this no-love state in the house makes them dull, unloving. They learn their first lesson of life from their parents, and the parents are unloving and there is constant jealousy and fighting and anger. And the children go on seeing the ugly faces of their parents.

Their very hope is destroyed. They can't believe that love is going to happen in their life if it has not happened in their parents' lives. And they see other parents, other families, also. Children are very perceptive; they go on looking all around and observing. When they see that there is no possibility of love, they start feeling that love is only in poetry— it exists only for poets, visionaries, it has no actuality in life. And once you have learned the idea that love is just poetry, then it will never happen because you have become closed to it.

To see it happen is the only way to let it happen later on in your own life. If you see your father and mother in deep love, in great love, caring for each other, with compassion for each other, with respect for each other—then you have seen love happening. Hope arises. A seed falls into your heart and starts growing. You know it is going to happen to you, too.

If you have not seen it, how can you believe it is going to happen to you too? If it didn't happen to your parents, how can it happen to you? In fact, you will do everything to prevent it happening to you—otherwise it will look like a betrayal of your parents.

This is my observation of people: Women go on saying deep in the unconscious, "Look, Mom, I am suffering as much as you suffered." Boys go on saying to themselves later on, "Dad, don't be worried, my life is as miserable as yours. I have not gone beyond you, I have not betrayed you. I remain the same miserable person as you were. I carry the chain, the tradition. I am your representative, Dad, I have not betrayed you. Look, I am doing the same thing as you used to do to my mother—I am doing it to the mother of my children. And what you used to do to me, I am doing to my children. I am bringing them up in the same way you brought me up."

Now the very idea of bringing up children is nonsense. You can help at the most, you cannot "bring them up." The very idea of building up children is nonsense—not only nonsense, very harmful, immensely harmful. You cannot build . . . A child is not a thing, not like a building. A child is like a tree. Yes, you can help. You can prepare soil, you can put in fertilizers, you can water, you can watch whether sun reaches the plant or not—that's all. But it is not that you are building up the plant, it is coming up on its own. You can help, but you cannot bring it up and you cannot build it up.

Children are immense mysteries. The moment you start building them up, the moment you start creating patterns and characters around them, you are imprisoning them. They will never be able to forgive you. But this is the only way they will learn, and they will do the same thing to their children, and so on. Each generation goes on giving its neurosis to the new people that come to the earth. And the society persists with all its madness, misery.

No, a different kind of thing is needed now. Man has come of age and the family is a thing of the past; it really has no future. The commune will be the thing that can replace the family, and it will be far more beneficial.

But in a commune only meditative people can be together. Only when you know how to celebrate life can you be together; only when you know that space I call meditation can you be together, can you be loving. The old nonsense of monopolizing love has to be dropped, only then can you live in a commune. If you go on carrying your old ideas of monopoly—that your woman should not hold somebody else's hand and your husband should not laugh with anybody else—if you carry these nonsensical things in your mind then you cannot become part of a commune.

If your husband is laughing with somebody else, it is good. Your husband is laughing—laughter is always good. With whom it happens doesn't matter—laughter is good, laughter is a value. If your woman is holding somebody else's hand, good! Warmth is flowing—the flow of warmth is good, it is a value. With whom it is happening is immaterial.

And if it is happening to your woman with many people, it will go on happening with you, too. If it has stopped happening with anybody else, then it is going to stop with you, too. The whole old idea is so stupid! It is as if the moment your husband goes out, you say to him, "Don't breathe anywhere else. When you come home you can breathe as much as you want, but only when you are with me can you breathe. Outside hold your breath, become a yogi. I don't want you to breathe anywhere else." Now this looks stupid—but then why should love not be like breathing?

Love *is* breathing. Breathing is the life of the body and love is the life of the soul. It is far more important than breathing. Now when your husband goes out, you make it a point that he should not laugh with anybody else, at least not with any other woman. He should not be loving to anybody else. So for twenty-three hours he is unloving, then for one hour when he is in bed with you, he pretends to love? You have killed his love, it is flowing no more. If for twenty-three hours he has to remain a yogi, holding his love, afraid, do you think he can relax suddenly for one hour? It is impossible. You destroy the man, you destroy the woman, and then you are fed up, bored. Then you start feeling, "He does not love me!" and it is you who created the whole thing. Then he starts feeling that you don't love him, and you are no longer as happy as you used to be before.

When people meet on a beach, when they meet in a garden, when they are on a date, nothing is settled and everything is liquid; both are very happy. Why? Because they are free. The bird on the wing is one thing, and the same bird in a cage is another thing. They are happy because they are free.

Man cannot be happy without freedom, and your old family structure destroyed freedom. And because it destroyed freedom, it destroyed happiness; it destroyed love.

It has been a kind of survival measure. Yes, it has somehow protected the body, but it has destroyed the soul. Now there is no need for it. We have to protect the soul, too. That is far more essential and far more important.

There is no future for the family, not in the sense that it has been understood up to now. There is a future for love and love relationships. "Husband" and "wife" are going to become ugly and dirty words.

And whenever you monopolize the woman or the man, naturally you monopolize the children, also. I agree totally with Dr. Thomas Gordon, who says, "I think all parents are potential child-abusers, because the basic way of raising children is through power and authority. I think it is destructive when many parents have the idea: 'It is my kid, I can do what I want to do with my kid.' It is violent, it is destructive." A child is not a thing, it is not a chair, is not a car. You cannot do whatsoever you want to do with him. He comes through you, but he does not belong to you. He belongs to existence. You are at the most a caretaker; don't become possessive.

But the whole family idea is one of possession—possess property, possess the woman, possess the man, possess children. And possessiveness is poison; hence I am against the family. But I am not saying that those who are really happy in their families—flowing, alive, loving—have to destroy it. No, there is no need. Their family is already a commune, a small commune.

And of course a bigger commune will be far better, with more possibilities, more people. Different people bring different songs, different people bring different life styles, different people bring different breezes, different people bring different rays of light—and children should be showered with as many different life styles as possible, so they can choose, so they can have the freedom to choose.

And they should be enriched by knowing so many women that they are not obsessed by the mother's face or the mother's style. Then they will be able to love many more women, many more men. Life will be more of an adventure.

A mother visiting a department store took her son to the toy department. Spying a gigantic rocking horse, he climbed upon it and rocked back and forth for almost an hour.

"Come on, son," the mother pleaded, "I have to go home to get your father's dinner ready." The little lad refused to budge, and all her efforts were unavailing. The department store manager also tried to coax the little fellow, without meeting with any success. Eventually, in desperation, they called for the store psychiatrist.

Gently he walked over and whispered a few words in the boy's ear, and immediately the lad jumped off and ran to his mother's side.

"How did you do it?" the mother asked incredulously. "What did you say to him?"

The psychiatrist hesitated for a moment, then said, "All I said was, 'If you don't jump off that rocking horse at once, son, I will knock the stuffing out of you!' "

People learn sooner or later that fear works, that authority works, that power works. And children are so helpless and they are so dependent on the parents that you can make them afraid. It becomes your technique to exploit them and oppress them, and they have nowhere to go.

In a commune they will have many places to go. They will have many uncles and many aunts and many people—they will not be so helpless. They will not be in your hands as much as they are right now. They will have more independence, less helplessness. You will not be able to coerce them so easily.

And all that they see in the home is misery. Sometimes, yes I know, sometimes the husband and wife are loving, but whenever they are loving it is always in private. Children don't know about it. Children see only the ugly faces, the ugly side. When the mother and the father are loving, they are loving behind closed doors. They keep quiet, they never allow the children to see what love is. The children see only their conflict—nagging, fighting, hitting each other, in gross and subtle ways, insulting each other, humiliating each other. Children go on seeing what is happening.

A man is sitting in his living room reading the newspaper when his wife comes over and slaps him.

"What was that for?" asked the indignant husband.

"That is for being a lousy lover."

A little while later the husband goes over to where the wife is sitting watching TV and he gives her a resounding smack.

"What was that for?" she yelled at him.

To which he answered, "For knowing the difference."

This goes on and on, and the children go on watching what is happening. Is this life? Is this what life is meant for? Is this all there is? They start losing hope. Before they enter into life they are already failures; they have accepted failure. If their parents, who are so wise and powerful, cannot succeed—what hope is there for them? It is impossible.

And they have learned the tricks—tricks of being miserable, tricks of being aggressive. Children never see love happening. In a commune there will be more possibilities. Love should come out into the open a little more. People should know that love happens. Small children should know what love is. They should see people caring for each other.

But it is a very ancient idea, an old idea—that you can fight in public but you cannot be loving in public. Fight is okay. You can murder, that is allowed. In fact when two persons are fighting, a crowd will stand there to see what is happening, and everybody will enjoy it! That's why people go on reading and enjoying murder stories, suspense stories, detective stories.

Murder is allowed, love is not allowed. If you are loving in public it is thought to be obscene. Now this is absurd—love is obscene and murder is not obscene? Lovers are not to be loving in public, and generals can go on walking in public showing all their medals? These are the murderers and these medals are for the murder! Those medals show how much they have murdered, how many people they have killed. That is not obscene?

That should be the obscene thing. Nobody should be allowed to fight in public. It is obscene; violence is obscene. How can love be obscene? But love is thought to be obscene. You have to hide it in darkness. You have to make love so nobody knows. You have to make it so silently, so stealthily . . . naturally you can't enjoy it much. And people don't become aware of what love is. Children, particularly, have no way of knowing what love is.

In a better world, with more understanding, love will be all over. Children will see what caring is. Children will see what joy it brings when you care for somebody. Love should be accepted more, violence should be rejected more. Love should be available more. Two persons making love should not be worried that no one should know. They should laugh, they should sing, they should scream in joy, so that the whole neighborhood knows that somebody is being loving to somebody—somebody is making love.

Love should be such a gift. Love should be so divine. It is sacred.

You can publish a book about a man being killed, that's okay, that is not pornography—to me, that is pornography. You cannot publish a book about a man lovingly holding a woman in deep, naked embrace— that is pornography. This world has existed against love up till now. Your family is against love, your society is against love, your state is against love. It is a miracle that love has still remained a little, it is unbelievable that love still goes on—not as it should be, it is just a small drop, not an ocean. But that it has survived so many enemies is a miracle. It has not been destroyed completely—it is a miracle.

My vision of a commune is of loving people living together with no antagonism toward each other, with no competition with each other, with love that is fluid, more available, with no jealousy and no possession. And the children will belong to all because they belong to existence—everybody takes care of them. And they are such beautiful people, these children; who will not take care of them? And they have so many possibilities to see so many people loving, and each person lives in his own way. They will become more rich. And I tell you that if these children exist in the world, none of them will read *Playboy*; there will be no need. And none of them will read Vatasayana's *Kama Sutra*, there will be no need. Nude pictures will disappear. They simply show starved sex, starved love. The world will become almost nonsexual, it will be so loving.

Your priest and your policeman have created all kinds of obscenity in the world. They are the source of all that is ugly. And your family has played a great part. The family has to disappear. It has to disappear into a bigger vision of a commune, of a life not based on small identities, more floating.

In a commune, somebody will be a Buddhist, somebody will be a Hindu, somebody will be a Jaina, somebody will be a Christian, and somebody will be a Jew. If families disappear, churches will disappear automatically, because families belong to churches. In a commune there will be all kinds of people, all kinds of religion, all kinds of philosophies floating around, and the child will have the opportunity to learn. One day he goes with one uncle to the church, another day he goes with another uncle to the temple, and he learns all that is there and he can have a choice. He can choose and decide to what religion he would like to belong. Nothing is imposed.

Life can become a paradise here and now. The barriers have to be removed. The family is one of the greatest barriers.

QUESTIONS

- *You said that love can make you free. But ordinarily we see that love becomes attachment, and instead of freeing us it makes us more bound. So tell us something about attachment and freedom.*

Love becomes attachment because there is no love. You were just playing, deceiving yourself. The attachment is the reality; the love was just foreplay. So whenever you fall in love, sooner or later you discover you have become an instrument—and then the whole misery begins. What is the mechanism? Why does it happen?

Just a few days ago a man came to me and he was feeling very guilty. He said, "I loved a woman. I loved her very much. The day she died I was weeping and crying but suddenly I became aware of a certain freedom within me, as if some burden had left me. I felt a deep breath, as if I had become free."

That moment he became aware of a second layer of his feeling. Outwardly he was weeping and crying and saying, "I cannot live without her. Now it will be impossible, life will be just like death." But deep down, he said, "I became aware that I am feeling very good, that now I am free."

A third layer began to feel guilt. It said to him, "What are you doing?" And the dead body was lying there just before him, he said to me, and he began to feel a great deal of guilt. He said to me, "Help me. What has happened to my mind? Have I betrayed her so soon?"

Nothing has happened, no one has betrayed. When love becomes attachment, it becomes a burden, a bondage. But why does love become an attachment? The first thing to be understood is that if love becomes an attachment, you were just in an illusion that it was love. You were just fooling yourself and thinking that this was love. Really, you were in need of attachment. And if you go still deeper, you will find that you were also in need of becoming a slave.

There is a subtle fear of freedom, and everyone wants to be a slave. Everyone, of course, talks about freedom, but no one has the courage to be really free because when you are really free you are alone. If you have the courage to be alone, then only can you be free.

But no one is courageous enough to be alone. You need someone. Why do you need someone? You are afraid of your own loneliness. You become bored with yourself. And really, when you are lonely nothing seems meaningful. With someone you are occupied, and you create artificial meanings around you.

You cannot live for yourself, so you start to live for someone else. And the same is the case with the someone else also—he or she cannot live alone, so he is in search to find someone. Two persons who are afraid of their own loneliness come together and they start a play—a play of love. But deep down they are searching for attachment, commitment, bondage.

So sooner or later, whatsoever you desire happens. This is one of the most unfortunate things in this world. Whatsoever you desire comes to happen. You will get it sooner or later and the foreplay will disappear. When its function is done, it will disappear. When you have become a wife and husband, slaves to each other, when marriage has happened, love will disappear because love was just an illusion in which two persons could become slaves to each other.

Directly you cannot ask for slavery; it is too humiliating. And directly you cannot say to someone, "Become my slave." He will revolt! Nor can you say, "I want to become a slave to you." So you say, "I cannot live without you." But the meaning is there; it is the same. And when this—the real desire—is fulfilled, love disappears. Then you feel bondage, slavery, and then you start struggling to become free.

Remember this. It is one of the paradoxes of the mind: Whatsoever you get you will get bored with, and whatsoever you do not get you will long for. When you are alone you will long for some slavery, some bondage. When you are in bondage you will begin to long for freedom. Really, only slaves long for freedom—and free people try again to be slaves. The mind goes on like a pendulum, moving from one extreme to the other.

Love doesn't become attachment. Attachment was the need; love was just the bait. You were in search of a fish named attachment; love was just the bait to catch the fish. When the fish is caught, the bait is thrown. Remember this, and whenever you are doing something, go deep within yourself to find out the basic cause.

If there is real love, it will never become attachment. What is the mechanism for love to become attachment? The moment you say to your lover or beloved, "Love only me," you have started possessing. And the moment you possess someone you have insulted him deeply, because you have made him into a thing.

When I possess you, you are not a person then, but just one more item amongst my furniture—a thing. Then I use you, and you are my thing, my possession, so I won't allow anyone else to use you. It is a bargain in which I am possessed by you, and you make me a thing. It is the bargain that now no one else can use you. Both partners feel bound and enslaved. I make a slave of you, then you in return make a slave of me.

Then the struggle starts. I want to be a free person, and still I want you to be possessed by me; you want to retain your freedom and still possess me—this is the struggle. If I possess you, I will be possessed by you. If I do not want to be possessed by you, I should not possess you. Possession should not come in between. We must remain individuals and we must move as independent, free consciousnesses. We can come together, we can merge into each other, but no one possesses. Then there is no bondage and then there is no attachment.

Attachment is one of the ugliest things. And when I say ugliest, I do not mean only religiously, I mean aesthetically, also. When you are attached, you have lost your aloneness; you have lost everything. Just to feel good that someone needs you and someone is with you, you have lost everything—you have lost yourself.

But the trick is that you try to be independent and you make the other a possession—and the other is doing the same.

So do not possess if you do not want to be possessed. Jesus said somewhere, "Judge ye not, so that ye should not be judged." It is the same: "Possess ye not so that ye should not be possessed." Do not make anyone a slave; otherwise you will become a slave.

So-called masters are always slaves of their own slaves. You cannot become a master of someone without becoming a slave— that is impossible. You can only be a master when no one is a slave to you.

This seems paradoxical, because when I say you can only be a master when no one is a slave to you, you will say, "Then what is the mastery? How am I a master when no one is a slave to me?" But I say, only then are you a master. Then no one is a slave to you and no one will try to make a slave out of you.

To love freedom, to try to be free, means basically that you have come to a deep understanding of yourself. Now you know that you are enough unto yourself. You can share with someone, but you are not dependent. I can share myself with someone. I can share my love, I can share my happiness, I can share my bliss, my silence, with someone. But that is a sharing, not a dependence. If no one is there, I will be just as happy, just as blissful. If someone is there, that is also good and I can share.

When you realize your inner consciousness, your center, only then will love not become an attachment. If you do not know your inner center, love will become an attachment. If you know your inner center, love will become devotion. But you must first be there to love, and you are not.

Right now you are not. When you say, "When I love someone it becomes an attachment," you are saying you are not. So whatever you do goes wrong, because the doer is absent. The inner point of awareness is not there, so whatsoever you do goes wrong. First be, and then you can share your being. And that sharing will be love. Before that, whatsoever you do will become an attachment.

And lastly, if you are struggling against attachment, you have taken a wrong turn. You can struggle—so many monks, recluses, *sannyasins* are doing that. They feel that they are attached to their house, to their property, to their wives, to their children, and they feel caged, imprisoned. They escape, they leave their homes, they leave their wives, they leave their children and possessions and they become beggars and escape to a forest, to a loneliness. But go and observe them. They will become attached to their new surroundings.

I was visiting a friend who was a recluse living under a tree in a deep forest, but there were other ascetics, also. One day it happened that I was staying with this recluse under his tree, and a new seeker came while my friend was absent. He had gone to the river to take a bath. Under his tree the new *sannyasin* started meditating.

The man came back from the river, and he pushed that new man away from the tree and said, "This is my tree. You go and find another, somewhere else. No one can sit under my tree." This man had left his house, his wife, his children—now the tree had become a possession: "You cannot meditate under my tree."

You cannot escape so easily from attachment. It will take new forms, new shapes. You will be deceived, but it will be there. So do not fight with attachment, just try to understand why it is there. And then know the deep cause: Because you are *not*, this attachment is there.

Inside, your own self is so much absent that you try to cling to anything in order to feel safe. You are not rooted, so you try to make anything your roots. When you are rooted in your self, when you know who you are, what this being is which is in you, and what this consciousness is which is in you, then you will not cling to anyone.

▪ *My boyfriend feels less and less like making love, and this makes me upset and frustrated, even to the point where I act aggressive toward him. What can I do?*

First thing: A moment always comes in life when one of the partners will not feel like having sex. It happens to every couple. When one person does not want to have sex, the other clings to it more than ever. The other starts feeling that if there is no sex, the relationship will disappear.

The more you ask for it, the more afraid he will feel. The

relationship will disappear not because sex has disappeared, but because you go on demanding and he feels nagged continuously. And he does not feel like making love—he can either force himself and then he will feel bad, or if he goes his own way, he feels bad that he is making you unhappy; he feels guilty.

One thing has to be understood—that sex has nothing to do with love. At the most it is a beginning. Love is greater than sex, higher than sex. Love can flower without sex.

[The questioner interrupts, "But he'll never say he loves me."]

No, you are making him afraid, because if he says that he loves you, you are ready there asking for sex. In your mind, love is almost synonymous with sex; that I can see. That's why he has become even afraid to touch and hug you. If he hugs you, touches you, you are ready.

You are making him afraid and you are not seeing the point. You are pushing him away unknowingly. He will become afraid to even talk to you, because he talks and again the situation comes up, and argument, and this and that.

You cannot argue about love. You cannot convince anybody about love. If he doesn't feel it, he doesn't. He loves you; otherwise he would leave you. And you love him, but you have a wrong understanding about sex.

My understanding is this, that love starts growing for the first time when the hectic, feverish sex has gone, when it has by and by slowed down. Then love becomes more and more settled, finer, superior. Something delicate starts happening. But you are not allowing it to happen. He is ready to love you, but you are clinging to sex. You go on pulling him down. That pulling him down may destroy the whole relationship.

I can understand, because the feminine mind always clings to sex only when the man is not interested. If the man is interested, the woman is completely uninterested. I see this every day. If the man is after you, you play the game that you are uninterested. When the man is not interested you become afraid, and then the whole role changes. Then you start playing the game that you need it, that without it you will go crazy; that you cannot live without it. All that is just nonsense! Nobody has ever gone mad without it.

If you love the person, your energy will be transformed. If you don't love the person, then drop out. If you love the person, the energy has a chance now to transform to a higher reality. Use that opportunity. And nagging is not going to help. It will make everything more ugly and it will do just the opposite of what you want.

■ *My sex life has become very quiet lately—not that I don't want sex or that I am not courageous enough to approach women, but it just doesn't happen. I can enjoy being with a woman, but when it comes to sex the energy changes—it almost feels like falling asleep. What am I doing wrong?*

What is happening to you is not a curse, it is a blessing. It is just your old mind that is interpreting it as if something is going wrong. Everything is going right, the way it should go. Sex has to disappear into a peaceful, playful rejoicing. Into a harmony of two silent beings—not meeting in their bodies but meeting in their very souls. It is going to happen to every meditator. Don't force yourself to do anything against what is happening on its own accord. Any forcing on your part will be a hindrance in your spiritual growth.

This is something very important to remember, and this will explain to you why all the religions have gone against sex. It was a misunderstanding—but a very natural misunderstanding. Everybody who has been in meditation goes through the transformation of the energies—the energies that are going downward start moving upward, opening your higher centers of consciousness, bringing new skies to your being. But you are unacquainted with them, they are unknown to you; hence, one may get frightened. And if it is happening only to one partner, then there is going to be trouble. Both the partners in meditation have to be transforming simultaneously—only then can they keep pace with each other. Otherwise they are going to fall apart.

This created the idea of celibacy. Because in marriage it was found continuously that if one partner became interested in meditation, the marriage was jeopardized. It was better not to get involved, not to hurt somebody else's feelings, and remain alone. But this was a wrong decision.

The right decision would have been that if one partner in a marriage or in a friendship is growing, he should help the other also to move into the new spaces. He should not leave the other partner behind. This would have been a tremendous revolution in human consciousness; but because religions had chosen celibacy, the whole world remained without meditation.

And those who had chosen celibacy—it was a chosen thing, it had not happened to them—became perverted sexually. They were not beyond sex, hence celibacy. They tried the other way: celibacy first, thinking that then would come the transformation. It does not work that way. Transformation has to be first. Then, without any inhibition, without fighting with sex, without condemning sex, a transformation comes on its own. But it does not come by celibacy, it comes by meditation. And it does not come by repression, it comes by a loving atmosphere. The celibate lives in an atmosphere of repression, inhibition, perversion; his whole atmosphere is psychologically sick. This was one fundamental point where all religions went wrong.

Secondly, every meditator has found that sex starts disappearing into something tremendously different—from biology into something spiritual. Rather than creating a bondage, a possessiveness, it opens up doors of freedom. All relationships disappear and one feels, in his aloneness, absolute contentment; a fulfillment that one could not even have dreamed of.

But because meditators found this happening, without any exception, the people who wanted to meditate inferred wrongly that perhaps repressing sex is going to help them in transforming their energies. Hence all organized religions started teaching a life of condemnation, renunciation; a life which is basically negative. This was a misunderstanding.

Through repressing sex you can pervert the energy but you cannot convert it. Conversion comes as you become more silent, as your heart becomes more harmonious, as your mind becomes more and more peaceful. As you start coming closer and closer to your being, to your very center, a transformation that is not your doing happens on its own accord. The energy that you had known as sexual becomes your very spirituality. It is the same energy, just the direction has changed. It is not going downward, it is moving upward.

What is happening to you is going to happen to every seeker—without exception. Hence your question is going to be everybody's question sooner or later. And whenever it happens, the partner who is left behind should not feel offended but blissful and happy that at least to his beloved, or to his friend, a beautiful experience is happening, and hope to join him or her as soon as possible. Your effort should be to go deeper into meditation so you can keep company with your partner, and you can go on dancing together toward the ultimate goal of life.

But remember, as you will grow in your spirituality your sexuality is going to disappear. There will be a new kind of love—a purity, a deep innocence, with no possessiveness, with no jealousy; but with all the compassion in the world, to help each other in the inner growth.

So you should not feel that something has gone wrong with you; something has suddenly gone right with you. You were not alert; you have been caught unawares.

Little Hymie was walking along the street with little Betty, aged four. As they were about to cross the street, little Hymie remembered his mother's teaching.

"Let me hold your hand," he offered gallantly.

"Okay," replied Betty. "But I want you to know you are playing with fire."

Any relationship between man and woman is playing with fire—and particularly if you also start being a meditator. Then you are surrounded by a wildfire, because so many changes are going to happen for which you are not prepared, and cannot be prepared. You are going to travel in an unknown territory every moment, every day. And there will be many times when either you will be left behind, or your partner will be left behind—and this will be a deep anguish to both.

In the beginning, when it starts, the natural inference will be that the relationship is finished, that you are no longer in love. Certainly you are no longer in the love that you were before—that old love is no longer possible. That was animal love, and it is good that it is gone. Now a higher quality, something more divine is going to take place. But you have to help each other.

These are the real, difficult times—when you come to know whether you love your partner, and whether your partner loves you, when these great gaps arise between you and you feel you are going far away from each other. These are the crucial moments, a fire test, when you should try to bring the other person who is left behind, closer to you. You should help the other person to be meditative.

The natural idea will be to bring yourself down so the other is not offended. That's an absolutely wrong attitude. You are not helping the other, you are hurting yourself. A good opportunity is being lost. When you could have pulled the other toward heights, you have descended yourself.

Don't be worried that the other will be offended. You make every effort to bring the other also to the same space, to the same meditative mind, and the other will be grateful, not offended. But these are not the moments when you should part from each other. These are the moments when you should make every effort to keep the contact with the other, with as much compassion as possible. Because if love cannot help the other in transforming the animal energies into higher spiritual energies, then your love is not love—not worth calling love.

And the same problems are going to be faced and encountered by everyone—so when a problem arises, never think twice. Ask the question fearlessly, howsoever stupid you look in asking it. Because it is going to help not only you; it is going to help many others who are also struggling in the same situation but have not been courageous enough to bring it forth. They are trying on their own, somehow, to settle the situation.

It is not a question of settling. It is good that it has lost its old, settled state. It is good that it is unsettled, that trouble has arisen. Now it depends on you and on your intelligence, how you use the opportunity—in favor of your growth, or against it. Asking the question may help you.

So two things . . . first, remember you are fortunate that sex seems to be going away from your life. Secondly, don't think that the other person is feeling offended. Expose your heart to the other person. Don't try to bring yourself to the position of the other but try in every possible way to hold the hand of the other, and take her, or him, to the higher stage, where you are suddenly finding yourself.

Only in the beginning will it be difficult; soon it will become very easy. When there are two persons growing together, many times gaps will arise because people cannot keep pace with each other; everybody has his own speed, everybody has his own unique growth pattern. But if you love, you can wait a little till the other arrives, and then, hand in hand, you can move further.

I want my people particularly not to think ever of celibacy. If celibacy comes by itself, that's another matter; you are not responsible for it. And then it will never bring any perversion, then it will bring a great conversion of energies.

- *How can I know if detachment or indifference is growing within?*

It is not difficult to know. How do you know when you have a headache, and how do you know when you don't have a headache? It is simply clear. When you are growing in detachment you will become healthier, happier; your life will become a life of joy. That is the criterion of all that is good.

Joy is the criterion. If you are growing in joy, you are growing and you are going toward home. With indifference there is no possibility that joy can grow. In fact, if you have any joy, that will disappear.

Happiness is health, and, to me, religiousness is basically hedonistic. Hedonism is the very essence of religion. To be happy is all. So remember, if things are going right and you are moving in the right direction, each moment will bring more joy—as if you are going toward a beautiful garden. The closer you come, the air will be fresher, cooler, more fragrant. That will be the indication that you are moving in the right direction. If the air becomes less fresh, less cool, less fragrant, then you are moving in the opposite direction.

The existence is made out of joy. That is its very stuff. Joy is the stuff existence is made of. So whenever you are moving toward becoming more existential, you will become more and more full of joy, delight, for no reason at all. If you are moving into detachment, love will grow, joy will grow, only attachments will drop—because attachments bring misery, because attachments bring bondage, because attachments destroy your freedom.

But if you are becoming indifferent . . . Indifference is a pseudo coin; it only *looks* like detachment. Nothing will be growing in it. You will simply shrink and die. Go and see: There are so many monks in the world—Catholic, Hindu, Jaina, Buddhist—watch them. They don't give a radiant feeling, they don't have the aura of fragrance, they don't look more alive than you are; in fact, they look less alive, crippled, paralyzed. Controlled, of course, but not in a deep, inner discipline; controlled but not conscious. Following a certain conscience that society has given to them but not yet aware, not yet free, not yet individuals. They live as if they are already in their graves, just waiting to die. Their life becomes morose, monotonous, sad—it is a sort of despair.

Beware. Whenever something goes wrong there are indications in your being. Sadness is an indicator, depression is an indicator. Joy, celebration, is also an indicator. More songs will happen to you if you are moving toward detachment. You will be dancing more and you will become more loving.

Remember, love is not attachment. Love knows no attachment and that which knows attachment is not love. That is possessiveness, domination, clinging, fear, greed—it may be a thousand and one things, but it is not love. In the name of love other things are parading, in the name of love other things are hiding behind but on the container the label LOVE is stuck. Inside you will find many sorts of things, but not love at all.

Watch. If you are attached to a person, are you in love? Or are you afraid of your aloneness, so you cling? Because you cannot be alone, you use this person so as not to be alone. Then you are afraid. If the person moves somewhere else or falls in love with someone else then you will kill this person and you will say, "I was so attached." Or you may kill yourself and you will say, "I was so attached that I could not live without her or without him."

It is sheer foolishness. It is not love, it is something else. You are afraid of your aloneness, you are not capable of being with yourself, you need somebody to distract you. And you want to possess the other person, you want to use the other person as a means for your own ends. To use another person as a means is violence.

Immanuel Kant has made it one of his fundamentals of moral life—it is. He used to say that to treat a person as a means is the most immoral act there is. It is, because when you treat another person as a means—for your gratification, for your sexual desire, for your fear, or for something else—when you use another person as a means you are reducing the other person to a thing. You are destroying his or her freedom, you are killing his or her soul.

The soul can grow only in freedom—love gives freedom. And when you give freedom, you are free; that's what detachment is. If you enforce bondage on the other, you will be imprisoning yourself at the same time. If you bind the other, the other will bind you; if you define the other, the other will define you; if you are trying to possess the other, the other will possess you.

That's how couples go on fighting for domination for their whole life. The man in his own way, the woman in her own way, both struggle. It is a continuous nagging and fighting. And the man thinks that in some ways he controls the woman and the woman thinks that in some ways she controls the man. Control is not love.

Never treat any person as a means. Treat everybody as an end in himself, in herself—then you don't cling, then you are not attached. You love, but your love gives freedom—and, when you give freedom to the other, you are free. Only in freedom does your soul grow. You will feel very, very happy.

The world has become a very unhappy place—not because the world is an unhappy place but because we have done something wrong to it. The same world can become a celebration.

You ask, *How can I know if detachment or indifference is growing within?* If you are feeling happy, if you are feeling happy with whatsoever is growing, more centered, more grounded, more alive than before, then go headlong into it. Then there is no fear. Let happiness be the touchstone, the criterion—nothing else can be the criterion.

Whatsoever the scriptures say is not a criterion unless your heart is throbbing with happiness. Whatsoever I say cannot be the criterion for you unless your heart is throbbing with happiness. The moment you are born, a subtle indicator is placed within you. It is part of life that you can always know what is happening, you can always feel whether you are happy or unhappy. Nobody asks how to know whether he is happy or unhappy. Nobody has ever asked. When you are unhappy, you know; when you are happy, you know. Then it is an intrinsic value. You know it, you are born knowing it, so let that intrinsic indication be used and it will never falsify your life.

■ *In your vision of a model society, would there be one large commune, or a series of communes? If there were more than one, what would be their relationship to one another? Do you imagine people of different communes being able to be interdependent, sharing ideas and skills?*

The question raises a very important thing, the concept of interdependence. Man has lived in dependence, and man has desired and fought for independence, but nobody looks into the reality—that dependence and independence are both extremes.

Reality is exactly in the middle; it is interdependence. Everything is interdependent. The smallest blade of grass and the biggest star both are interdependent. This is the whole foundation of ecology. Because man has behaved without understanding the reality of interdependence, he has destroyed so much of the organic unity of life. He has been cutting his own hands, his own legs, without knowing.

Forests have disappeared, millions of trees are being cut every day. Scientists are giving warnings—but nobody is ready to listen—that if all trees disappear from the earth, man cannot live. We are in a deep interexchange. Man goes on breathing in oxygen and throwing out carbon dioxide; trees go on inhaling carbon dioxide and exhaling oxygen. You cannot exist without the trees, nor can the trees exist without you.

This is a simple example; otherwise life is interwoven in a thousand and one ways. Because many trees have disappeared, so much carbon dioxide has gathered in the atmosphere that it has raised the temperature on the whole earth by four degrees. To you it may seem insignificant—four degrees—but it is not insignificant. Soon this temperature will be enough to melt so much ice that every ocean will rise higher. So the cities which are on the coast of the oceans—and all the great cities are there—will be flooded with water.

If the temperature goes on increasing, as is the possibility, because nobody is listening . . . Trees are being cut, without any understanding, for useless things—for third-rate newspapers you need newsprint, and you are destroying life. There is a possibility that if the eternal ice of the Himalayas starts melting, which has never happened in the whole past, then all the oceans will rise twenty feet higher and will drown almost the whole earth. They will destroy all your cities—Bombay and Calcutta, New York, London, and San Francisco. Perhaps a few primitive people who live high in the mountains may survive.

Such is the interdependence that when your first astronauts reached the moon, we became aware for the first time that the whole earth is surrounded by a thick sheet of ozone, which is a form of oxygen. That layer of ozone surrounds the whole earth like a blanket. It has been because of this ozone blanket that life has become possible on this planet, because ozone does not allow in the death rays that come from the sun. It allows in only the life rays and prevents the death rays; it returns them.

But in our stupidity to reach to the moon, we have made holes in the blanket. And the efforts continue. Now we are trying to reach Mars! Each time a rocket goes beyond the atmosphere of the earth, that is two hundred miles beyond, it creates great holes. Through those holes, death rays have started entering in. Now scientists are saying that these death rays will increase the rate of cancer by almost thirty percent; and other diseases are not counted, small diseases are not counted.

The stupid politicians are not listening. And if you call them stupid then you are jailed, you are punished; false allegations are made against you. But I don't see what else to call them. Stupid seems to be the most gentle and the most cultured word for them. They don't deserve it; they deserve something worse.

Life is a deep interdependence.

My vision of a commune is that nations disappear, big cities disappear, because they don't allow enough space for every human being—and every human being has a certain psychological need for a territorial imperative, just like other animals. In big cities, man is continuously moving in a crowd. That creates great anxiety, tension, agony, and does not allow him any time to relax, any time, any place, to be himself—to be alone, to be with the trees, which are life-giving sources, to be with the ocean, which is a life-giving source.

My vision of a new world, the world of communes, means no

nations, no big cities, no families, but millions of small communes spread all over the earth in thick forests, lush green forests, in mountains, on islands. The smallest commune manageable, which we have already tried, can be of five thousand people, and the biggest commune can be of fifty thousand people. From five thousand to fifty thousand—more than that will become unmanageable; then again comes the question of order and law, and the police, and the court, all have to be brought back.

Small communes... five thousand seems to be the perfect number, because we have tried that. Everybody knows everybody else, all are friends. There is no marriage—children belong to the commune. The commune has hospitals, schools, colleges. The commune takes care of the children; parents can visit them. It is simply insignificant whether the parents are living together or they have separated. For the child, they both are available; he can visit them, they can visit him.

All the communes should be interdependent, but they will not exchange money. Money should be dissolved. It has done tremendous harm to humanity. Now it is time to say goodbye to it! These communes should exchange things. You have more milk products; you can give them to another commune, because you need more clothes, and that commune can provide you with more clothes—a simple barter system, so no commune becomes rich.

Money is a very strange thing. You can accumulate it; that is the strangest secret of money. You cannot accumulate milk products, you cannot accumulate vegetables. If you have more vegetables you have to share with some commune that does not have enough vegetables. But money can be accumulated. And if one commune becomes richer than the other commune, then from the back door comes the poverty and the richness and the whole nightmare of capitalism, and the classes of the poor and the rich, and the desire to dominate. Because you are rich, you can enslave other communes. Money is one of the enemies of man.

Communes will be exchanging. They will be broadcasting on

their radio stations that such and such a product is available from them. Anybody who has certain other products that they need can contact them, and things can be exchanged in a friendly way; there is no haggling, there is no exploitation. But the commune should not become too big, because bigness is also dangerous. A commune's criterion of bigness should be that everybody knows everybody else; that should be the limit. Once that limit is crossed, the commune should divide itself into two. Just as two brothers separate, when a commune becomes big enough it divides itself into two communes, two sister communes.

And there will be a deep interdependence, sharing ideas and skills, without any of the attitudes that grow out of possessiveness, like nationalism and fanaticism. There will be nothing to be fanatic about. There will be no reason for a nation.

A small group of people can enjoy life more easily, because to have so many friends, so many acquaintances, is a joy unto itself. Today in the big cities, you live in the same house and you don't know your neighbor. In one house, one thousand people may be living, and they are absolute strangers to each other. Living in a crowd, and yet being alone.

My idea of a commune is that of living in small groups, which gives you enough space, and yet living in a close, loving, relationship. Your children are taken care of by the commune, your needs are taken care of by the commune, your medical care is taken care of by the commune. The commune becomes an authentic family without any of the diseases that families have created in the past. It is a loose family and a constant movement.

There is no question of any marriage, and no question of any divorce. If two persons want to be together, they can be together and if one day they don't want to be together, that is perfectly good. It was their decision to be together; now they can choose other friends. In fact, in one life why not live many lives? Why not make it richer? Why should a man cling to a woman, or a woman cling to a man unless they enjoy each other so much that they want to be together for their whole life?

But looking at the world, the situation is clear. People would like to be independent from their families; children want to be independent from their families. Just the other day, one small boy in California did something unique and special. He wanted to go out and play. This was nothing special; all children should be allowed to go out and play. But the mother and father insisted, "No, don't go out; just play inside the house." And the boy shot both the mother and the father. He played inside the house! There is a limit, always listening to "no, no, no . . ."

In America the average rate of husbands and wives changing is three years. It is the same rate that people change their jobs; it is the same rate that people change cities. There seems to be something special about three years! It seems it is the limit one can tolerate. Beyond that, it becomes intolerable. So people change wives and husbands, people change cities, people change jobs.

But in a commune, there is no need to make any fuss. You can say goodbye any moment, and you can still remain friends because who knows? After two years you may fall in love again with the same man, with the same woman. In two years time you may have forgotten all the troubles, and you want to have a taste again; or perhaps you had fallen into the hands of a worse man and a worse woman, and you repent, and you want to go back! But it will be a richer life; you will have known many men and many women. Each man has his own uniqueness, and each woman has her own uniqueness.

Communes can also exchange people, if somebody wants to move into another commune, and the other commune is willing to accept. The other commune may say, "If somebody else wants to go into your commune, exchange is possible—because we don't want to raise our population." People can decide. You can go and advertise yourself; some woman may like you, some people may turn friends. Somebody may have been bored in that commune, and would like to change their commune . . .

The whole world should be one humanity, only divided by small communes on a practical basis: no fanaticism, no racism, no nationalism. Then, for the first time, we can drop the idea of wars. We can make life with honesty, worth living, worth enjoying; playful, meditative, creative, and give every man and every woman equal opportunity to grow and bring their potential to flowering.

PART FOUR

Aloneness

Every effort that has been directed toward avoiding loneliness has failed, and will fail, because it is against the fundamentals of life. What is needed is not something in which you can forget your loneliness. What is needed is that you become aware of your aloneness, which is a reality. And it is so beautiful to experience it, to feel it, because it is your freedom from the crowd, from the other. It is your freedom from the fear of being lonely.

CHAPTER FOURTEEN

Aloneness Is Your Nature

The first thing to realize is that whether you want or not, you are alone. Aloneness is your very nature. You can try to forget it, you can try not to be alone by making friends, having lovers, mixing in the crowd . . . But whatever you do remains just on the surface. Deep inside, your aloneness is unreachable, untouchable.

A strange accident happens to every human being: As he is born the very situation of his birth begins in a family. And there is no other way, because the human child is the weakest child in the whole of existence. Other animals are born complete. A dog is going to remain a dog his whole life, he is not going to evolve, grow. Yes, he will become aged, old, but he will not become more intelligent, he will not become more aware, he will not become enlightened. In that sense all the animals remain exactly at the point of their birth; nothing essential changes in them. Their death and their birth are horizontal—in one line.

Only man has the possibility of going vertical, upward, not just horizontal. Most of humanity behaves like other animals: Life is just growing old—not growing up. Growing up and growing old are totally different experiences.

Man is born in a family among human beings. From the very first moment he is not alone; hence, he gets a certain psychology of always remaining with people. In aloneness he starts feeling scared . . . unknown fears. He is not exactly aware of what he is afraid of, but as he ɔves out of the crowd something inside him becomes uneasy. To be with others he feels cozy, at ease, comfortable.

It is because of this reason he never comes to know the beauty of aloneness; the fear prevents him. Because he was born in a group he remains part of a group, and as he grows in age he starts making new groups, new associations, new friends. Already existing collectivities don't satisfy him—the nation, the religion, the political party—he creates his own new associations, Rotary Club, Lions Club. But all these strategies are just in service of one thing: never to be alone.

The whole life experience is of being together with people. Aloneness seems almost like a death. In a way it is a death; it is the death of the personality that you have created in the crowd. That is a gift of others to you. The moment you move out of the crowd you also move out of your personality.

In the crowd you know exactly who you are. You know your name, you know your degrees, you know your profession; you know everything that is needed for your passport, your identity card. But the moment you move out of the crowd, what is your identity, who are you? Suddenly you become aware that you are not your name—your name was given to you. You are not your race—what relationship has race with your consciousness? Your heart is not Hindu or Mohammedan; your being is not confined to any political boundaries of a nation; your consciousness is not part of any organization or church. Who are you?

Suddenly your personality starts dispersing. This is the fear: the death of the personality. Now you will have to discover freshly, you will have to ask for the first time who you are. You will have to start meditating on the question, Who am I?—and there is a fear that you may not be at all! Perhaps you were nothing but a combination of all the opinions of the crowd, that you were nothing but your personality.

Nobody wants to be nothing. Nobody wants to be nobody, and in fact everybody *is* a nobody.

There is a very beautiful story . . .

Alice has reached Wonderland. She came to meet the king and the king asked, "Alice, did you meet a messenger coming toward me?"

She said, "I met nobody."

The king said, "If you met Nobody, why has he not arrived yet?"

Alice was very much puzzled. She said, "You are not understanding me rightly. Nobody is nobody."

The king said, "That is obvious that Nobody is Nobody, but where is he? He should have reached here by this time. It simply means Nobody walks slower than you."

And naturally Alice was very much annoyed and forgot that she was talking to the king. She said, "Nobody walks faster than me."

Now the whole conversation goes on with that "nobody." She understands that he is saying, "Nobody walks slower than you."

". . . and I am a fast walker. I have come from the other world to Wonderland, a small world—and he is insulting me." Naturally she retorts, "Nobody walks faster than me!"

The king said, "If that is right, then why has he not arrived?"

And this way the discussion continues.

Everybody is a nobody.

So the first problem for a seeker is to understand exactly the nature of aloneness. It means nobodiness; it means dropping your personality, which is a gift to you from the crowd. As you move away, out of the crowd, you cannot take that gift with you in your aloneness. In your aloneness you will have to discover again, afresh, and nobody can guarantee whether you will find anybody inside or not.

Those who have reached to aloneness have found nobody there. I *really* mean nobody—no name, no form, but a pure presence, a pure life, nameless, formless. This is exactly the true resurrection, and it certainly needs courage. Only very courageous people have been able to accept with joy their nobodiness, their nothingness. Their nothingness is their pure being; it is a death and a resurrection both.

Just today my secretary was showing me a small, beautiful cartoon: Jesus hanging on the cross, looking at the sky, is saying, "It would have been better if alongside God the Father I had Allah the uncle. It would have been better; at least if God was not listening, Allah might have helped."

Having just God for his whole life he was very happy proclaiming, "I am the only begotten Son of God." And he never talked about God's family, his brother, his wife, his other sons and daughters. In the whole of eternity what has God been doing? He does not have a TV to waste time, to pass time. He does not have any possibility of having a movie hall. What does this poor fellow go on doing?

It is a well-known fact that in poor countries the population goes on exploding for the simple reason that the poor man has no other free entertainment. The only free entertainment is to produce children. Although it is in the long run very costly, right now there is no ticket, no problem, no standing in the queue . . .

What has God been doing for the whole of eternity? He has created only one son. Now on the cross Jesus realizes that it would have been better if God had a few brothers, sisters, uncles. "I could have asked help from somebody else if he is not listening to me." He is praying and he is angry, saying, "Why have you forgotten me? Have you given up on me?"—but there is no answer. He is waiting for the miracle. The whole crowd that has gathered to see the miracle by and by starts dispersing. It is too hot, and they are waiting unnecessarily. Nothing is going to happen; if something were going to happen it would have happened.

After six hours there were only three ladies left who still believed that a miracle might happen. One was Jesus' mother—naturally, mothers go on believing that their children are geniuses. Every mother, without exception, believes that she has given birth to a child who is a giant. Another woman who loved Jesus was a prostitute, Mary Magdalene. That woman, although she was a prostitute, must have loved Jesus. Even the disciples, the so-called apostles, who became second to Jesus in importance in the history of Christianity, all twelve escaped just out of fear of being caught and of being recognized—because they were always hanging around with Jesus, everywhere. You never can trust the crowd: If they were caught, they might have been crucified, if not crucified at least beaten, stoned to death. Only three women were left. The third was another woman who loved Jesus. It was love that remained in the last moments, in the form of these three women.

All those disciples must have been with Jesus just in order to get into paradise. It is always good to have good contacts, and you can't find a

better contact than the only begotten Son of God. Just behind hi
would also be able to enter through the gates of paradise. Their disci-
plehood was a kind of exploitation of Jesus; hence there was no courage.
It was cunning and clever, but not courageous.

Only love can be courageous. Do you love yourself? Do you love
this existence? Do you love this beautiful life, which is a gift? It has
been given to you without your being even ready for it, without your
deserving it, without your being worthy of it. If you love this existence,
which has given life to you, which goes on providing every moment
life and nourishment to you, you will find courage. And this courage
will help you to stand alone like a cedar of Lebanon—high, reaching
to the stars but alone.

In aloneness you will disappear as an ego and personality and you
will find yourself as life itself, deathless and eternal. Unless you are capable of being alone your search for truth will remain a failure.

Your aloneness is your truth. Your aloneness is your divineness.

The function of a master is to help you to stand alone. Meditation is
just a strategy to take away your personality, your thoughts, your mind,
your identity with the body, and leave you absolutely alone inside, just
a living fire. And once you have found your living fire, you will know
all the joys and all the ecstasies that human consciousness is capable of.

The old woman watched her grandson eat his soup with the wrong
spoon, grasp his knife by the wrong end, eat the main course with
his hands, and pour tea into the saucer and blow on it.

"Hasn't watching your mother and father at the dinner table
taught you anything?" she asked.

"Yes," said the boy, chewing with his mouth open, "never to
get married."

He has learned a great lesson! Remain alone.

It is really very difficult to be with others, but we are accustomed
from our very birth to be with others. It may be miserable, it may be
a suffering, it may be a torture but we are accustomed; at least it is well
known. One is afraid to step into the darkness beyond the territory, but

unless you go <u>beyond the territory of the collective mask</u>, you cannot find yourself.

Groucho Marx has made a beautiful statement for you to remember: "I find television very educating. Every time somebody turns on the set I go into the other room and read a book."

The teacher of a class of ten-year-olds is too shy to conduct the sex-education class and so she asks her class to make this a home-work project.

Little Hymie asks his father, who mumbles something about a stork. His grandmother says he came from a cabbage patch and his great-grandmother blushes and whispers that children come from the great ocean of existence.

The next day, little Hymie is called by the teacher to report on his project. Hymie says to the teacher, "I'm afraid there is some-thing wrong in our family. Apparently nobody has made love for three generations!"

In fact, very few people have loved at all. They have pretended, have been hypocrites deceiving not only others but have deceived themselves, too. You can love authentically only when you *are*. Right now you are only a part of a crowd, a cog in the machine. How can you love?—because you are not. <u>First, be</u>; first, know yourself.

In your aloneness you will discover what it is to be. And out of that awareness of your being love flows, and much more. Aloneness should be your only search.

And it does not mean that you have to go to the mountains. <u>You can be alone in the marketplace. It is simply a question of being aware, alert, watchful, remembering that you are only your watchfulness.</u> Then you are alone wherever you are. You may be in the crowd, you may be in the mountains; it makes no difference, you are just the same watchfulness. In the crowd you watch the crowd; in the mountains you watch the mountains. <u>With open eyes you watch existence; with closed eyes you watch yourself.</u> You are only one thing: the watcher.

<u>And this watcher is the greatest realization.</u> This is your buddha na-

ture; this is your enlightenment, your awakening. This should be your only discipline. Only this makes you a disciple, <u>this discipline of knowing your aloneness</u>. Otherwise, what makes you a disciple? You have been deceived on every point in life. You have been told that to believe in a master makes you a disciple—that is absolutely wrong; otherwise, everybody in the world is a disciple. Somebody believes in Jesus, somebody believes in Buddha, somebody believes in Krishna, somebody believes in Mahavira; everybody believes in somebody but nobody is a disciple, because to be a disciple does *not* mean to believe in a master. To be a disciple means to learn the discipline of being yourself, of being your true self.

In that experience is hidden the very treasure of life. In that experience you become for the first time an emperor; otherwise you will remain a beggar in the crowd. There are two kinds of beggars: poor beggars and rich beggars, but they are all beggars. Even your kings and your queens are beggars.

Only those people, very few people who have stood alone in their being, in their clarity, in their light, who have found their own light, who have found their own flowering, who have found their own space they can call their home, their eternal home—those few people are the emperors. This whole universe is their empire. They don't need to conquer it; it is already conquered.

<u>By knowing yourself you have conquered it.</u>

CHAPTER FIFTEEN

Strangers to Ourselves

We are born alone, we live alone, and we die alone. Aloneness is our very nature, but we are not aware of it. Because we are not aware of it we remain strangers to ourselves, and instead of seeing our aloneness as a tremendous beauty and bliss, silence and peace, at-easeness with existence, we misunderstand it as loneliness.

Loneliness is a misunderstood aloneness. Once you misunderstand your aloneness as loneliness, the whole context changes. Aloneness has a beauty and grandeur, a positivity; loneliness is poor, negative, dark, dismal.

Loneliness is a gap. Something is missing, something is needed to fill it, and nothing can ever fill it because it is a misunderstanding in the first place. As you grow older, the gap also grows bigger. People are so afraid to be by themselves that they do any kind of stupid thing. I have seen people playing cards alone; the other party is not there. They have invented games in which the same person plays cards from both sides.

Those who have known aloneness say something absolutely different. They say there is nothing more beautiful, more peaceful, more joyful than being alone.

The ordinary man goes on trying to forget his loneliness, and the meditator starts getting more and more acquainted with his aloneness. He has left the world; he has gone to the caves, to the mountains, to the forest, just for the sake of being alone. He wants to know who he is. In the crowd, it is difficult; there are so many disturbances. And those who have known their aloneness have known the greatest blissfulness possible to human beings—because your very being is blissful.

After being in tune with your aloneness, you can relate; then your relationship will bring great joys to you, because it is not out of fear. Finding your aloneness you can create, you can be involved in as many things as you want, because this involvement will not anymore be running away from yourself. Now it will be your expression; now it will be the manifestation of all that is your potential.

But the first basic thing is to know your aloneness absolutely.

So I remind you, don't misunderstand aloneness as loneliness. Loneliness is certainly sick; aloneness is perfect health. Your first and most primary step toward finding the meaning and significance of life is to enter into your aloneness. It is your temple; it is where your God lives, and you cannot find this temple anywhere else.

CHAPTER SIXTEEN

Solitary and Elect

Jesus said:
Blessed are the solitary and elect, for you shall find the kingdom; and
because you come from it you shall go there again.

—from the Gospel of St. Thomas

The deepest urge in man is to be totally free. Freedom, *moksha*, is
the goal. Jesus calls it the "kingdom of God"—to be like kings, just
symbolically, so that there is no fetter to your existence, no bondage,
no boundary; you exist as infinity, nowhere do you clash with anybody
else . . . as if you are alone.

Freedom and aloneness are two aspects of the same thing. That's why
the Jaina mystic Mahavira called his concept of freedom *"kaivalya."*
Kaivalya means to be absolutely alone, as if nobody else exists. When
you are absolutely alone, who will become a bondage to you? When
nothing else is there, who will be the other?

That's why those who are in search of freedom will have to find their
solitariness; they will have to find a way, means, a method to reach their
aloneness.

Man is born as part of the world, as a member of a society, of a
family, as part of others. He is brought up not as a solitary being, he is
brought up as a social being. All training, education, culture, consists of
how to make a child a fitting part of the society, how to make him fit

with others. This is what psychologists call "adjustment." And whenever somebody is solitary he looks maladjusted.

Society exists as a network, a pattern of many persons, a crowd. There you can have a little freedom—at the cost of much. If you follow the society, if you become an obedient counterpart to others, they will lease you a little world of freedom. If you become a slave, freedom is given to you. But it is a given freedom, it can be taken back any moment. And it is at a very great cost; it is an adjustment with others, so boundaries are bound to be there.

In society, in a social existence, nobody can be absolutely free. The very existence of the other will create trouble. Sartre says, "The other is hell," and he is right to a very great extent because the other creates tensions in you; you are worried because of the other. There is going to be a clash because the other is in search of absolute freedom, you are also in search of absolute freedom—everybody needs absolute freedom—and absolute freedom can exist only for one.

Even your so-called kings are not absolutely free, cannot be. They may have an appearance of freedom, but that is false. They have to be protected, they depend on others. Their freedom is just a facade. But still, because of this urge to be absolutely free, one wants to become a king, an emperor. The emperor gives a false impression that he is free.

One wants to become very rich, because riches also give a false impression that you are free. How can a poor man be free? His needs will be the bondage, and he cannot fulfill his needs. Everywhere he moves he comes to a wall which he cannot cross. Hence the desire for riches. Deep down is the desire to be absolutely free, and all other desires are created by it. But if you move in false directions, you can go on moving but you will never reach the goal because from the very beginning the direction has gone wrong—you missed the first step.

In Old Hebrew, the word *sin* is very beautiful. It means one who has missed the mark. There is no sense of guilt in it really; a sinner means one who has missed the mark, gone astray. And religion means to come back to the right path so you don't miss the goal.

The goal is absolute freedom; religion is just a means toward it. That's why you have to understand that real religion exists as an antisocial force.

Its very nature is antisocial, because in society absolute freedom is not possible.

Psychology, on the other hand, is in the service of the society. The psychiatrist goes on trying in every way to make you adjusted again to the society; he is in the service of the society. Politics, of course, is in the service of the society. It gives you a little freedom so that you can be made a slave. That freedom is just a bribe—it can be taken back any moment. If you think that you are really free, soon you can be thrown into prison.

Politics, psychology, culture, education, they all serve society. Religion alone is basically rebellious. But the society has fooled you, it has created its own religions: Christianity, Hinduism, Buddhism, Mohammedanism—these are social tricks. Jesus is antisocial. Look at Jesus—he was not a very respectable man, could not be. He moved with wrong elements, antisocial elements. He was a vagabond, he was a freak—had to be, because he would not listen to the society and he would not become adjusted to it. He created an alternate society, a small group of followers.

Ashrams have existed as antisocial forces—but not all ashrams, because society always tries to give you a false coin. If there are a hundred ashrams then there may be one—and that, too, only perhaps—that is a real ashram, because that one will exist as an alternative society, against this society, against this nameless crowd. Schools have existed—for example, Buddha's monasteries in Bihar—which try to create a society that is not a society at all. They create ways and means to make you really and totally free—no bondage on you, no discipline of any sort, no boundaries. You are allowed to be infinite, to be the all.

Jesus is antisocial, Buddha is antisocial—but Christianity is not antisocial, Buddhism is not antisocial. Society is very cunning; it immediately absorbs even antisocial phenomena into the social. It creates a facade, it gives you a false coin and then you are happy, just like small children who have been given a false, plastic breast, a pacifier. They go on sucking it and they feel they are being nourished. It will soothe them; of course, they will fall into sleep. Whenever a child is uneasy, this has to be done; a false breast has to be given. He sucks, believing that he is getting nutrition. He goes on sucking, and then sucking becomes a monotonous process; nothing is moving in, just sucking and it becomes like a mantra! Then he falls into sleep. Bored, feeling sleepy, he goes into sleep.

Buddhism, Christianity, Hinduism, and all other "-isms" that have become established religions, are just pacifiers. They give you consolation, they give you a good sleep, they allow a soothing existence in this torturing slavery all around; they give you a feeling that everything is okay, nothing is wrong. They are like tranquilizers. They are drugs.

It is not only LSD that is a drug, Christianity is, also—and a far more complex and subtle drug, which gives you a sort of blindness. You cannot see what is happening. You cannot feel how you are wasting your life, you cannot see the disease that you have accumulated through many existences. You are sitting on a volcano and they go on saying that everything is okay: "God in heaven and government on the earth—everything is okay." And the priests go on saying to you, "You need not be disturbed, we are here. Simply leave everything in our hands and we will take care of you in this world and in the other, also." And you *have* left it to them, that's why you are in misery.

Society cannot give you freedom. It is impossible, because society cannot manage to make everybody absolutely free. Then what to do? How to go beyond society? That's the question for a religious person. But it seems impossible. Wherever you move, society is there. You can move from one society to another, but society will be there. You can even go to the Himalayas—then you will create a society there. You will start talking with the trees, because it is so difficult to be alone. You will start making friends with the birds and animals, and sooner or later there will be a family. You will wait every day for the bird who comes in the morning and sings.

Now you don't understand that you have become dependent, the other has entered. If the bird doesn't come, you will feel a certain anxiety: What has happened to the bird? Why has he not come? Tension enters, and this is not in any way different from when you were worried about your wife or worried about your child. This is not in any way different, it is the same pattern—the other. Even if you move to the Himalayas you create society.

Something has to be understood: Society is not outside of you, it is something within you. And unless the root causes within you disappear, wherever you go the society will come into existence again and again and again. Even if you go to a hippie community, the society will come in; it will become a social force. If you go to an ashram, society will come in. It is not the society that follows you, it is you. You always create your society around you—you are a creator. Something in you exists as a seed, which creates the society. This shows really that unless you are transformed completely you can never go beyond society, you will always create your own society. And all societies are the same; the forms may differ, but the basic pattern is the same.

Why can't you live without society? There is the rub! Even in the Himalayas you will wait for somebody. You may be sitting under a tree and you will wait for someone, a traveler, a hunter, who passes by on the road. And if somebody comes by, you will feel a little happiness coming to you. Alone, you become sad—and if a hunter comes, you will gossip. You will ask, "What is happening in the world? Have you got the latest newspaper?" Or, "Give me news! I am hungry and thirsty for it."

Why? Roots have to be brought up into the light so that you can understand.

One thing, you need to be needed; you have a deep need to be needed. If nobody needs you, you feel useless, meaningless. If somebody needs you, he gives you significance; you feel important. You go on saying, "I have to look after the wife and the children," as if you are carrying them as a burden—you are wrong. You talk as if it is a great responsibility and you are just fulfilling a duty. You are wrong! Just think, if the wife is not there and the children have disappeared, what will you do? Suddenly you will feel your life has become meaningless, because they needed you. Small children, they waited for you, they gave you significance, you were important. Now that nobody needs you, you will shrink. Because when nobody needs you nobody pays attention to you; whether you are or not makes no difference.

The whole of psychoanalysis and its business depends just on listening. There is nothing much, there is really nothing much in psychoanalysis and the whole thing around it is almost complete hocus-pocus. But why does it go on? A man pays you so much attention—and not an ordinary man, a famous psychiatrist, well known, who has written many books. He has treated many well-known people, so you feel good. Nobody else listens to you, not even your wife. Nobody listens to you, nobody pays any attention to you; you move in the world as a nonentity, a nobody—and you pay so much to a psychiatrist. It is a luxury, only very rich people can afford it.

But why do they do what they do? They simply lie down on the couch and talk, and the psychoanalyst listens—but he *listens*, he pays attention to you. Of course you have to pay for it, but you feel good. Simply because the other is paying attention you feel good. You walk differently out of his office, your quality has changed. You have a dance in your feet, you can hum, you can sing. It may not be forever—next week you will have to come again to his office—but when somebody listens to you, pays attention to you, he is saying, "You are somebody, you are worth listening to." He doesn't seem bored. He may not say anything but even so, it is very good.

You have a deep need to be needed. Somebody must need you, otherwise you don't have any ground under your feet—society is your need. Even if somebody fights with you it is okay, better than being alone, because at least he pays attention to you—the enemy, you can think about him.

Whenever you are in love, look at this need. Look at lovers, watch, because it will be difficult if you yourself are in love. Then to watch is difficult because you are almost crazy, you are not in your senses. But watch lovers; they say to each other, "I love you," but deep down in their hearts they want to be loved. To love is not the thing, to be loved is the real thing—and they love just in order to be loved. The basic thing is not to love, the basic thing is to be loved.

That's why lovers go on complaining against each other, "You don't love me enough." Nothing is enough, nothing can ever be enough because the need is infinite. Hence the bondage is infinite. Whatsoever the lover is doing, you will always feel something more is possible; you can still hope more, you can still imagine more. And then that is lacking, and then you feel frustrated. And every lover thinks, "I love, but the other is not responding well," and the other thinks in the same terms. What is the matter?

Nobody loves. And unless you become a Jesus or a Buddha you cannot love, because only one whose need to be needed has disappeared can love.

In Kahlil Gibran's beautiful book, *Jesus the Son of Man*, he has created a fictitious but beautiful story—and sometimes fictions are more factual than facts. Mary Magdalene looks out of her window and sees Jesus sitting in her garden under a tree. The man is beautiful. She had known many men, she was a famous prostitute—even kings used to knock at her door, she was one of the loveliest flowers. But she had never known such a man—because a person like Jesus carries an invisible aura around him that gives him a beauty that is something of the other world; he doesn't belong to this world. There was a light around him, a grace, the way he walked, the way he sat, as if he were an emperor in the robes of a beggar. He looked so much of another world that Magdalene asked her servants to go and invite him, but Jesus refused. He said, "I am okay here. The tree is beautiful and very shady."

Then Magdalene had to go herself and ask, request Jesus—she could not believe that anybody would refuse her request. She said, "Come into my house and be my guest."

Jesus said, "I have already come into your house, I have already become a guest. Now there is no other need."

She could not understand. She said, "No, you come, and don't refuse me—nobody has ever refused me. Can't you do such a little thing? Become my guest. Eat with me today, stay with me this night."

Jesus said, "I have accepted. And remember: Those who say they accept you, they have never accepted you; and those who say to you that they love you, none of them has ever loved you. And I tell you, I love you and only I can love you." But he would not enter the house; when he had rested, he left.

What did he say? He said, "Only I can love you. Those others who go on saying that they love you, they can't love because love is not something you can do—it is a quality of your being."

Love happens when you have attained a crystallized soul, a self. With ego it never happens; the ego wants to be loved because that is a food it needs. You love so that you become a needed person. You give birth to children, not that you love children but just so that you are needed, so that you can go around and say, "Look how many responsibilities I am fulfilling, what duties I am carrying out! I am a father, I am a mother . . ." This is just to glorify your ego.

Unless this need to be needed drops you cannot be a solitary. Go to the Himalayas—you will create a society. And if this need to be needed drops, wherever you are, living in the marketplace, at the very hub of the city, you will be alone.

Now try to understand the words of Jesus: *Blessed are the solitary and elect, for you shall find the kingdom; and because you come from it you shall go there again.*

Penetrate each single word. *Blessed are the solitary . . .* Who is the solitary? One whose need to be needed has dropped; one who is completely content with himself as he is. One who does not need anybody to say to him, "You are meaningful." His meaning is within him; now his meaning does not come from others. He does not beg for it, he does not ask for it—his meaning comes from his own being. He is not a beggar and he can live with himself.

You cannot live with yourself. Whenever you are alone you become uneasy; immediately you feel inconvenience, discomfort, a deep anxiety. What to do? Where to go? Go to the club, go to the church or go to the theater—but go somewhere, meet the other. Or just go shopping. For people who are rich, shopping is the only game, the only sport; they go shopping. If you are poor you need not enter the shop, you can just move on the street looking at the windows. But go!

To be alone is very difficult, very unusual, extraordinary. Why this hankering?—because whenever you are alone, your whole meaning disappears. Go and purchase something from a shop; at least the salesman will give you meaning . . . not the thing, because you go on purchasing useless things. You purchase just for the sake of the purchase. But the salesman or the owner of the shop, they look at you as if you are a king. They behave as if they depend on you—and you know well that this is just a face. This is how shopkeepers behave. The salesman is not bothered about you at all; his smile is just a painted smile. He smiles at everybody, it is nothing particular for you. But you never look at these things. He smiles and greets and receives you as a welcome guest. You feel comfortable, you are somebody, there are people who depend on you; this shopkeeper was waiting for you.

You are in search all over of eyes that can give you a certain meaning. Whenever a woman looks at you she gives you meaning. Now psychologists have discovered that when you enter a room—in a waiting room at the airport, or at a station or in a hotel—if a woman looks twice at you, she is ready to be seduced. But if a woman looks once, don't bother her, just forget it. They have made films and they have been watching and this is a fact, because a woman looks twice only if she wants to be appreciated and looked at.

A man enters a restaurant—the woman can look once, but if he is not worthwhile she will not look another time. And woman-hunters know it well, they have known it for centuries! Psychologists have come to know just now. They watch the eyes—if the woman looks again she is interested. Now much is possible, she has given the hint: She is ready to move with you or play the game of love. But if she doesn't look at you again then the door is closed; better knock at some other door, this door is closed for you.

Whenever a woman looks at you, you become important, very significant; in that moment you are unique. That's why love gives so much radiance; love gives you so much life, vitality.

But this is a problem, because the same woman looking at you every day will not be of much help. That's why husbands become fed up with their wives, wives become fed up with their husbands—because how can you gain the same meaning from the same eyes again and again? You become accustomed to it: She is your wife, there is nothing to conquer. Hence the need to become a Byron, hence the need to become a Don Juan and move from one woman to another.

This is not a sexual need, remember, this is nothing related to sex at all—because sex goes deeper with one woman, in deep intimacy. It is not sex. It is not love, absolutely not, because love wants to be with one more and more, in a deeper and deeper way; love moves in depth. This is neither love nor sex, this is something else: an ego need. If you can conquer a new woman every day you feel very, very meaningful, you feel yourself a conqueror.

But if you are finished with one woman, stuck, and nobody looks at you, no other woman or man gives you meaning, you feel finished. That's why wives and husbands look so lifeless, lustless. You can just look and you can tell from far away whether the couple is wife and husband or not. If they are not you will feel a difference; they will be happy, laughing, talking, enjoying each other. If they are wives and husbands, then they are just tolerating each other.

Múlla Nasruddin's twenty-fifth wedding anniversary came, and he was going out of his house that day. His wife felt a little peeved, because she was expecting he would do something and he was just moving in a routine way. So she asked, "Nasruddin, have you forgotten what day it is?"

Nasruddin said, "I know."

Then she said, "Then do something unusual!"

Nasruddin thought and said, "How about two minutes of silence?"

Wherever you feel life is stuck, it shows that you may have been thinking it was love but it was not love, it was an ego need—a need to conquer, to be needed every day by a new man, a new woman, new people. If you succeeded, then you felt happy for a while because you were no ordinary man. This is the lust of the politician—to be needed by the whole country. What was Hitler trying to do? To be needed by the whole world!

But this need cannot allow you to become solitary. A politician cannot become religious—they move in opposite directions. That's why Jesus says, "It is very difficult for a rich man to enter into the kingdom of God. A camel may pass through the eye of a needle, but not a rich man into the kingdom of God." Why? Because a man who has been accumulating riches is trying to become significant through wealth. He wants to be somebody, and whosoever wants to be somebody, the door of the kingdom is closed for him.

Only nobodies enter there, only those who have attained to their nothingness, only those whose boats are empty; whose ego needs, they have come to understand, are futile and neurotic; whose ego needs they have come to penetrate and found to be useless—not only useless but harmful, also. Ego needs can make you mad, but they can never fulfill you.

Who is a solitary? One whose need to be needed has disappeared, who does not ask any meaning from you, from your eyes, from your responses. No! If you give your love he will be grateful, but if you don't give it there is no complaint. If you don't give, he is as good as ever. If you come to visit him he will be happy, but if you don't come he is as happy as ever. If he moves in a crowd he will enjoy it, but if he lives in a hermitage he will enjoy that, also.

You cannot make a solitary man unhappy, because he has learned to live with himself and be happy with himself. Alone, he is sufficient. That's why people who are related to each other never like the other to become religious—if the husband starts moving toward meditation the wife feels disturbed. Why? She may not even be aware of what is happening or why she feels disturbed. If the wife starts moving in the direction of religiousness the husband feels disturbed. Why?

An unconscious fear comes into the conscious. The fear is that she or he is trying to become sufficient unto herself or unto himself; this is the fear. So, if a wife is given the choice, "Would you like your husband to become a meditator or a drunkard?" she will choose a drunkard rather than a meditator. Given the choice, "Would you like your wife to become a *sannyasin* or to move on wrong ways and go astray?" a husband will choose the latter.

A *sannyasin* means one who is sufficient unto himself, who does not need anybody, who is not in any way dependent. And that gives fear—then you become useless. Your whole existence has been around his need, that he needed you. Without you he was nothing, without you his life was futile, a desert; only with you did he flower. But if you come to know that he can flower in his solitariness, then there will be disturbance because your ego will be hurt.

Who is a solitary? Jesus says *blessed are the solitary* . . . People who can live with themselves as easily as if the whole world were there with them, who can enjoy themselves just like small children.

Very small children can enjoy themselves. Freud has a particular term for them: *polymorphous*. A small child enjoys himself, he plays with his own body, he is autoerotic, he sucks his own thumb. If he needs somebody else, that need is only for the body. You give the milk, you turn him over, you change the clothes—physical needs. He has really no psychological needs yet. He is not worried what people are thinking about him, whether they think him beautiful or not. That's why every child is beautiful—because he does not bother about your opinion.

No ugly child is ever born, and all children become, by and by, ugly. It is very difficult to find an old man beautiful—rare. It is very difficult to find a child ugly—rare. All children are beautiful, all old men become ugly. What is the matter? When all children are born beautiful they should die beautiful! But life does something . . .

All children are self-sufficient—that is their beauty; they exist as light unto themselves. All old men are useless, they have come to realize that they are not needed. And the older they grow the more the feeling comes that they are not needed. The people who needed them have disappeared; the children are grown, they have moved with their own families. The wife is dead, or the husband is dead. Now the world does not need them; nobody comes to their home, nobody pays respect. Even if they go for a walk, nobody recognizes who they are. They may have been great executives, bosses in offices, presidents in banks, but now nobody recognizes them. Nobody even misses them. Not needed, they feel futile; they are just waiting for death. And nobody will bother . . . even if they die, nobody is going to bother. Even death becomes an ugly thing.

Even if you can think that when you die millions of people will weep for you, you will feel happy—thousands and thousands will go to pay their homage when you are dead.

It happened once. One man in America planned it—and he is the only man in the whole history of the world to have done it. He wanted to know how people would react when he was dead. So before his death, when doctors said that within twelve hours he would die, he declared his death. And he was a man who owned many circuses, exhibitions, advertising agencies, so he knew how to advertise the fact. In the morning his agent declared to all the press, to the radio, to the television, that he was dead. So articles were written, editorials were written, phone calls started coming, and there was much commotion. And he read everything; he really enjoyed it!

People are always good when you die; you become an angel immediately because nobody thinks it worth saying anything against you when you are dead. When you are alive, nobody will say anything for you. Remember, when you are dead they will be happy—at least you have done one good thing: You have died!

Everybody was paying respects to this man, and this and that, and photographs had come into the newspapers—he enjoyed it perfectly. And then he died, completely at ease that things were going to be beautiful.

Not only do you need others in your life—even in your death . . . Think about your death: only two or three persons, your servants and a dog following you for the last goodbye. Nobody else, no newspapermen, no photographers, nothing—even your friends are not there. And everybody is feeling very happy that the burden is gone. Just thinking about it, you will become sad. Even in death the need to be needed remains. What type of life is this? Just others' opinions are important, not you? Your existence doesn't mean anything?

When Jesus says *blessed are the solitary* he means this: a man who has come to remain absolutely happy with himself, who can be alone on this earth and there will be no change of mood, the climate will not change. If the whole world disappears into a third world war—it can happen any day—and you are left alone, what will you do? Except to immediately commit suicide, what will you do? But a solitary can sit under a tree and become a buddha without the world. The solitary will be happy, and he will sing and he will dance and he will move—his mood will not change. You cannot change the mood of a solitary, you cannot change his inner climate.

Jesus says, *Blessed are the solitary and elect* ... And these are the elect people, because those who need a crowd will be thrown again and again into the crowd—that is their need, that's their demand, that's their desire. Existence fulfills whatever you ask, and whatever you are is just a fulfillment of your past desires. Don't blame it on anybody else—it is what you have been praying for. And remember it, this is one of the dangerous things in the world—whatsoever you desire will be fulfilled.

Think before you desire a thing. There is every possibility it will be fulfilled, and then you will suffer. That's what happens to a rich man. He was poor, then he desired riches, and desired and desired, and now it is fulfilled. Now he is unhappy, now he is crying and weeping and he says, "My whole life has gone accumulating worthless things, and I am unhappy!" But this was his desire. If you desire knowledge, it will be fulfilled. Your head will become a great library, containing many scriptures. But then in the end you will weep and cry and scream, "Only words and words and words, and nothing substantial. And I have wasted my whole life."

Desire with full awareness, because every desire is bound to be fulfilled sometime or other. It may take a little more time because you are always standing in a queue; many others have desired before you, so it may take a little time. Sometimes your desire of this life may be fulfilled in another life, but desires are always fulfilled; this is one of the dangerous laws. So before you desire, think! Before you demand, think! Remember well that it is going to be fulfilled someday—and then you will suffer.

A solitary becomes an elect; he is the chosen, the chosen one of existence. Why?—because a solitary never desires anything of this world. He does not need to. He has learned whatever was to be learned from this world; this school is finished, he has passed through it, transcended it. He has become like a high peak, which remains alone in the sky—he has become the elect, the Gourishankar, the Everest. A Buddha, a Jesus, they are high peaks, solitary peaks. That's their beauty; they exist alone.

The solitary is the elect. What has the solitary chosen? He has chosen only his own being. And when you choose your own being, you have chosen the being of the whole universe—because your being and the universal being are not two things. When you choose yourself you have chosen God, and when you choose God, God has chosen you—you have become the elect.

Blessed are the solitary and elect, for you shall find the kingdom; and because you come from it you shall go there again.

A solitary, a *sannyasin*—that's what *sannyasin* means, a solitary being, a wanderer, absolutely happy in his aloneness. If somebody walks by his side it is okay, it is good. If somebody leaves it is also okay, it is good. He never waits for anybody and he never looks back. Alone, he is whole. This beingness, this wholeness, makes you a circle. And the beginning and the end meet, the alpha and the omega meet.

A solitary is not like a line. You are like a line—your beginning and end will never meet. A solitary is like a circle, his beginning and end meet. That's why Jesus says, *Because you come from it you shall go there again*—you will become one with the source, you have become a circle.

There is another saying of Jesus: "When the beginning and the end have become one, you have become God." You may have seen a picture—it is one of the oldest seals of the secret societies in Egypt—of a snake eating its own tail. That's what the beginning and end meeting means, that's what rebirth means, that's what becoming like children means: moving in a circle, back to the source; reaching there, from where you have come.

CHAPTER SEVENTEEN

The Lion and the Sheep

Aloneness is the ultimate reality. One comes alone, one goes alone; and between these two alonenesses we create all kinds of relationships and fighting, just to deceive ourselves—because in life, also, we remain alone. But aloneness is not something to be sad about; it is something to rejoice in. There are two words—the dictionary will say they have the same meaning, but existence gives them totally opposite meanings. One word is *loneliness* and the other word is *aloneness*. They are not synonymous.

Loneliness is a negative state, like darkness. Loneliness means you are missing someone; you are empty, and you are afraid in this vast universe. Aloneness has a totally different meaning: It does not mean that you are missing someone, it means that you have found yourself. It is absolutely positive.

Finding oneself, one finds the meaning of life, the significance of life, the joy of life, the splendor of life. Finding oneself is the greatest finding in man's life, and this finding is possible only when you are alone. When your consciousness is not crowded by anything, by anybody, when your consciousness is utterly empty—in that emptiness, in that nothingness, a miracle happens. And that miracle is the foundation of all religiousness.

The miracle is that when there is nothing else for your consciousness to be conscious of, the consciousness turns upon itself. It becomes a circle. Finding no obstacle, finding no object, it comes back to the source. And the moment the circle is complete, you are no longer just an ordinary human being; you have become part of the godliness that surrounds existence. You are no longer yourself; you have become part of the whole universe—your heartbeat is now the heartbeat of the universe itself.

This is the experience mystics have been searching for all their lives, down the ages. There is no other experience that is more ecstatic, more blissful. This experience transforms your whole outlook: Where there used to be darkness, now there is light; where there used to be misery, there is bliss; where there used to be anger, hate, possessiveness, jealousy, there is only a beautiful flower of love. The whole energy that was being wasted in negative emotions is no longer wasted; it takes a positive and creative turn.

On the one hand you are no longer your old self; on the other hand you are, for the first time, your authentic self. The old is gone, the new has arrived. The old was dead; the new belongs to the eternal, the new belongs to the immortal.

It is because of this experience that the seers of the Upanishads have declared man to be *amritasya putrah*—"sons and daughters of immortality."

Unless you know yourself as eternal beings, part of the whole, you will remain afraid of death. The fear of death is simply because you are not aware of your eternal source of life. Once the eternity of your being is realized, death becomes the greatest lie in existence. Death has never happened, never happens, never will happen, because that which is, remains always—in different forms, on different levels, but there is no discontinuity. Eternity in the past and eternity in the future both belong to you. And the present moment becomes a meeting point of two eternities: one going toward the past, one going toward the future.

The remembrance of your aloneness has not to be only of the mind; your every fiber of being, your every cell of the body should remember it—not as a word, but as a deep feeling. Forgetfulness of yourself is the only sin there is, and to remember yourself is the only virtue.

Gautama Buddha emphasized one single word continually for forty-two years, morning and evening; the word is *sammasati*—it means "right remembering." You remember many things—you can become an *En-cyclopedia Britannica*; your mind is capable of remembering all the libraries of the world—but that is not the right remembering. There is only one right remembering—the moment you remember yourself.

Gautama Buddha used to illustrate his point with the ancient story of a lioness who was jumping from one hillock to another hillock, and between the two hillocks a big flock of sheep was moving. The lioness was pregnant, and gave birth while she was jumping. Her cub fell into the flock of sheep, was brought up by the sheep, and naturally, he be-lieved himself also to be a sheep. It was a little strange because he was so big, so different—but perhaps he was just a freak of nature. He was brought up as a vegetarian.

He grew up, and one day an old lion who was in search of food came close to the flock of sheep—and he could not believe his eyes. In the midst of the sheep, there was a young lion in its full glory, and the sheep were not afraid. He forgot about his food; he ran after the flock of sheep . . . and it was becoming more and more puzzling, because the young lion was also running away with the sheep. Finally he got hold of the young lion. He was crying and weeping and saying to the old lion, "Please, let me go with my people!"

But the old lion dragged him to a nearby lake—a silent lake without any ripples, it was just like a pure mirror—and the old lion forced him to see his reflection in the lake, and also the reflection of the old lion. There was a sudden transformation. The moment the young lion saw who he was, there was a great roar—the whole valley echoed the roar of the young lion. He had never roared before because he had never thought that he was anybody other than a sheep.

The old lion said, "My work is done; now it is up to you. Do you want to go back to your own flock?"

The young lion laughed. He said, "Forgive me, I had completely forgotten who I am. And I am immensely grateful to you that you helped me to remember."

Gautama Buddha used to say, "The master's function is to help you remember who you are." You are not part of this mundane world; your home is the home of the divine. You are lost in forgetfulness; you have forgotten that inside you God is hidden. You never look inside—because everybody looks outside, you also go on looking outside.

To be alone is a great opportunity, a blessing, because in your aloneness you are bound to stumble upon yourself and for the first time remember who you are. To know that you are part of the divine existence is to be free from death, free from misery, free from anxiety; free from all that has been a nightmare to you for many many lives.

Become more centered in your deep aloneness. That's what meditation is: becoming centered in one's own aloneness. The aloneness has to be so pure that not even a thought, not even a feeling disturbs it. The moment your aloneness is complete, your experience of it will become your enlightenment. Enlightenment is not something that comes from outside; it is something that grows within you.

To forget your self is the only sin. And to remember your self, in its utter beauty, is the only virtue, the only religion. You need not be a Hindu, you need not be a Mohammedan, you need not be a Christian—all that you need to be religious is to be yourself.

And in fact, we are not separate, even now—nobody is separate; the whole existence is one organic unity. The idea of separation is because of our forgetfulness. It is almost as if every leaf of the tree started thinking it is separate, separate from other leaves . . . but deep down they are nourished by the same roots. It is one tree; the leaves may be many. It is one existence; the manifestations may be many.

Knowing oneself, one thing becomes absolutely clear: No man is an island—we are a continent, a vast continent, an infinite existence without any boundaries. The same life runs through all, the same love fills every heart, the same joy dances in every being. Just because of our misunderstanding, we think we are separate.

The idea of separation is our illusion. The idea of oneness will be our experience of the ultimate truth. Just a little more intelligence is needed and you can come out of the gloom, the misery, the hell in which the whole of humanity is living. The secret of coming out of this hell is to remember yourself. And this remembrance will become possible if you understand the idea that you are alone.

You may have lived with your wife or with your husband for fifty years; still, you are two. Your wife is alone, you are alone. You have been trying to create a facade that "We are not alone," that, "We are a family," that "We are a society," that "We are a civilization," that "We are a culture," that "We are an organized religion," that "We are an organized political party." But all these illusions are not going to help.

You have to recognize, howsoever painful it appears in the beginning, that "I am alone and in a strange land." This recognition, for the first time, is painful. It takes away all our illusions—which were great consolations. But once you have dared to accept the reality, the pain disappears. And just hidden behind the pain is the greatest blessing of the world: You come to know yourself.

You are the intelligence of existence; you are the consciousness of existence; you are the soul of existence. You are part of this immense godliness that manifests in thousands of forms: in the trees, in the birds, in the animals, in human beings . . . but it is the same consciousness in different stages of evolution. And the man who recognizes himself and feels that the God he was searching and looking for all over the world resides within his own heart, comes to the highest point of evolution. There is nothing higher than that.

It makes your life for the first time meaningful, significant, religious. But you will not be a Hindu, and you will not be a Christian, and you will not be a Jew; you will be simply religious. By being a Hindu or a Mohammedan or a Christian or a Jaina or a Buddhist, you are destroying the purity of religiousness—it needs no adjectives.

Love is love—have you ever heard about Hindu love? Mohammedan love? Consciousness is consciousness—have you ever thought about Indian consciousness or Chinese consciousness? Enlightenment is enlightenment; whether it happens in the white body or in the black body, whether it happens in the young man or in the old man, whether it happens in a man or in a woman, it does not make any difference. It is the same experience, the same taste, the same sweetness, the same fragrance.

The only person who is not intelligent is one who is running around all over the world in search of something, not knowing exactly what. Sometimes thinking perhaps it is money, sometimes thinking perhaps it is power, sometimes thinking perhaps it is prestige, sometimes thinking perhaps it is respectability.

The intelligent man first searches his own being before he starts a journey in the outer world. That seems to be simple and logical—at least first look inside your own house before you go searching all over the world. And those who have looked within themselves have found it, without any exception.

Gautama Buddha is not a Buddhist. The word *buddha* simply means the awakened one, who has come out of sleep. Mahavira, the Jaina, is not a Jaina. The word *jaina* simply means one who has conquered—conquered himself. The world needs a great revolution where each individual finds his religion within himself. The moment religions become organized they become dangerous; they become really politics with a false face of religion. That's why all the religions of the world go on trying to convert more and more people to their religion. It is the politics of numbers; whoever has more numbers will be more powerful. But nobody seems to be interested in bringing millions of individuals to their own selves.

My work here consists of taking you out of any kind of organized effort—because truth can never be organized. You have to go alone on the pilgrimage, because the pilgrimage is going to be inside. You cannot take anybody with you. And you have to drop everything that you have learned from others, because all those prejudices will distort your vision—you will not be able to see the naked reality of your being. The naked reality of your being is the only hope of finding God.

God is your naked reality—undecorated, without any adjective. It is not confined by your body, not confined by your birth, not confined by your color, not confined by your sex, not confined by your country. It is simply not confined by anything. And it is available, so close:

Just one step inside and you have arrived.

You have been told for thousands of years that the journey to God is very long. The journey is not long, God is not far away. God is in your breath, God is in your heartbeat, God is in your blood, in your bones, in your marrow—just a single step of closing your eyes and entering within yourself.

It may take a little time because old habits die hard. Even if you close your eyes, thoughts will go on crowding you. Those thoughts are from the outside and the simple method, which has been followed by all the great seers of the world, is just to watch your thoughts— just to be a witness. Don't condemn them, don't justify them, don't rationalize them. Remain aloof, remain indifferent, let them pass— they will be gone.

And the day your mind is absolutely silent, with no disturbance, you have taken the first step that takes you to the temple of God.

The temple of God is made of your consciousness. You cannot go there with your friends, with your children, with your wife, with your parents.

Everybody has to go there alone.

QUESTIONS

- *Never belonged, never been on the "inside," never felt "at one" with another. Why such a loner all my life?*

Life is a mystery, but you can reduce it to a problem. And once you make a mystery a problem you will be in difficulty, because there can be no solution to it. A mystery remains a mystery; it is insoluble—that's why it is called a mystery.

Life is not a problem. And that is one of the most basic mistakes we all go on committing: We immediately put a question mark. And if you put a question mark on a mystery, you will be searching for the answer your whole life and you will not find it, and naturally it brings great frustration.

My observation of the questioner is that she is a born meditator. Rather than making it a problem, rejoice! Not to belong is one of the greatest experiences of life. To be utterly an outsider, never feeling to be a part anywhere, is a great experience of transcendence.

An American tourist went to see a Sufi master. For many years he had heard about him, had fallen in deep love with his words, his message. Finally he decided to go to see him. When he entered his room he was surprised—it was an utterly empty room! The master was sitting; there was no furniture at all! The American could not conceive of a living space without any furniture. He immediately asked, "Where is your furniture, sir?"

And the old Sufi laughed and he said, "And where is yours?"

And the American said, "Of course I am a tourist here. I cannot go on carrying my furniture!"

And the old man said, "So am I a tourist for only just a few days, and then I will be gone, just as you will be gone."

This world is just a pilgrimage—of great significance, but not a place to belong to, not a place to become part of. Remain a lotus leaf.

This is one of the calamities that has happened to the human mind: We make a problem out of everything. Now this should be something of immense joy to you. Don't call yourself a "loner." You are using a wrong word, because the very word connotes some condemnation. You are alone, and the word "alone" has great beauty. You are not even lonely. To be lonely means you are in need of the other; to be alone means you are utterly rooted in yourself, centered in yourself. You are enough unto yourself.

You have not yet accepted this gift of existence, hence you are unnecessarily suffering. And this is my observation: Millions of people go on suffering unnecessarily.

Look at it from another perspective. I am not giving you an answer, I never give any answers. I simply give you new perspectives to see, new angles.

Think of yourself as a born meditator who is capable of being alone, who is strong enough to be alone, who is so centered and rooted that the other is not needed at all. Yes, one can relate with the other, but it never becomes a relationship. To relate is perfectly good. Two persons who are both alone can relate, two persons who are both alone cannot be in relationship.

Relationship is the need of those who cannot be alone. Two lonely persons fall into a relationship. Two alone persons relate, communicate, commune, and yet they remain alone. Their aloneness remains uncontaminated; their aloneness remains pure. They are like peaks, Himalayan peaks, high in the sky, the clouds. No two peaks ever meet, yet there is a kind of communion through the wind and through the rain and through the rivers and through the sun and through the stars. Yes, there is a communion; much dialogue goes on. They whisper to each other, but their aloneness remains absolute, they never compromise.

Be like an alone peak high in the sky. Why should you hanker to belong? You are not a thing! Things belong!

You say, *"Never belonged, never been on the inside."*

There is no need! To be an insider in this world is to get lost. The worldly is the insider; a Buddha is bound to remain an outsider. All Buddhas are outsiders. Even if they are in the crowd they are alone. Even if they are in the marketplace they are not there. Even if they relate they remain separate. There is a kind of subtle distance that is always there.

And that distance is freedom, that distance is great joy, that distance is your own space. And you call yourself a loner? You must be comparing yourself with others: "They are having so many relationships, they are having love affairs. They belong to each other, they are insiders—and I am a loner. Why?" You must be creating anguish unnecessarily.

My approach always is: Whatsoever existence has given to you must be a subtle necessity of your soul, otherwise it would not have been given in the first place.

Think more of aloneness. Celebrate aloneness, celebrate your pure space, and great song will arise in your heart. And it will be a song of awareness, it will be a song of meditation. It will be a song of an alone bird calling in the distance—not calling to somebody in particular, but just calling because the heart is full and wants to call, because the cloud is full and wants to rain, because the flower is full and the petals open and the fragrance is released . . . unaddressed. Let your aloneness become a dance.

I am utterly happy with you. If you stop creating problems for yourself . . . I don't see that there are real problems. The only problem is, people go on creating problems! Problems are never solved, they are only dissolved. I am giving you a perspective, a vision. Dissolve your problem! Accept it as a gift of God, with great gratitude, and live it. And you will be surprised: What a precious gift, and you have not even appreciated it yet. What a precious gift, and it is lying there in your heart, unappreciated.

Dance your aloneness, sing your aloneness, live your aloneness!

And I am not saying don't love. In fact, only a person who is capable of being alone is capable of love. Lonely persons cannot love. Their need is so much that they cling—how can they love? Lonely persons cannot love, they can only exploit. Lonely persons pretend to love; deep down they want to get love. They don't have it to give, they have nothing to give. Only a person who knows how to be alone *and* joyous is so full of love that he can share it. He can share it with strangers.

And all are strangers, remember. Your husband, your wife, your children, all are strangers. Never forget it! You don't know your husband, you don't know your wife. You don't know even your child; the child that you have carried in your womb for nine months is a stranger.

This whole life is a strange land; we come from some unknown source. Suddenly we are here, and one day suddenly we are gone, back to the original source. This is a few days' journey; make it as joyous as possible. But we do just the opposite—we make it as miserable as possible. We put our whole energies into making it more and more miserable.

▪ *Why does my sadness feel more real than my happiness? I want so much to be real and authentic, not to wear any masks, but this seems to mean so much rejection by others. Is it possible to be so alone?*

It is important to understand. It is the case with most of the people. Your sadness is certainly more real because it is yours, it is authentic. Your happiness is shallow; it is not yours, it depends on something, somebody. And anything that makes you dependent, however happy you can feel for a few moments, soon the honeymoon is over—sooner than you had ever expected.

You are happy because of your girlfriend, your boyfriend. But they are individual beings; they may not agree on all points with you. In fact, mostly what happens is that whatever the husband likes, the wife dislikes; whatever the wife likes, the husband dislikes. Strange . . . because it is almost universal. There is some reason in it. Deep down they hate each other, for the simple reason that they are dependent on each other for gaining happiness, and nobody likes dependence. Slavery is not the intrinsic desire of human beings. If a woman or a man gives you joy, and you become dependent, you are at the same time creating a deep hate—because of dependence. You cannot leave the woman because she makes you happy, and you cannot leave your hatred of the woman because she makes you dependent.

So all so-called love relationships are very strange, complicated phenomena. They are love-hate relationships. The hate needs to be expressed some way or other. That's why whatever your wife likes, you don't like; whatever your husband likes, you don't like. On every small thing husbands and wives are fighting. Which movie to go to?—and there is an immense fight. Which restaurant to go to?—and immediately there is a fight. This is the hatred that is moving underneath the facade of happiness. Happiness remains shallow, very thin; just scratch it a little bit and you will find its opposite.

But sadness is more authentic, because it is not dependent on anybody. It is yours, absolutely yours—this should give you a great insight, that your sadness can help you more than your happiness. You have never looked at sadness closely. You try to avoid seeing it, in many ways. If you feel sad, you go to a movie; if you feel sad, you start the television. If you feel sad, you go and play with your friends, you go to a club. You start doing something so that you do not have to see the sadness. This is not the right approach.

When you are sad, it is a momentous phenomenon, very sacred, something of your own. Get acquainted with it, go deeper into it, and you will be surprised. Sit silently, and be sad. Sadness has its own beauties.

Sadness is silent, it is yours. It is coming because you are alone. It is giving you a chance to go deeper into your aloneness. Rather than jumping from one shallow happiness to another shallow happiness and wasting your life, it is better to use sadness as a means for meditation. Witness it. It is a friend! It opens the door of your eternal aloneness.

There is no way not to be alone. You can delude yourself, but you cannot succeed. And we are deluding ourselves in every way—in relationship, in ambition, in becoming famous, in doing this, in doing that. We are trying to convince ourselves that we are not alone, that we are not sad. But, sooner or later, your mask wears out—it is false, it cannot remain forever—then you have to wear another mask. In one small life, how many masks do you wear? And how many have melted away, changed? But you go on continuing the old habit.

If you want to be an authentic individual, use sadness; don't escape from it. It is a great blessing. Sit silently with it, rejoice in it. There is nothing wrong in being sad. And the more you become acquainted with it and its subtle nuances, you will be surprised—it is a great relaxation, a great rest, and you come out of it rejuvenated, refreshed, younger, livelier. And once you have tasted it, you will seek those beautiful moments of sadness again and again. You will wait for them, you will welcome them, and they will open new doors of your aloneness . . .

Alone you are born, alone you will die. Between these two alonenesses you can deceive yourself that you are not alone, that you have a wife, a husband, children, money, power. But between these two alonenesses you *are* alone. Everything is just to keep yourself engaged in something or other, so that you don't become aware of it.

From my very childhood I have never been associating with people. My whole family was very much concerned: I was not playing with children, and I have never played with them. My teachers were concerned: "What do you go on doing when all the children are playing? You sit under the tree just by yourself." They thought something was wrong with me.

And I told them, "You need not be worried. The reality is that something is wrong with you, and wrong with all your children. I am perfectly happy to be alone."

Slowly, slowly they accepted that that's how I am; nothing can be done about it. They tried in every way to help me to mix with other children of my age. But I enjoyed being alone so much that it looked almost neurotic to play football.

And I told my teacher, "I don't see any point in it. Why unnecessarily hit the football from here to there? There is no point. And even if you make the goal, so what? What is achieved out of it? And if these people love making goals so much, then rather than having one football, have eighteen footballs. Give everybody one, and he makes as many goals as he wants, nobody prevents him. Let them have goals to their hearts' content! This way it is too difficult—why make it unnecessarily difficult?"

And my teacher said, "You don't understand at all that that will not be a game, if eighteen footballs are given to the children and everybody is making goals as many times as he wants. That will not help."

I said, "I don't understand, that by creating hindrances and preventing people . . . They fall and they have fractures and all kinds of nonsense. And not only that—when there are matches, thousands of people gather to see them. It seems these people don't know that life is so short—and they are watching a football match! And they are so excited, jumping, shouting—to me, it is absolutely neurotic. I would rather sit under my tree."

I had my tree, a very beautiful tree, behind my school building. It became known that it was my tree, so nobody would go there. I used to sit there whenever there was time for play, or time for any kind of neurotic activity—"extracurricular" activities. And I found so much under that tree that whenever I used to go back to my town, I never went to see the principal—his office was close to the tree; just behind his office was the tree—but I used to go to the tree just to thank it, to show my gratitude. The principal would come out, and he would say, "This is strange. You come to the town—you never come to me, you never come to the school, but you always come to this tree."

I said, "I have experienced much more under that tree than under your guidance and that of all kinds of mad teachers that you have. They have not given anything to me—in fact, whatever they gave to me I had to get rid of. But what this tree has given to me is still with me."

And you will be surprised—it happened twice, so it cannot be just coincidence. In 1970 I stopped going to the town, because I gave a promise to my grandmother: "I will come only while you are alive. When you are gone, I have nothing to come here for." I was informed that when I stopped going to the town, the tree died. I thought it must have been an accident, just a coincidence; it could not be connected with me. But it happened twice . . .

When I became a professor in the university, there was a line of beautiful trees. I used to park my car under one tree. And it had always been my privilege—I don't know why—that wherever I sat in the common room for the professors, nobody would sit on the chair I used, nobody would sit even by the side of the chair. They thought me a little dangerous.

A man who has no friends, a man who has strange thoughts, a man who is against all religions, against all traditions, a man who can oppose single-handedly people like Mahatma Gandhi, who is worshipped by the whole country—they thought, "It is better to keep away from this man. He can put some idea in your mind, and you may be in some difficulty."

I used to park my car under that one tree. Nobody else parked their cars in that place; even if I was not coming, the place remained empty. All the other trees died, only my tree—it had become known as my tree—remained gorgeous.

After I resigned from the university, the vice-chancellor said to me, one year later, "It is strange; that tree has died. Since you stopped coming to the university something has happened."

I understand that there is some synchronicity. If you silently sit with a tree . . . the tree is silent, you are silent . . . and two silences cannot remain separate, there is no way to divide them.

You are all sitting here. If you are all thinking thoughts, you are separate. But if you are all silent, then suddenly there is something like a collective soul.

Perhaps those two trees missed me. Nobody came close to them again, nobody with whom they could communicate. They died because they could not get any warmth from anybody. I had tremendous love and respect for those trees.

Whenever you feel sad, sit by the side of a tree, by the side of the river, by the side of a rock, and just relax into your sadness without any fear. The more you relax, the more you will become acquainted with the beauties of sadness. Then sadness will start changing its form; it will become a silent joy, uncaused by anybody outside you. That will not be shallow happiness, which can be taken away very easily.

And getting deeper into your aloneness, one day you will find not only joy—joy is only midway. Happiness is very superficial, depends on others; joy is in the middle, does not depend on anyone. But going deeper you will come to the state of bliss—that's what I call enlightenment.

Use anything and you will come to enlightenment—but use something authentic, which is yours. And then you have a bliss that is yours twenty-four hours a day. It is simply radiating from you. You can share it now, you can give it to whomever you love. But it is an unconditional gift. And nobody can make you miserable.

This is my effort, to make you independently blissful. That does not mean that you have to renounce the world. That does not mean that you have to leave your wife, your girlfriend, your love for food—even for ice cream; it has nothing to do with that. Your blissfulness is with you whatever you are doing. It will enhance every activity, it will enrich every act that you do. Your love will have a totally different flavor. Now there will not be any hate hiding behind it; it will be simply love. There will not be even the expectation that something should be returned to you. You don't need anything. Giving is such a benediction, there is no need. You are so rich inside that nothing can make you richer.

And you can go on sharing bliss. The more you share it, the more you have it, so nothing can make you poorer. This is the only miracle that I know of.

■ *As I move deeper into meditation and looking into who I really am, I am having trouble maintaining any relationship. Is this something to be expected, or have I gone wrong somewhere?*

When you move on an inner pilgrimage the energies turn inward, the same energies that were moving outward, and suddenly you find yourself alone like an island. The difficulty arises because you are not really settled in being yourself, and all relationships look like a dependence, a bondage. But this is a passing phase; don't make it a permanent attitude. Sooner or later when you are settled inside again, you will be overflowing with energy and will want to move into a relationship again.

So for the first time that mind becomes meditative, love appears to be like a bondage. And in a way it is true, because a mind that is not meditative cannot really be in love. That love is false, illusory—more of an infatuation, less like love. But you have nothing to compare it with unless the real happens, so when meditation starts, the illusory love by and by dissipates, disappears. Don't be disheartened. And don't make it a permanent attitude; these are two possibilities.

If you become disheartened because your love life is disappearing and you cling to it, that will become a barrier in your inner journey. Accept it—now the energy is seeking a new path and for a few days it will not be available for the outward movement, for activities.

If somebody is a creator and he meditates, all creativity will disappear for the time being. If you are a painter, suddenly you will not find yourself in it. You can continue, but by and by you will have no energy and no enthusiasm. If you are a poet, poetry will stop. If you are a man who has been in love, that energy will simply disappear. If you try to force yourself to move into a relationship, to be your old self, that enforcement will be very, very dangerous. Then you are doing a contradictory thing: On one hand you are trying to go in, on the other you are trying to go out. It is as if you are driving a car, pressing the accelerator and at the same time pressing the brake. It can be a disaster because you are doing two opposite things together.

Meditation is only against false love. The false will disappear, and that's a basic condition for the real to appear. The false must go, the false must vacate you completely; only then are you available for the real. So for a few days forget all relationships.

The second thing, which is also a very great danger, is that you can make it a style of life. It has happened to many people. They are in the monasteries—old monks, orthodox religious people who have made not being in a love relationship a lifestyle. They think that love is against meditation, and meditation is against love— that's not true. Meditation is against false love, but is totally with true love.

Once you are settled, when you can go in no further, you have reached the core of your being, the bottom rock, then you are centered. Suddenly energy is available but now there is nowhere to go. The outer journey stopped when you started meditating, and now the inner journey is also complete. You are settled, you have reached home. This energy will start overflowing. It is a totally different type of movement, the quality of it is different because it has no motivation. Before, you were moving toward others with a motivation; now there will be none. You will simply be moving toward others because you have so much to share.

Before you were moving as a beggar, now you will be moving like an emperor. Not that you are seeking some happiness from somebody—that you have already. Now the happiness is too much, the cloud is so full it would like to rain. The flower is so full that it would like to ride on the winds as fragrance and go to the very corners of the world. It is a sharing, a new type of relationship has come into existence. To call it a relationship is not right because it is no longer a relationship; rather, it is a state of being. Not that you love, but that you *are* love.

So don't be disheartened, or make it a style of life; it is just a passing phase. Renunciation is a passing phase—celebration is the goal of life. Renunciation is just a means. There are moments when you have to renounce, just as when you are ill and the doctor says to fast. Fasting is not going to be a style of life. Renounce food, and once you are healthy enjoy it again—and you will be able to enjoy it more than ever. Don't make fasting your life—it was a passing phase, it was needed.

Just fast a little with love and relationships, and soon you will be capable of moving again, again overflowing, and moving without motivation. Then love is beautiful. And it is never beautiful before that; it is always ugly. Howsoever you try, it always turns sour. Both people may be trying hard to make a beautiful thing out of it, but it is not in the nature of things; something ugly comes in. Every love affair is always on the rocks. Just wait . . .

Two Women and a Monk

A Zen story:

There was an old woman in China who had supported a monk for over twenty years. She had built a hut for him, and she fed him while he was meditating.

One day she decided to find out just what progress he had made in all this time.

She obtained the help of a girl rich in desire, and said to her, "Go and embrace him, and then ask him suddenly, 'What now?' "

The girl called upon the monk and immediately started caressing him, and asking him what he was going to do about it.

"An old tree grows on a rock in winter," replied the monk somewhat poetically, "nowhere is there any warmth."

The girl returned and related what he had said.

"To think I fed that fellow for twenty years!" exclaimed the old woman in anger. "He showed no consideration for your need, no disposition to explain your condition. He need not have responded to passion, but at least he should have experienced some compassion."

She at once went to the hut of the monk and burned it down.

An ancient proverb says, *Sow a thought, reap an act. Sow an act, reap a habit. Sow a habit, reap a character. Sow a character, reap a destiny.*

And I say to you: Sow nothing, and reap meditation or love.

Sowing nothing—that's what meditation is all about. And its natural consequence is love. If, at the end of the journey of meditation, love has not flowered then the whole journey has been futile. Something went wrong somewhere. You started but you never reached.

Love is the test. For the path of meditation, love is the test. They are two sides of one coin, two aspects of the same energy. When one is there, the other has to be there. If the other is not there, then the first is also not there.

Meditation is not concentration. A man of concentration may not reach to love; in fact, he will not. A man of concentration may become more violent because concentration is a training to remain tense, concentration is an effort to narrow down the mind. It is deep violence with your consciousness. And when you are violent with your own consciousness you cannot be nonviolent with others. Whatsoever you are with yourself, you are going to be with others.

Let this be a fundamental rule of life, one of the most fundamental: Whatsoever you are toward yourself, you will be toward others. If you love yourself, you will love others. If you are flowing within your being, you will be flowing in relationships, also. If you are frozen inside, you will be frozen outside, also. The inner tends to become the outer; the inner goes on manifesting itself in the outer.

Concentration is not meditation; concentration is the method of science. It is scientific methodology. A man of science needs the deep discipline of concentration, but a man of science is not expected to be compassionate. There is no need. In fact, a man of science becomes more and more violent with nature—all scientific progress is based on violence toward nature. It is destructive because, in the first place, the scientific man is destructive to his own expanding consciousness. Rather than expanding his consciousness he narrows it down, makes it exclusive, one-pointed. It is a coercion, violence.

So remember, meditation is not concentration—but neither is meditation contemplation. It is not thinking. Maybe you are thinking about God—even then, it is thinking. If there is "about," there is thinking. You may be thinking about money, you may be thinking about God—it basically makes no difference. Thinking continues, only objects change. So if you are thinking about the world, or about sex, nobody will call it contemplation. If you are thinking about God, virtue, if you are thinking about Jesus, Krishna, Buddha, then people will call it contemplation. But Zen is very strict about it—it is not meditation, it is still thinking. You are still concerned with the other.

In contemplation the other is there, although of course not so exclusively as it is in concentration. Contemplation has more fluidity than concentration. In concentration the mind is one-pointed; in contemplation the mind is oriented toward one subject, not toward one point. You can go on thinking about it, you can go on changing and flowing with the subject but still, on the whole, the subject remains the same.

Then what is meditation? Meditation is just being delighted in your own presence; meditation is a delight in your own being. It is very simple—a totally relaxed state of consciousness where you are not doing anything. The moment doing enters, you become tense; anxiety enters immediately. How to do? What to do? How to succeed? How not to fail? You have already moved into the future.

If you are contemplating, what can you contemplate? How can you contemplate the unknown? How can you contemplate the unknowable? You can contemplate only the known. You can chew it again and again, but it is the known. If you know something about Jesus, you can think again and again; if you know something about Krishna, you can think again and again. You can go on modifying, changing, decorating—but it is not going to lead you toward the unknown. And God is the unknown.

Meditation is just to be, not doing anything—no action, no thought, no emotion. You just are, and it is a sheer delight. From where does this delight come when you are not doing anything? It comes from nowhere—or, it comes from everywhere. It is uncaused, because the existence is made of the stuff called joy. It needs no cause, no reason. If you are unhappy you have a reason to be unhappy; if you are happy you are simply happy—there is no reason for it. Your mind tries to find a reason because it cannot believe in the uncaused because it cannot control the uncaused—with the uncaused, the mind simply becomes impotent. So the mind goes on finding some reason or other. But I would like to tell you that whenever you are happy, you are happy for no reason at all; whenever you are unhappy, you have some reason to be unhappy—because happiness is just the stuff you are made of. It is your very being, it is your innermost core. Joy is your innermost core.

Look at the trees, look at the birds, look at the clouds, look at the stars . . . and if you have eyes you will be able to see that the whole of existence is joyful. Everything is simply happy. Trees are happy for no reason; they are not going to become prime ministers or presidents and they are not going to become rich and they will never have any bank balance. Look at the flowers—for no reason. It is simply unbelievable how happy flowers are.

The whole existence is made of the stuff called joy. Hindus call it *satchitanand, ananda,* joy. That's why no reason, no cause is needed. If you can just be with yourself, not doing anything, just enjoying yourself, just being with yourself, just being happy that you are, just being happy that you are breathing, just being happy that you are listening to the birds—for no reason—then you are in meditation. Meditation is being here now. And when one is happy for no reason, that happiness cannot be contained within you. It goes on spreading to others, it becomes a sharing. You cannot hold it, it is so much, it is so infinite. You cannot hold it in your hands, you have to allow it to spread.

This is what compassion is. Meditation is being with yourself and compassion is overflowing with that being. It is the same energy that was moving into passion that becomes compassion. It is the same energy that was narrowed down into the body or into the mind. It is the same energy that was leaking from small holes.

What is sex? Just a leakage of energy from a small hole in the body. Hindus call these—exactly—holes. When you are flowing, overflowing, when you are not moving through the holes, all walls disappear. You have become the whole. Now you spread. You cannot do anything about it.

It is not that you have to be compassionate, no. In the state of meditation you *are* compassion. Compassion is as warm as passion—hence the word *compassion.* It is very passionate but the passion is unaddressed, and the passion is not in search of any gratification. The whole process has become just the reverse. First you were seeking some happiness somewhere—now you have found it and you are expressing it. Passion is a search for happiness; compassion is an expression of happiness. But it is passionate, it is warm, and you have to understand it because it has a paradox in it.

The greater a thing, the more paradoxical it is, and this meditation and compassion is one of the highest peaks, the uttermost peak. So there is bound to be a paradox.

The paradox is that a man of meditation is very cool, not cold; cool yet warm, not hot. Passion is hot, it is almost feverish. It has a temperature. Compassion is cool yet warm, welcoming, receptive, happy to share, ready to share, waiting to share. If a person of meditation becomes cold, he has missed. Then he is just a man of repression. If you repress your passion you will become cold. That's how the whole humanity has become cold—passion has been repressed in everyone.

From the very childhood your passion has been crippled and repressed. Whenever you started becoming passionate, there was somebody—your mother, your father, your teacher, the police—there was somebody who immediately became suspicious of you. Your passion was curbed, repressed: "Don't do it!" Immediately you shrank within yourself. And by and by you learned that to survive it is better to listen to people who are around you. It is safer.

So what to do? What is a child supposed to do when he feels passionate, when he feels full of energy and he wants to jump and run and dance and his father is reading the newspaper? It is rubbish, but he is reading his newspaper and he is a very important man, he's the master of the house. What to do? The child is doing something really great—in him it is God who is ready to dance—but the father is reading his newspaper so there has to be silence. He cannot dance, he cannot run, he cannot scream.

He will repress his energy; he will try to be cold, collected, controlled. Control has become such a supreme value, and it is of no value at all.

A controlled person is a dead person. A controlled person is not necessarily a disciplined person; discipline is totally different. Discipline comes out of awareness; control comes out of fear. People who are around you are more powerful than you, they can punish you, they can destroy you. They have all the power to control, to corrupt, to repress. And the child has to become diplomatic. When sex energy arises, the child is in difficulty. The society is against it; the society says it has to be channeled—and it is flowing all over the child—it has to be cut.

In the schools what are we doing? In fact, the schools are not so much instruments for imparting knowledge as instruments of control. For six, seven hours a day a child is sitting there. This is to curb his dancing, to curb his singing, to curb his joy; this is to control him. Sitting for six, seven hours every day in an almost prisonlike atmosphere, by and by the energy deadens. The child becomes repressed, frozen. Now there is no streaming, the energy does not come, he lives at the minimum—that's what we call control. He never goes to the maximum.

Psychologists have been searching and they have come to recognize a great factor in human misfortune—that is, that ordinarily people live only ten percent. They live ten percent, they breathe ten percent, they love ten percent, they enjoy ten percent—ninety percent of their life is simply not allowed. This is sheer waste! One should live at the hundred percent capacity, only then is flowering possible.

So meditation is not control, it is not repression. If somehow you have got the wrong idea and you are repressing yourself, then you will become very controlled—but then you will be cold. Then you will become more and more indifferent, not detached. Indifferent, noncaring, unloving—you will almost commit suicide. You will be alive at the minimum. You can be called just so-so alive. You will not be burning from both ends, your flame will be very dim. Much smoke will be there but almost no light.

It happens to people who are on the path of meditation—Catholics, Buddhists, Jainas—that they become cold, because to control comes easily. Awareness is very arduous. Control is very easy because control needs only a cultivation of habits. You cultivate habits, then those habits possess you and you need not worry. Then you go on with your habits, they become mechanical and you live a robot life. You may look like a Buddha but you will not be. You will be just a dead stone statue.

If compassion has not arisen in you, then apathy will arise. Apathy means absence of passion; compassion means transformation of passion. Go and watch Catholic monks, Jaina monks, Buddhist monks, and you will see very apathetic figures—dull, stupid, nonradiant, closed, afraid, continuously anxious.

Controlled persons are always nervous because deep down turmoil is still hidden. If you are uncontrolled, flowing, alive, then you are not nervous. There is no question of being nervous—whatsoever happens, happens. You have no expectations for the future, you are not performing. Then why should you be nervous? If you go to Catholic, Jaina, Buddhist monks, you will find them very nervous—maybe not so nervous in their monasteries, but if you bring them out to the world, you will find them very, very nervous because on each step there is temptation.

A man of meditation comes to a point where there is no temptation left. Try to understand it. Temptation never comes from without; it is the repressed desire, repressed energy, repressed anger, repressed sex, repressed greed, that creates temptation. Temptation comes from within you, it has nothing to do with the without. It is not that a devil comes and tempts you, it is your own repressed mind that becomes devilish and wants to take revenge. To control that mind one has to remain so cold and frozen that no life energy is allowed to move into your limbs, into your body. If energy is allowed to move, those repressions will surface.

That's why people have learned how to be cold, how to touch others and yet not touch them, how to see people and yet not see them. People live with clichés—"Hello, how are you?" Nobody means anything by it, these words are just to avoid the real encounter of two persons. People don't look into each other's eyes, they don't hold hands, they don't try to feel each other's energy. They don't allow each other to pour. Very afraid, somehow just managing. Cold and dead. In a straitjacket.

A man of meditation has learned how to be full of energy, at the maximum, optimum. He lives at the peak, he makes his abode at the peak. Certainly he has a warmth, but it is not feverish, it only shows life. He is not hot, he is cool, because he is not carried away by desires. He is so happy, that he is no longer seeking any happiness. He is so at

home, he is not going anywhere, he is not running and
very cool.

is a dictum: *agere sequitur esse*—to do follows to be; action
t is tremendously beautiful. Don't try to change your ac-
d out your being, and action will follow. The action is secondary; being is primary. Action is something that you do; being is
something that you are. Action comes out of you, but action is just a fragment. Even if all of your actions are collected together they will not be
equal to your being because all actions collected together will be your
past. What about your future? Your being contains your past, your future,
your present; your being contains your eternity. Your actions, even if all
collected, will just be of the past. Past is limited, future is unlimited. That
which has happened is limited; it can be defined, it has already happened.
That which has not happened is unlimited, indefinable. Your being contains eternity, your actions contain only your past.

So it is possible that a man who has been a sinner up to this moment
can become a saint the next. Never judge a man by his actions, judge
a man by his being. Sinners have become saints and saints have fallen
and become sinners. Each saint has a past and each sinner has a future.

Never judge a man by his actions. But there is no other way, because
you have not known even your own being—how can you see the being
of others? Once you know your own being you will learn the language,
you will know the clue of how to look into another's being. You can
see into others only to the extent that you can see into yourself. If you
have seen yourself through and through, you become capable of seeing
into others through and through.

So, a few things before I enter into this beautiful story.

If by your meditations you are becoming cold—beware. If your meditation is making you more warm, more loving, more flowing—good,
you are on the right path. If you are becoming less loving, if your
compassion is disappearing and apathy is settling inside you—then the
sooner you change your direction the better. Otherwise you will become a wall.

Don't become a wall. Remain alive, throbbing, streaming, flowing,
melting.

Of course there are problems. Why have people become walls? Because walls can be defined. They give you a boundary, a definite shape and form—what Hindus call *nam roop*, name and form. If you are melting and flowing you don't have boundaries; you don't know where you are and where you end and where the other begins. You go on being together with people so much that all the boundaries by and by become dreamlike. And one day they disappear.

That is how reality is. Reality is unbounded. Where do you think you stop? At your skin? Ordinarily we think, "Of course, we are inside our skins and the skin is our wall, the boundary." But your skin could not be alive if the air was not surrounding it. If your skin is not constantly breathing the oxygen that is being supplied by the surroundings, your skin cannot be alive. Take away the atmosphere and you will die immediately. Even if your skin has not been scratched you will die. So that cannot be your boundary.

There are two hundred miles of atmosphere all around the earth—is that your boundary? That, too, cannot be your boundary. This oxygen and this atmosphere and the warmth and the life cannot exist without the sun. If the sun ceases to exist, or drops dead . . . One day it is going to happen. Scientists say that some day the sun will cool down and drop dead. Then suddenly this atmosphere will not be alive. Immediately you will be dead. So is the sun your boundary? But now physicists say this sun is connected to some central source of energy that we have not yet been able to find but is suspected—because nothing is unrelated.

So where do we decide where our boundary is? An apple on the tree is not you. Then you eat it, it becomes you. So it is just waiting to become you. It is you potentially, it is your future you. Then you have defecated and you have dropped much rubbish out of the body. Just a moment before, it was you. So where do you decide? I am breathing—the breath inside me is me, but just a moment before it may have been your breath. It must have been because we are breathing in a common atmosphere. We are all breathing into each other; we are members of each other. You are breathing in me, I am breathing in you.

And it is not only so with breathing, it is exactly so with life. Have you watched? With certain people you feel very alive, they come just bubbling with energy. And something happens in you, a response, and you are also bubbling. And then there are people . . . just their face and one feels one will flop down! Just their presence is enough poison. They must be pouring something into you that is poisonous. And when you come around a person and you become radiant and happy and suddenly something starts throbbing in your heart, and your heart beats faster, this man must have poured something into you.

We are pouring into each other. That's why, in the East, *satsang* has become very, very important. To be with a person who has known, just to be in his presence, is enough—because he is constantly pouring his being into you. You may know or you may not know. You may recognize it today or you may not recognize it today, but someday or other the seeds will come to flower.

We are pouring into each other. We are not separate islands. A cold person becomes like an island and it is a misfortune, it is a great misfortune because you could have become a vast continent and you decided to become an island. You decided to remain poor, when you could have become as rich as you wanted to be.

Don't be a wall and never try to repress, otherwise you *will* become a wall. Repressed people have masks, faces. They are pretending to be somebody else. A repressed person is carrying the same world as you are—just an opportunity is needed, a provocation, and immediately the real will come out. That's why monks disappear from the world—because there are too many provocations, too many temptations. It is difficult for them to remain contained, to hold on. So they go to the Himalayas or to the caves, they retire from the world so that even if ideas, temptations, desires arise, there is no way to fulfill them.

But this is not a way of transformation.

The people who become cold are the people who were very hot. The people who take vows of remaining celibate are the people who were extremely sexual. The mind turns from one extreme to another very easily. It is my observation that many people who are too obsessed with food one day or other become obsessed with fasting. It has to happen because you cannot stay in one extreme long. You are doing too much of it, soon you will get fed up with it, tired of it. Then there is no other way, you have to move to the other extreme.

The people who have become monks are very worldly people. The market was too much, they had moved too much in the market, then the pendulum moved to the other extreme. Greedy people renounce the world. This renunciation is not of understanding—it is just greed upside-down. First they were holding, holding . . . now suddenly they see the pointlessness of it, the futility of it and they start throwing it. First they were afraid to lose a single penny, now they are afraid to keep a single penny, but the fear continues. First they were too greedy about this world, now they are too greedy about the other world, but the greed is there. These people one day or other are bound to join a monastery—then they become great celibates, great renouncers. But it does not change their nature.

Except for awareness, nothing changes a person, nothing at all. So don't try to pretend. That which has not happened, has not happened. Understand it, and don't try to pretend and don't try to make others believe that it has happened, because nobody is going to lose in this deception except you.

People who try to control themselves have chosen a very foolish way. Control will not happen, but they will become cold. That is the only way a man can control himself—to become frozen so that energy does not arise. People who take vows of celibacy will not eat much; in fact, they will starve their bodies. If more energy is created in the body then there will be more sex energy, and then they don't know what to do with it. So Buddhist monks eat only once a day—and then not enough. They eat only enough that bodily needs are fulfilled, very minimum needs, so no energy is left. This type of celibacy is not celibacy. When you are flowing with energy and the energy starts transforming itself into love, then a celibacy, a *brahmacharya*, which is beautiful, happens.

The sweet old lady came into the store and bought a package of mothballs. The next day she was back for another five packets. Another day passed and she came in for a dozen more.

"You must have a lot of moths," said the salesman.

"Yes," replied the old dear, "and I have been throwing these things at them for three days now and I have only managed to hit one!"

Through control you will not even be able to hit one! That is not the way. You are fighting with leaves, branches, cutting them here and there. That is not the way to destroy the tree of desire; the way is to cut the roots. And roots can be cut only when you have reached to the roots of desire. On the surface there are only branches—jealousy, anger, envy, hatred, lust. They are just on the surface. The deeper you move, the more you will understand: They are all coming out of one root and that root is unawareness.

Meditation means awareness. It cuts the very root. Then the whole tree disappears on its own accord. Then passion becomes compassion.

I have heard about a very great Zen master who had become old and almost blind at the age of ninety-six and no longer able to teach or work about the monastery. The old man then decided it was time to die because he was of no use to anybody, he could not be of any help. So he stopped eating.

When asked by his monks why he refused his food, he replied that he had outlived his usefulness and was only a bother to everybody.

They told him, "If you die now"—it was January—"when it is so cold, everybody will be uncomfortable at your funeral and you will be an even greater nuisance. So please eat."

This can happen only in a Zen monastery, because disciples love the master so deeply, their respect is so deep, that there is no need for any formality. Just see what they were saying. They were saying, "If you die now, and it is January, see, it is so cold, everybody will be uncomfortable at the funeral and you will be an even greater nuisance. So please eat."

He thereupon resumed eating. But when it became warm again he stopped, and not long after he quietly toppled over and died.

Such compassion! One lives then for compassion; one dies then for compassion. One is even ready to choose a right time to so that nobody is bothered and one need not be a nuisance.

I have heard about another Zen master who was going to die.

He said, "Where are my shoes? Bring them."

Somebody asked, "Where are you going? The doctors say you are going to die."

He said, "I am going to the cemetery."

"But why?"

He said, "I don't want to trouble anybody. Otherwise you will have to carry me on your shoulders."

He walked to the cemetery and died there.

Tremendous compassion! What manner of man is this, not to give even that much trouble to anybody? And these people helped thousands. Thousands were grateful to them, thousands became full of light and love because of them. Yet they would not like to bother anybody. If they are useful they would like to live and help, if they are not useful then it is time to leave and go.

Now, the story.

There was an old woman in China who had supported a monk for over twenty years. She had built a hut for him, and she fed him while he was meditating.

It is a miracle that has happened in the East—the West is still unable to understand it. For centuries in the East, if somebody was meditating, the society would feed him. It was enough that he was meditating. Nobody would think that he was a burden on the society—"Why should we work for him?" Just because he was meditating was enough, because the East came to know that if even one man becomes enlightened, his energy is shared by all; if even one man comes to flower in meditation, his fragrance becomes part of the whole society. And the gain is so tremendous that the East has never said, "Don't sit there and meditate. Who is going to feed you, who is going to clothe you, and who is going to give you shelter?" Thousands and thousands—Buddha had ten thousand *sannyasins* moving with him, but people were happy to feed them, to shelter them, to clothe them, to look after them, because they were meditating.

Now it is very, very impossible in the West to think that way. Even in the East it is becoming difficult. In China monasteries were closed, meditation halls were converted into hospitals or school rooms. Great masters disappeared. They were forced to work in the fields or in the factories. Nobody is allowed to meditate, because a great understanding is lost—the whole mind is full of materialism, as if matter is all that exists.

If a man in a town becomes enlightened, the whole town is benefited. It is not a waste to support him. For nothing you are going to get such tremendous treasure! People were happy to help.

For twenty years this woman helped a monk who was meditating and meditating and meditating and doing nothing. He was sitting in Zazen. She built a hut for him, she looked after him, she took every care. One day when she had become very old and was going to die she wanted to know whether meditation had flowered or not, or whether this man had been simply sitting and sitting and sitting. Twenty years is a long enough time, the woman was getting old and was going to die, so she wanted to know whether she had been serving a man of real meditation or just a hocus-pocus.

One day she decided to find out . . .

The woman must have been of great understanding herself because the examination, the test that she tried, was full of understanding.

One day she decided to find out just what progress he had made in all this time.

If meditation is progressing then the *only* criterion of its progress is love, the *only* criterion of its progress is compassion.

She obtained the help of a girl rich in desire, and said to her, "Go and embrace him, and then ask him suddenly, 'What now?' "

Three are the possibilities. One: If for twenty years he had not touched a beautiful woman, the first possibility was that he would be tempted, would be a victim, would forget all about meditation and would make love with this girl. The other possibility was that he would remain cold, controlled and would not show any compassion toward this girl. He would simply hold himself back, hard, so that he could not be tempted. And the third possibility was that if meditation had come to fruition, he would be full of love, understanding, compassion and he would try to understand this girl and would try to help her. She was just a test for these possibilities.

If the first was the possibility, then all his meditation was simply a waste. If the second was the possibility then he had fulfilled the ordinary criterion of being a monk but he had not fulfilled the real criterion of being a man of meditation. If the second was the possibility then it simply showed that he was a behaviorist, that he had made a habit, controlled his behavior.

You must have heard the name of Pavlov the Russian behaviorist. He said there is no consciousness in man or in animals or anywhere— the whole thing is just a mind mechanism. You can train the mind mechanism and then it starts working in that way—it is all a question of conditioning. Mind functions as a conditioned reflex. If you put food before your dog he immediately comes running, his tongue hanging forward, dripping. He starts to salivate. Pavlov tried. Whenever he gave food to the dog he would ring a bell. By and by, the bell and the food became associated. Then one day he simply rang the bell and the dog came running, tongue hanging out, dripping.

Now this is absurd, no dog has ever been known to react to a ringing bell in this way. The bell is not food. But now the association has conditioned the mind. Pavlov says man can be changed in the same way. Whenever sex arises in you, punish yourself. Go for a seven-day fast, flog your body, stand in the cold the whole night, or beat yourself, and by and by the body will learn a trick. Whenever sex arises, it will repress it automatically because of the fear of the punishment. Reward and punishment—this is the way to condition the mind if you follow Pavlov.

This monk must have been doing that—many are doing that. Almost ninety-nine percent of people in the monasteries are doing that, just reconditioning their minds and bodies. But consciousness has nothing to do with it. Consciousness is not a new habit; consciousness is to live a life with awareness, not confined to any habit, not possessed by any mechanism—above the mechanism.

And she said to her, "Go and embrace him, and then ask him suddenly, 'What now?' "

Suddenly is the clue to the whole thing. If you give a little time then the mind can start working in the conditioned way for which it has been prepared. So don't give any time: Go in the middle of the night when he will be alone meditating. Just go inside the hut—he must have been living outside the town, alone—go inside the hut and simply start caressing him, embracing him, kiss him. And then immediately ask, "What now?" Watch his reaction, what happens to him, what he says, what colors pass on his face, what his eyes indicate, how he reacts and responds to you.

The girl called upon the monk and immediately started caressing him, and asking him what he was going to do about it.

"An old tree grows on a cold rock in winter," replied the monk some-what poetically, "nowhere is there any warmth."

He has conditioned his dog; he has conditioned his body-mind. Twenty years is a long enough time to condition. Even this sudden attack could not break his habitual pattern. He remained controlled. He must have been a man of tremendous control. He remained cold, with not even a flicker of energy, and he said, *"An old tree grows on a cold rock in winter."* Not only was he controlled and cold—he was so controlled, he remained so cold that in such a dangerous situation, provocative, seductive, he could use poetic words to reply. The conditioning must have gone very, very deep, to the roots.

"An old tree grows on a cold rock in winter," replied the monk somewhat poetically, "nowhere is there any warmth."

That's all he said.

The girl returned and related what he had said.
"To think I fed that fellow for twenty years!" exclaimed the old woman
in anger.

His meditation had not flowered. He had become cold and dead, corpselike; he had not become enlightened or a buddha.

"He showed no consideration for your need . . ."

A man of compassion always thinks about you, about your need. He remained coldly self-centered. He simply said something about himself— "An old tree grows on a cold rock in winter, nowhere is there any warmth." He did not utter a single word about the woman. He did not even ask, "Why did you come? Why? What do you need? And why have you chosen me out of so many people? Sit down." He should have listened to her. She must be in a deep need. Nobody comes in the middle of the night to a withered-away monk who has been sitting in meditation for twenty years. Why had she come? He did not pay any attention to her.

Love always thinks of the other; ego only thinks of oneself. Love is always considerate; ego is absolutely inconsiderate. Ego has only one language and that is of self. Ego always uses the other; love is ready to be used, love is ready to serve.

"He showed no consideration for your need, no disposition to explain your
condition."

When you go to a man of compassion and he looks at you, he looks deeply into your heart. He tries to find out what your problem is, why you are in such a situation, why you are doing the thing that you are doing. He forgets himself. He simply becomes focused on the person who has come to him—that person's need, problem, anxiety, is his consideration. He tries to help. Whatsoever he can do he will do.

"He need not have responded to passion . . ."

That's true. A man of compassion cannot respond in a passionate way. He is not cold, but he is cool. He can give you his warmth, nourishing warmth, but he cannot give you any fever. He has none. Remember the difference between a feverish body and a warm body. A feverish body is not healthy, a warm body is simply healthy. In passion, people become feverish. Have you watched yourself deep in passion? You are almost a raving maniac, mad, wild, doing something you don't know why—and in a great fever, with the whole body trembling, in a cyclone with no center.

A man of warmth is simply healthy. Just as when a mother takes her child to her breast and the child feels the warmth—surrounded by the warmth, nourished by it, welcomed by it. So when you enter into the aura of a compassionate man you enter a motherlike warmth, you enter into a very nourishing energy field. In fact, if you come to a man of compassion, your passion will simply disappear. His compassion will be so powerful, his warmth will be so great, his love will be showering on you so much that you will become cool, you will become centered.

"He need not have responded to passion, but at least he should have experienced some compassion."
She at once went to the hut of the monk and burned it down.

It was just a symbolic gesture that those twenty years that he was meditating there—during which they had been hoping that he had been progressing—had been a waste.

It is not enough just to be a monk superficially, just to be a monk repressed and cold—coldness is an indication of repression, a very deep repression.

That's what I have been telling you: If you move into meditation, compassion and love will come automatically, on their own accord. They follow meditation like a shadow. So you need not be worried about any synthesis—the synthesis will come. It comes by itself, you don't have to bring it. You choose one path. Either you follow the path of love, devotion, dancing, dissolve yourself completely into your love toward the divine. That path is of dissolving, no awareness is needed. You are needed to be drunk, completely drunk with God, you will need to become a drunkard. Or, choose the path of meditation. There you are not needed to be dissolved into anything. You are needed to become very crystallized, you are needed to become very integrated, alert, aware.

Follow the path of love and one day, suddenly, you will see that meditation has flowered within you—thousands of white lotuses. And you have not done anything for them, you were doing something else and they flowered. When love or devotion comes to its climax, meditation flowers. And the same happens on the path of meditation. Just forget all about love, devotion. You simply become aware, sit silently, enjoy your being—that's all. Be with yourself, that's all. Learn how to be alone—that's all. And remember, a person who knows how to be alone is never lonely. People who don't know how to be alone, they are lonely.

On the path of meditation, aloneness is sought, desired, hoped for, prayed for. Be alone. So much so that not even in your consciousness does any shadow of the other move. On the path of love, get so dissolved that only the other becomes real and you become a shadow and by and by you completely disappear. On the path of love, God remains, you disappear; on the path of meditation, God disappears, you appear. But the total and the ultimate result is the same. A great synthesis happens.

Never try to synthesize these two paths in the beginning. They meet in the end, they meet at the peak, they meet in the temple.

One of Rabbi Moshe's disciples was very poor. He complained to the zaddik that his wretched circumstances were an obstacle to learning and praying.

"In this day and age," said Rabbi Moshe, "the greatest devotion, greater than learning and praying, consists in accepting the world exactly as it happens to be."

The person who is moving into meditation, or who is moving on the path of love, will be helped if he accepts the world as it is. Worldly people never accept the world as it is—they are always trying to change it. They are always trying to make something else, they are always trying to fix things into a different order, they are always trying to do something outside. The religious person accepts whatsoever is on the outside as it is. He is not disturbed, he is not distracted by the outside. His whole work consists of moving inside. One moves through love, another moves through meditation, but both move inside. The religious world is the world of the within. And the within is the beyond.

In Latin *sin* has two meanings: one is "missing the target," and another that is even more beautiful—"without." Sin means to be without, to be outside yourself. Virtue means to be within—to be inside yourself.

Soon after the death of Rabbi Moshe, Rabbi Mendel of Kotyk asked one of his disciples, "What was most important to your teacher?"

The disciple thought and then replied, "Whatever he happened to be doing at the moment."

The moment is the most important thing.

Embracing the Paradox

It is beautiful to be alone, it is also beautiful to be in love, to be with people. And they are complementary, not contradictory. When you are enjoying others, enjoy, and enjoy to the full; there is no need to bother about aloneness. And when you are fed up with others, then move into aloneness and enjoy it to the full.

Don't try to choose—if you try to choose you will be in difficulty. Every choice is going to create a division in you, a kind of split in you. Why choose? When you can have both, why have one?

My whole teaching consists of two words, "meditation" and "love." Meditate so that you can feel immense silence, and love so that your life can become a song, a dance, a celebration. You will have to move between the two, and if you can move easily, if you can move without any effort, you have learned the greatest thing in life.

It has been one of the greatest problems down the ages: meditation and love, aloneness and relationship, sex and silence. Only the names are different; the problem is one. And down the ages man has suffered much because the problem has not been understood rightly—people have chosen.

Those who have chosen relationship are called the worldly, and those who have chosen aloneness are called the monks, the otherworldly. But both suffer, because they remain half, and to be half is to be miserable. To be whole is to be healthy, happy; to be whole is to be perfect. To remain half is miserable because the other half goes on sabotaging, the other half goes on preparing to take revenge. The other half can never be destroyed because it is *your* other half! It is an essential part of you; it is not something accidental that you can discard.

It is like a mountain deciding that "I will not have any valleys around me." Now, without the valleys, the mountain cannot be. The valleys are part of the mountain's being; the mountain cannot exist without the valleys; they are complementary to each other. If the mountain chooses to be without valleys, there will be no mountain any more. If the valley chooses to be without the mountain, there will be no valley, either. Or, you will become a pretender—the mountain will pretend that there is no valley. But the valley is there—you can hide the valley, you can drown it deep into your unconscious, but it remains, it persists, it is existential, there is no way to destroy it. In fact, mountain/valley are one thing, so are love and meditation, so are relationship and aloneness. The mountain of aloneness rises only in the valleys of relationship.

In fact, you can enjoy aloneness only if you can enjoy relationship. It is relationship that creates the need for aloneness, it is a rhythm. When you have moved in deep relationship with somebody, a great need arises to be alone. You start feeling spent, exhausted, tired—joyously tired, happily tired, but each excitement is exhausting. It was tremendously beautiful to relate, but now you would like to move into aloneness so that you can again gather yourself together, so that again you can become overflowing, so that again you become rooted in your own being.

In love you moved into the other's being, you lost contact with yourself. You became drowned, drunk. Now you will need to find yourself again. But when you are alone, you are again creating a need for love. Soon you will be so full that you would like to share, you will be so overflowing that you would like somebody to pour yourself into, to whom to give of yourself.

Love arises out of aloneness. Aloneness makes you overfull, love receives your gifts. Love empties you so that you can become full again. Whenever you are emptied by love, aloneness is there to nourish you, to integrate you. And this is a rhythm.

To think of these two things as separate has been the most dangerous

stupidity that man has suffered from. A few people become worldly—
they are spent, they are just exhausted, empty. They don't have any
space of their own. They don't know who they are; they never come
across themselves. They live with others, they live for others. They are
part of a crowd; they are not individuals. And remember: Their life of
love will not be of fulfillment—it will be half, and no half can ever be
a fulfillment. Only the whole is fulfilled.

And then there are the monks who have chosen the other half. They
live in the monasteries. The word *monk* means one who lives alone; the
word comes from the same root as *monogamy, monotony, monastery, monopoly*. It means one, alone.

The monk is one who has chosen to be alone—but soon he is overfull, ripe, and knows nowhere to pour himself. Where to pour himself?
He cannot allow love, he cannot allow relationship; he cannot go and
meet and mix with people. Now his energies start getting sour. Any
energy that stops flowing becomes bitter. Even nectar, stagnant, becomes
poison—and vice versa; even poison, flowing, becomes nectar.

To flow is to know what nectar is and to become stagnant is to know
what poison is. Poison and nectar are not two things but two states of
the same energy. Flowing it is nectar; frozen it is poison. Whenever
some energy is there, and there is no outlet for it, it goes sour. It becomes bitter, it becomes sad, it becomes ugly. Rather than giving you
wholeness and health it makes you ill. All monks are ill; all monks are
bound to be pathological.

The worldly people are empty, bored, exhausted, dragging themselves
somehow, in the name of duty, in the name of the family, in the name
of the nation—all sacred cows—somehow dragging toward death, just
waiting for death to come and deliver them. They will know their rest
only in their graves. They will not know any rest in life—and a life that
knows no rest is not a life, really. It is like music that has no silence in
it—then it is just noise, nauseating; it will make you sick.

Great music is a synthesis between sound and silence. And the greater
the synthesis, the deeper the music goes. The sound creates silence, and
the silence creates receptivity to receive sound, and so on and so forth.
Sound creates more love for music, more capacity to become silent.

Listening to great music you will always feel prayerful, something whole. Something integrates in you. You become centered, rooted. The earth and the sky meet, they are no longer separate. The body and the soul meet and merge, they lose their definitions.

And that is the great moment, the moment of the mystic union.

It is an ancient battle, and foolish, utterly foolish, so please beware: Don't create any battle between sex and silence. If you create a battle, your sex will be ugly, sick, and your silence will be dull and dead. Let sex and silence meet and merge. In fact the greatest moments of silence are those which are followed by love, great love, peaks of love. And the peaks of love are always followed by great moments of silence and aloneness. Meditation leads into love. Love leads into meditation. They are partners. It is impossible to divide them. It is not a question of creating a synthesis—it is impossible to divide them. It is a question of understanding, seeing that they are indivisible. The synthesis is already there, it is already the case. They are one! Two aspects of the same coin. You need not synthesize them, they never have existed separately. And man has tried, and tried hard, but has always failed.

Religiousness has not yet become the noesphere of the earth; religiousness has not yet become a very vital, tidal force in the world. And what is the reason?—this division. Either you have to be worldly or you have to be otherworldly, choose! And the moment you choose, you miss something. Whichever you choose, you are going to be a loser.

I say, don't choose. I say, live both in their togetherness. Of course it needs art to live both. It is simple to choose and be attached to one. Any idiot can do it—in fact, only idiots do it. A few idiots have chosen to be worldly and a few other idiots have chosen to be otherworldly. The man of intelligence would like both. And that's what *sannyas* is all about. You can have the cake and eat it, too—that is intelligence.

Be alert, aware, intelligent. See the rhythm and move with the rhythm, without any choice. Remain choicelessly aware. See both the extremes. On the surface they look opposite, contradictory, but they are not. Deep down there is a complementariness. It is the same pendulum that goes to the left and to the right. Don't try to fix it at the left or at the right; if you fix it you have destroyed the whole clock. And that's what has been done up to now.

Accept life in all its dimensions.

And I understand the problem; the problem is simple, well known. The problem is that when you start relating, you don't know how to be alone—that simply shows unintelligence. It is not that relationship is wrong, it simply shows that you are still not intelligent enough, so relationship becomes too much and you don't find any space to be alone and you feel exhausted and tired. Then one day you decide relationship is bad, it is meaningless: "I want to become a monk. I will go to a Himalayan cave and live there alone." And you will dream great dreams of being alone. How beautiful it will be—nobody encroaching on your freedom, nobody trying to manipulate you; you don't have to think of the other at all.

Jean-Paul Sartre says, "The other is hell." That simply shows that he has not been able to understand the complementariness of love and meditation. "The other is hell"—yes, the other becomes hell if you don't know how to be alone sometimes. Amidst all kinds of relationships, the other becomes hell. It is tedious, tiring, exhausting, boring. The other loses all beauty, because the other has become known. You are well acquainted; now there is no surprise any more. You have known the territory perfectly well; you have traveled in the territory so long that there is no surprise any more. You are simply fed up with the whole thing.

But you have become attached, and the other has become attached to you. The other is also in misery, because you are her or his hell, just as he or she is your hell. Both are creating hell for each other and both are clinging to each other, afraid to lose because . . . anything is better than nothing. At least something is there to hold onto, and one can still hope that tomorrow things will be better. Today they are not better, but tomorrow things are going to be better. One can still hope and one goes on hoping. One lives in despair and goes on hoping.

Then sooner or later one starts feeling it would be better to be alone. But if you go into aloneness, for a few days it will be tremendously beautiful, as it is beautiful with the other—for a few days. Just as there is a honeymoon in relationship, there is a honeymoon in meditation, too. For a few days you will feel so free, just to be yourself, nobody there to demand, nobody there to expect anything from you. If you want to get up early in the morning, you can get up; if you don't want to get up early in the morning, you can go on sleeping. If you want to do something, okay; if you don't want to do anything, there is nobody to force you. For a few days you will feel so tremendously happy—but only for a few days. Soon you will become tired of it. You will be overflowing and have nobody to receive your love. You will be ripe, and the energy needs to be shared. You will become heavy, you will become burdened with your own energy. You would like somebody to welcome your energy, to receive your energy. You would like to be unburdened. Now, aloneness will look not like aloneness but loneliness. Now there will be a change—the honeymoon is finished. Aloneness will start turning into loneliness. You will have a great desire to find the other. In your dreams the other will start appearing.

Go and ask the monks what they dream. They dream only about women; they cannot dream about anything else. They dream of somebody who can unburden them. Ask the nuns—they dream only about men. And the thing can become pathological. You must be aware of the Christian history. Nuns and monks start dreaming even with open eyes. The dream becomes such a substantial reality that you need not wait for the night. Even in the day, the nun is sitting there and she sees the devil coming, and the devil is trying to make love to her. You will be surprised: Many times it happened in the Middle Ages that nuns were burned at the stake because they confessed that they had made love to the devil. They themselves confessed, and it was not only that they had made love to the devil they even became pregnant by the devil—a false pregnancy, just hot air in the belly, but their bellies started becoming bigger and bigger. A psychological pregnancy. And they described the devil in such detail—that devil was their own creation. And the devil followed them day and night . . . And so was the case with the monks.

This choice of being alone has created a very sick humanity. And the people who live in the world are not happy, and the monks are not happy—nobody seems to be happy. The whole world is a constant misery, and you can choose—from one misery to another, you can choose this-worldly misery or that-worldly misery, but it is misery all the same. For a few days you will feel good.

I am bringing you a new message. The message is no longer to choose—remain choicelessly alert in your life, and become intelligent rather than changing circumstances. Change your psychology, become more intelligent. More intelligence is needed to be blissful! And then you can have aloneness together with relationship.

Make your woman or your man also alert to the rhythm. People should be taught that nobody can love twenty-four hours a day; rest periods are needed. And nobody can love on order. Love is a spontaneous phenomenon. Whenever it happens, it happens, and whenever it doesn't happen it doesn't happen. Nothing can be done about it. If you *do* anything, you will create a pseudo phenomenon, an acting.

Real lovers, intelligent lovers, will make each other alert to the phenomenon: "When I want to be alone that does not mean that I am rejecting you. In fact, it is because of your love that you have made it possible for me to be alone." And if your woman wants to be left alone for one night, for a few days, you will not feel hurt. You will not say that you have been rejected, that your love has not been received and welcomed. You will respect her decision to be alone for a few days. In fact, you will be happy! Your love was so much that she is feeling empty; now she needs rest to become full again.

This is intelligence.

Ordinarily, you think you are rejected. You go to your woman and if she is not willing to be with you, or not very loving to you, you feel great rejection. Your ego is hurt. This ego is not a very intelligent thing—all egos are idiotic. Intelligence knows no ego; intelligence simply sees the phenomenon, tries to understand why the woman does not want to be with you. Not that she is rejecting you—you know she has loved you so much, she loves you so much, but this is a moment she wants to be alone. And if you love her, you will leave her alone; you will not torture her, you will not force her to make love to you. And if the man wants to be alone, the woman will not think, "He is no longer interested in me, maybe he has become interested in some other woman." An intelligent woman will leave the man alone so he can again gather together his being, so that again he has energy to share. And this rhythm is like day and night, summer and winter; it goes on changing.

If two persons are really respectful—and love is always respectful, it reveres the other; it is a very worshipful, prayerful state—then slowly, slowly you will understand each other more and more and you will become aware of the other's rhythm and your rhythm. And soon you will find that out of love, out of respect, your rhythms are coming closer and closer. When you feel loving, she feels loving; this settles. This settles on its own, it is a synchronicity.

Have you watched, ever? If you come across two real lovers, you will see many things similar in them. Real lovers become as if they are brothers and sisters. You will be surprised—even brothers and sisters are not so alike. Their expression, their way of walking, their way of talking, their gestures—two lovers become alike and yet so different. This naturally starts happening. Just being together, slowly, slowly they become attuned to each other. Real lovers need not say anything to the other— the other immediately understands, intuitively understands.

If the woman is sad, she may not say it is so, but the man understands and leaves her alone. If the man is sad, the woman understands and leaves him alone—finds some excuse to leave him alone. Stupid people do just the opposite. They never leave each other alone—they are constantly with each other, tiring and boring each other, never leaving any space for the other to be.

Love gives freedom and love helps the other to be himself or herself. Love is a very paradoxical phenomenon. In one way it makes you one soul in two bodies; in another way it gives you individuality, uniqueness. It helps you to drop your small selves but it also helps you to attain to the supreme self. Then there is no problem: Love and meditation are two wings, and they balance each other. And between the two you grow, between the two you become whole.

About the Author

OSHO'S teachings defy categorization, covering everything from the individual quest for meaning to the most urgent social and political issues facing society today. His books are not written but transcribed from audio and video recordings of extemporaneous talks given to international audiences over a period of thirty-five years. Osho has been described by the *Sunday Times* in London as one of the "1,000 Makers of the Twentieth Century," and by American actor Tom Robbins as "the most dangerous man since Jesus Christ."

About his own work, Osho has said that he is helping to create the conditions for the birth of a new kind of human being. He has often characterized this new human being as "Zorba the Buddha"—capable both of enjoying the earthly pleasures of a Zorba the Greek and the silent sreenity of a Gautam Buddha. Running like a thread through all aspects of Osho's work is a vision that encompasses both the timeless wisdom of the East and the highest potential of Western science and technology.

Osho is also known for his revolutionary contribution to the science of inner transformation, with an approach to meditation that acknowledges the accelerated pace of contemporary life. His unique "Active Meditations" are designed to first release the accumulated stresses of body and mind, so that it is easier to experience the thought-free and relaxed state of meditation.

Meditation Resort

OSHO MEDITATION RESORT

The Osho Meditation Resort is a place where people can personally experience a new way of living with more alertness, relaxation, and fun. Located about one hundred miles southeast of Mumbai in Pune, India, the resort offers a variety of programs to thousands of people who visit each year from more than a hundred countries around the world.

Originally developed as a summer retreat for Maharajas and wealthy Briitish colonialists, Pune is now a thriving modern city that is home to a number of universities and high-tech industries. The Meditation Resort spreads over forty acres in a tree-lined suburb known as Koregaon Park. The resort campus provides accommodation for a limited number of guests, in a new "Guesthouse," and there is a plentiful variety of nearby hotels and private apartments available for stays of a few days up to several months.

All resort programs are based in the Osho vision of a qualitatively new kind of human being, who is able both to participate creatively in everyday life and to relax into silence and meditation. Most programs take place in modern, air-conditioned facilities and include a variety of individual sessions, courses, and workshops covering everything from creative arts to holistic health treatments, personal transformation and therapy, esoteric sciences, the "Zen" approach to sports and recreation, relationship issues, and significant life transitions for men and women. Individual sessions and group workshops are offered throughout the year, alongside a full daily schedule of meditations. Outdoor cafés and restaurants within the resort grounds serve both traditional Indian fare and a choice of international dishes, all made with organically grown vegetables from the resort's own farm. The campus has its own private supply of safe, filtered water.

For more information:

www.osho.com

a comprehensive Web site in several languages that includes an on-line tour of the Meditation Resort and a calendar of its course offerings, a catalog of books and tapes, a list of Osho information centers worldwide, and selections from Osho's talks.

Osho International
New York
Email: oshointernational@oshointernational.com
www.osho.com/oshointernational

FURTHER READINGS

SEX MATTERS

Sex Matters begins with selections from the revolutionary classic, *From Sex to Superconsciousness*, where Osho explains how sex is nature's way of offering a glimpse of what it feels like to be free from time, free from thoughts, and completely present in the here and now. Osho also illuminates how religious institutions, by condemning sex and trying to enforce celibacy, have not only repressed man's spiritual growth but have actually contributed to the spread of sexual perversion and exploitation.

"*Sex Matters* rediscovers the human, and rewards rather than punishes one for being in that state. It is a wondrous revelation that will give peace, confidence, and courage all at the same time."
— Eugene Kennedy, author of *The Unhealed Wound: The Church, the Priesthood, and the Question of Sexuality*

ISBN 0-312-26160-8 Hardcover $25.95/$38.95 Canadian

AUTOBIOGRAPHY OF A SPIRITUALLY INCORRECT MYSTIC

This delightful glimpse into the life of one of the most outrageous twentieth-century spiritual leaders answers some of the criticisms leveled at him for his seemingly outrageous behavior and his iconoclastic tendencies. He proves a fascinating man: a prolific writer and lecturer, highly educated, and deeply passionate about his own search for truth.

"[H]is autobiography is entertaining, insightful and for some, perhaps, even enlightening." — *Booklist*

Includes a 16-page black & white photo insert

ISBN 0-312-28071-8 Paperback $14.95/$21.95 Canadian

THE INSIGHT SERIES

Osho's Insight Series aims to shine light on concious behaviors that prevent individuals from being their true selves. With an artful mix of compassion and humor, Osho seduces his audience into confronting what they would most like to avoid, which in turn provides the key to true insight and power.

ISBN 0-312-27563-3
Paperback $11.95/$17.95 Canadian

ISBN 0-312-20517-1
Paperback $11.95/$17.95 Canadian

ISBN 0-312-20519-8
Paperback $11.95/$17.95 Canadian

ISBN 0-312-27566-8
Paperback $11.95/$17.95 Canadian

ISBN 0-312-27567-6
Paperback $11.95/$17.95 Canadian

ISBN 0-312-20561-9
Paperback $11.95/$17.95 Canadian

 ST. MARTIN'S GRIFFIN